STATE DEPARTMENT

COUNTERINTELLIGENCE

STATE DEPARTMENT COUNTERINTELLIGENCE

Leaks, Spies, and Lies

ROBERT DAVID BOOTH

BROWN BOOKS
PUBLISHING GROUP

State Department Counterintelligence: Leaks, Spies, and Lies

Brown Books Publishing Group
16250 Knoll Trail Drive, Suite 205
Dallas, Texas 75248
www.BrownBooks.com
(972) 381-0009

A New Era in Publishing™

ISBN 978-1-61254-372-7 (PB)
LCCN 2014949310

Printed in the United States
10 9 8 7 6 5 4 3 2 1

For more information or to contact the author, please go to www.LeaksSpiesAndLies.com

To Maria, my mother;

Lori, my wife;

and

Chloe, my daughter.

CONTENTS

PART 3
LEAKS AND LOSSES

PART 4
INSIDE THE CASTLE

INTRODUCTION

Gentlemen don't read each other's mail.

—Henry L. Stimson
Secretary of State, 1929

Counterintelligence Then and Now

In August 1914, as President Woodrow Wilson publicly pledged to maintain US neutrality, the opening salvos of a world war erupted across Europe. German secret agents had already traveled to America to sabotage industrial targets, foment labor strikes at munitions plants, and promote pacifistic propaganda in the news media. Wholly one-third of the American population was foreign born or of foreign parentage—a ready-made army of fifth columnists, or so the German high command hoped. One audacious scheme called for German agents to operate a biological warfare laboratory secretly in the outskirts of Washington, DC. Its purpose was to produce anthrax delivery systems to infect American horses and mules heading to the battlefields of northern France. Other disinformation campaigns, sabotage plots, and cases of espionage, while less ambitious, were more successful.

Imperial Germany's secret operatives needed genuine US passports that could be easily altered to cross the Atlantic successfully and operate clandestinely in the United States.

Authentic-looking travel documentation was absolutely essential in escaping detection by the British security services and America's fledgling counterintelligence agencies. At the time, the United States and its military lacked an organized, cohesive counterintelligence program. The Federal Bureau of Investigation (FBI) didn't exist, and other federal agencies were ill-prepared to deal with the phenomenon of passport fraud tied to espionage. Moreover America had no federal statutes on the books to arrest and convict foreign spies operating in the country. Those would come later in the form of the Espionage Act of 1917.

By 1916, it was clear that the Kaiser's General Staff Political Section was actively engaged in numerous schemes to target unwary US citizens, both in the United States and Germany, to obtain US passports for its spies. To combat the new threat, Secretary of State Robert Lansing created the Secret Intelligence Bureau in order to investigate and identify individuals who were residing in the United States under false claims of US citizenship.

Joseph "Bill" Nye was appointed the first chief special agent of the Department of State, and his mission was to assist the secretary of state on all intelligence and security matters relating to the department. With a small staff of special agents and secretaries, Nye implemented changes that injected safeguards into the passport issuance program by requiring more extensive proof of US citizenship, including photographs. Secretary Lansing also authorized Agent Nye to wiretap the German ambassador's telephone line to provide daily transcripts. Two field offices were opened: one in Washington, DC, and the other in New York City, since the Secret Intelligence Bureau agents had to work closely with their US Secret Service and Postal Inspection Service counterparts monitoring the activities of German diplomats and suspected spies.

By the mid-1920s, the Secret Intelligence Bureau, now commonly called "the Force," was capitalizing on its investigative expertise in dealing with German passport fraud. It collaborated with the newly created FBI to identify and deport Russian NKVD agents who attempted to enter the United States illegally to engage in espionage. The US government was so worried about Bolshevik subversive activities that for many years American communists were denied passports. The US government feared that if American citizens traveled to Russia for revolutionary training and willingly turned over their valid passports to NKVD agents, those same passports would be used by Russian agents to enter the United States under the original owner's identity. Secret Intelligence Bureau agents also conducted background investigations for applicants seeking employment with the department and were responsible for the protection of official guests of the United States and distinguished visitors attending international conferences on American soil, a responsibility shared with the US Secret Service.

In 1929, Secretary of State Henry L. Stimson uttered his now famous statement: "Gentlemen don't read each other's mail." With that, he disbanded the cryptanalytic branch, the code breaking unit of the State Department. In 1919, at the conclusion of World War I, the League of Nations had been created to prevent future wars through collective security, disarmament, and settling international disputes by arbitration—a gentlemen's club of good old boys and square shooters, or so it thought. However, the League did not foresee the likes of Hitler and Mussolini, who refused to play by the rules despite the fact they were members in good standing. The League closed its doors in failure in 1933 during the run-up to World War II when there were more than a couple of dubious gentlemen acting in bad faith on the world stage.

Perhaps Secretary Stimson simply could not deign to believe that gentlemen could be so unprincipled. In any event, the work of the department's cryptanalytic branch was assumed by the US Army's Signal Intelligence Service. While never part of the Secret Intelligence Bureau, the cryptanalytic branch's demise eliminated an important intelligence resource for the department.

Following the end of World War II, the Secret Intelligence Bureau was renamed the Office of Security (SY). A small number of its agents were assigned to manage the security operations of the larger European embassies while their domestic colleagues continued to investigate passport and visa fraud, protect visiting foreign dignitaries, and conduct pre-employment investigations.

Given espionage concerns, the Office of Security created a counterintelligence arm to combat foreign spies, especially those of the NKVD. Department officials, including Alger Hiss, Noel Field, Laurence Duggan, and Michael Straight, were investigated in the mid to late 1940s on suspicion of spying for the Soviet Union. From 1960 to 1975, SY expanded its presence through security officers assigned to our embassies and assumed the dignitary protection responsibilities for foreign heads of state visiting the United States, all the while vigorously conducting counterintelligence investigations. In the late eighties and early nineties, three State Department officials were investigated for spying for a foreign power. Steven Lalas was convicted of spying for Greece, and Geneva Jones was convicted of passing classified information to an African journalist. The third, Felix Bloch, the deputy chief of mission at the US embassy in Vienna, escaped prosecution after being warned by the Russian KGB (Komitet Gosudarstvennoy Bezopasnosti—Committee for State Security)* via a coded telephone conversation to cease his clandestine activities. Bloch's protector was none other than the notorious FBI traitor Robert Hanssen, who alerted the SVR (Sluzhba Vneshney Razvedki—the Russian Foreign Intelligence Service) to the intelligence community's interest in Bloch.

The department's Office of Security changed its name in 1985 to the Bureau of Diplomatic Security. The special agents of the bureau were properly part of the Diplomatic Security Service, a subset of professionals in the bureau, but the names were often used interchangeably. The letters DS or Diplomatic Security were commonly used as shorthand for anything or anyone associated with either organization.

DS now has over eighteen hundred special agents and many more civil service employees and contractors who are responsible for the physical, operational, and personal protection of department employees assigned to the department's 285 diplomatic facilities overseas, including our diplomatic facilities in war-torn Baghdad and Kabul, as well as its domestic offices and operations throughout the US, including passport offices, Foreign Missions offices, and its own twenty-five field offices.

Today the DS Counterintelligence Division (DS/CI) conducts a robust counterintelligence program designed to deter, detect, and neutralize the efforts of foreign intelligence services targeting

*During the time period covered by this book, the Russian intelligence service had two names, KGB (1954-1991) and SVR (1991-present). For consistency, I use the term "SVR" throughout the remaining text.

Department of State personnel, facilities, and diplomatic missions worldwide. It conducts aggressive counterintelligence inquiries and counterespionage investigations with other US government agencies. All counterespionage investigations are conducted in close coordination with the FBI in accordance with its statutory mandate to prosecute instances or allegations of suspected espionage. The division also provides counterintelligence and security awareness briefing sessions for US government personnel traveling overseas, including Cabinet level officials and their staffs on official visits to foreign countries. Most recently, the division has provided support to the US embassy in Baghdad in a highly successful effort to identify attempts to infiltrate the US embassy with workers affiliated with terrorist groups and foreign intelligence agencies.

In addition, the division relies on a cadre of security engineers to mitigate attempts by foreign intelligence services to technically penetrate Department of State office buildings and certain residences. These efforts range from detecting a simple listening device in a wall to countering the most sophisticated electronic eavesdropping devices and systems. To this end, audio countermeasures inspections are routinely conducted by the engineers in controlled access areas and other sensitive working spaces within department facilities worldwide.

One DS mission that has not changed over the past ninety or so years is the protection of classified foreign affairs information from unauthorized disclosures by its own employees.

Unlike espionage, leaks to media organizations are fairly common events and are most often used as vehicles for promoting opposing policy views in and outside the department. For whatever motives and rationales, the employees disclosing such information have violated both their oaths of office and nondisclosure agreements. These unauthorized disclosures are rarely treated as criminal offenses but rather as administrative inquiries involving a breach of regulations subject to disciplinary action

Make no mistake, the State Department and its employees working in the US and abroad continue to remain a coveted target for many foreign intelligence services. The end of the Cold War has not changed this dynamic. As long as other countries attempt to secure advantage by discovering and stymieing America's sensitive foreign relations, there will be an ever-present risk to our national security. While the Information Age with its sophisticated technology has opened up new methods of acquiring secrets, the human spy is still the best source of a nation's plans and intentions. The human agent provides critical perspective, context, and sense to things.

The twelve Russian "sleeper" spies deported back to Russia in the summer of 2010 serve only to remind Americans of the continuing intelligence threat in the United States. What is not well known is the number of State Department employees who had "casual" contact with those twelve "sleepers." And there's no shortage of these characters knocking on the State Department's door. Regrettably, we've opened it too often and let them inside.

Bona Fides with a Little Braggadocio

On October 7, 1974, as I took my oath of allegiance and swore to support and defend the Constitution of the United States against all enemies foreign and domestic, I never expected to investigate unauthorized disclosures of classified information. As a newly minted, twenty-one- year-old special agent with the State Department's Office of Security, I envisioned protecting foreign dignitaries, conducting criminal investigations, and serving as a security officer at one of many diplomatic posts overseas.

After an initial ten-month orientation tour in the Washington Field Office, I spent the next six years as a security officer in our diplomatic facilities in Beijing, Geneva, and Tokyo. The assignments offered unique experiences. For example, while serving in the People's Republic of China, I was the first US government official to debrief one of the twenty-two US servicemen who defected to North Korea after our first post-WWII conflict in Asia. The former serviceman had settled in China, worked in a small factory, and married a Chinese citizen. He'd come to the US mission to obtain a passport to visit his mother in the United States.

In Switzerland, I oversaw the investigation into the theft of the US Marine Corps Ball funds stolen from a locked safe inside the US Mission's Marines' very own office. In Japan, I assisted my CIA colleagues in clandestinely ex-filtrating an SVR clandestine intelligence officer operating under Russian journalist cover back to the United States before the Soviets realized he had defected. All of these experiences, as well as routine security duties, helped shape my professional life.

After I returned to the United States in 1980, I was assigned to the protective security details for secretaries of state Edmund Muskie and Alexander Haig and began a non-eventful eighteen-month tour as a glorified bodyguard for two totally different and interesting men. I wouldn't suggest the assignment was boring, but I could now count the number of angels dancing on the head of that pin with my eyes closed, which they were much of the time. But my routine professional life was about to change.

From 1982 to 1986, I was assigned to the Special Investigations Branch (SIB), where I participated in numerous investigations involving leaks of information, losses of classified materials, and suspected instances of espionage. By 1985, I discovered the overlooked or otherwise hidden fifty-year history of how classified State Department documents had been disclosed to the media, purportedly lost inside foreign embassies, planes, trains, and hotels or compromised by foreign intelligence services. In some instances, secrets were compromised by design; in others, by accident. But all cases shared a common denominator: the culpable State Department officer always attempted to conceal his or her guilt with a web of lies. The incidences of convenient amnesia and prevarication in the department were especially high when employees were confronted with their sins. The long-forgotten names of those State Department employees implicated in these cases were detailed in newspaper clippings buried in the official investigative files. The files also revealed that State Department secrets were being lost and betrayed with little, if any, negative repercussions for the offending officers.

During my tour in SIB, I witnessed firsthand how aggressively the US media pursued department staffers and seniors alike in search of a sexy foreign affairs story, an exclusive sprinkled with heretofore secret information. I saw how articles published by the *Wall Street Journal* had a negative impact on our foreign relations with a particular South American country. I led an investigation into why an article from the May 1983 edition of the *Atlantic* contained sentences lifted verbatim from secret State Department cables, which earned one of our embassies a verbal rebuke from a country's ministry of foreign affairs. I attempted to determine which government official had slipped columnist Robert Novak a sensitive department document, which he used as a basis for his 1984 "Evans and Novak" article, affectionately dubbed the "Dear Misha" letter. (Novak later gained notoriety by using sensitive information leaked by Deputy Secretary of State Richard Armitage for his July 2003 article outing Valerie Plame as a CIA employee.)

Over the course of my tour as a regional security officer in Port-au-Prince, Haiti, from 1986 to 1987, I investigated the murder of Paul Alexander, an American doctor working in Haiti, the stabbing of a US embassy political officer's spouse inside the consular section's parking lot, the rape of a young Peace Corps volunteer near Jacmel, the wounding of a Peace Corps volunteer in the leg, the stabbing death of one of our residential guards, and three specific death threats made against embassy officers by local Haitians. These incidents were in addition to a heavy workload of passport and visa fraud violations, personnel security investigations, and the ever-present threat of civil disorder with consequences for the safety of the embassy and its staff. I even supervised a protective detail of three DS agents for Ambassador McKinley for 120 days after he received a death threat from the "Haitian Liberation Organization"—a fun and exciting assignment!

As a result of my tour in Haiti, background in overseas training, and fluency in French, I returned to Port-au-Prince in February 1997 to help supervise US security agents contracted to protect Haitian president Jean-Bertrand Aristide and train Haitian security officers in assuming their future role as protectors of their nation's leaders—a department ghost of Christmas future in Baghdad, Monrovia, Kabul, and elsewhere.

In 1990, I returned to SIB as chief and supervised approximately fifty unauthorized disclosure cases and personally interviewed scores of department officers who had leaked classified department information to the press or managed to lose custody of classified documents. I worked closely with the FBI to identify employees who had inadvertently or willfully provided classified information to a host of unauthorized recipients.

From 1992 to 1995, I served as a security officer at the American embassy in Paris and had the opportunity to establish the bone fides of a clandestine SVR officer, talk to a former Russian naval officer seeking US protection from the French intelligence services, identify two US-citizen Soviet penetration agents who were previously assigned to the embassy, help translate for the French police in its investigation of a US citizen who was the victim of a sexual assault, and assist the United States Secret Service's protection for President Clinton on his visit to France to celebrate the fiftieth anniversary of the end of World War II.

In late 1996, I was offered the position of deputy director of the Division of Counterintelligence (DS/CI) with the department's Bureau of Diplomatic Security. Highlights of my seven-year tenure included being intimately involved in the discovery of a Russian-placed listening device inside the State Department in 1999 and assisting the FBI in its investigation of Robert Philip Hanssen before his arrest in 2001. The division worked closely with colleagues in the CIA, DOD, FBI, and NSA to identify US government employees providing secret information to foreign intelligence services. In January 2002, as I prepared for my impending retirement slated for later that year, a personnel decision delayed the arrival of the new DS/CI director until late 2002. As a result, I gladly agreed to serve as the acting director for the interim nine months.

As September approached, I reminisced about the many intriguing criminal and security cases that humbled and baffled me over the previous twenty-eight years. I found it disappointing that DS's fascinating history of successes and failures to safeguard government secrets remained largely unheralded and unknown to the public. Adding to my feelings were the numerous books and articles authored by retired government officials lauding their personal or agency's contributions to historical events while largely overlooking or minimizing DS's accomplishments. The seed was sown to write this book.

My retirement from the State Department was shortly followed by the Valerie Plame/"Scooter" Libby leak saga. Given the public debate, I felt qualified to offer my personal opinions on the subject and wrote an op-ed piece entitled "Full Disclosure on Leaks" that was printed in the October 22, 2003 edition of the *New York Times*. Fortunately my friends were generous in their reviews of the piece despite the fact I had openly moved to the enemy's camp to make some points.

Less than a year after the op-ed article, the Justice Department announced that Donald W. Keyser, the State Department's principal deputy assistant secretary of state for East Asian and Pacific affairs, had been detained by FBI special agents in the company of two Taiwanese clandestine intelligence officers. Coincidentally Keyser and I had been professional colleagues in the United States Liaison Office in Beijing from 1976 to 1977 and the US embassy in Tokyo from 1979 to 1980. Professional contact, though sparse, continued over the next twenty-five years. Keyser would soon face serious repercussions as a result of his relationships with these foreign intelligence agents. Then in 2004, the Bureau of Diplomatic Security brought me back two days a week as a consultant with the Division of Counterintelligence, where I reunited with my DS* and FBI colleagues. I would later play a pivotal role in a multiyear counterespionage investigation into a Cuban agent working for the State Department, arguably Fidel Castro's most damaging US citizen spy.

My book doesn't purport to be a comprehensive compilation of all State Department unauthorized disclosures or espionage cases. It's obviously written from my experiences of the past thirty-five years working for the department. Naturally some of my own warts and bias have crept into the writing, but I've done my best to portray the incidents as accurately as possible.

Simply stated, the book is one insider's account of State Department leaks, spies, and lies, the bureaucratic machinations that went along with them, and how they have adversely affected our national security. I hope you enjoy the read.

---

*The title for the security and law enforcement component of the State Department in 1917—the Security Intelligence Bureau—was changed in 1946 to the Office of Security. In 1985, by an act of Congress, the Bureau of Diplomatic Security (and within it the Diplomatic Security Service) was established as the successor to the Office of Security. For consistency, I use the term "DS" throughout the remaining text.

PART ONE

A Decidedly Cuban Connection

Yes, with a capital "Y," was the answer given in English when asked in 2006 if Cuba would continue to send its spies to the United States.

—Ricardo Alarcón
president of Cuba's National Assembly

If true, I can't help but admire their [Kendall and Gwendolyn Myers] disinterested and courageous conduct on behalf of Cuba.

—Fidel Castro
former president of the Republic of Cuba,
June 6, 2009

CHAPTER ONE

He was arguably Fidel Castro's most valuable spy within the State Department, operating undetected and with impunity for decades before we discovered him. We had been hunting him for years. Now he was about to escape.

The suspect, one Kendall Myers, had become suspicious and decided to retire from the department. Fearful that he was still being monitored by federal investigators in his retirement, Kendall and Gwendolyn, his wife and accomplice, completely divorced themselves from their clandestine life and devoted themselves to the pleasures of learning to sail their Swedish-made thirty-eight-foot Malmo sailboat complete with mahogany-lined living and sleeping quarters. The investigation by the FBI and DS had ground to a halt. By the early spring of 2009, after almost eighteen months of intensive, expensive, and exhaustive surveillance and with no obvious indications of espionage activities, the FBI decided there was nothing left to do but take a high-risk gamble.

After extensive consultation with the US Intelligence Community (IC), the FBI designed a bold, ingenious ploy: Kendall would be approached by an undercover FBI asset posing as a Cuban Foreign Intelligence Service (CuIS) agent. The meet would take place outside the Washington, DC, campus of the Johns Hopkins School of Advanced International Studies (SAIS) where he lectured.

On April 15, after much FBI preparation, IC trepidation, Justice Department hesitation, and DS exultation, the FBI undercover asset, codenamed "EK," approached Kendall on his birthday as he prepared to teach a SAIS class. It was a quiet, drizzly evening on the urban campus. Kendall, a man in his early seventies who stood six feet six inches tall, bespectacled, with a receding white hairline and a moustache that draped over a constant smile, looked every bit the professor he was. After introducing himself to his target, EK offered Kendall a Cuban Cohiba cigar and said that a Cuban agent known to Kendall had "sent me to contact you" and "to get some information" because of the "change that is taking place in Cuba and the new [Obama] administration."

EK suggested they meet in an hour at the Doubletree Hotel, located a few blocks away, to continue their conversation. To the collective delight of those of us listening in, Kendall not only agreed but also soon called Gwendolyn and excitedly told her that she had to drop everything and immediately come to the hotel for an important meeting. When she asked what was so important, he told her that she would soon find out.

An hour later, over a couple of beers in the hotel lounge, Kendall and EK casually talked about the new administration's potential approach to Cuba and who might be the future South American policymakers. Among other things, Kendall revealed espionage tradecraft and methods.

Kendall said, "We have nicknames. We never use real names, even the double names." In response to EK's questions about receiving messages in Morse code, he replied, "Yes, that's right."

Kendall said the last time that he and Gwendolyn visited Cuba was ten years before and added, "We've been meeting in third countries" (with CuIS agents) and that the last country was Mexico, "like three years ago, four years ago."

When Gwendolyn spoke, she confirmed that she and Kendall still had the same shortwave Sony radio to receive messages and said, "You gave us the money to buy [the radio] a hundred years ago, and it still works beautifully . . . although I haven't listened to it in a while."

Those of us listening grew nervous at the following bits of ominous conversation. Kendall stated that "the problem with this country, there's just too many North Americans," and that "it would be nice" to travel to Cuba "in the near future" on their sailboat. He added that they "already have the charts . . . , the maps, and a cruising guide [GPS]." Kendall later said that it was his and Gwendolyn's "idea to sail home."

So home was Havana, not Washington, DC. Were they preparing for an expedited departure from the US? How soon? Along with the other investigators and prosecutors, I knew that all of our efforts depended on acting quickly, or Kendall and Gwendolyn Myers would slip away. We had to tie them convincingly to specific violations of federal espionage laws, including the unauthorized transmission of classified materials to a foreign agent.

And if we could not do it fast, the American couple who had compromised the US government's diplomatic initiatives with Cuba for the last two decades, not to mention hundreds of millions of dollars' worth of technical operations—the couple who were personally given medals for their work by Castro himself following a midnight dinner in Havana lasting over five hours—would indeed be sailing home.

★★★

It was 1999. The National Security Agency (NSA) code breakers pressed their headphones to their ears as they strained to isolate every sound transmitted from a radio site in Santiago, Cuba. The CuIS was attempting to relay a coded message to a prized penetration agent in Washington, DC. The female announcer, nicknamed "Havana Anna," began the broadcast by calling out *Atencion! Atencion!*, followed by a series of 150 five-number groups the IC had dubbed the "Spanish Numbers." The high-frequency shortwave transmissions were painstakingly recorded on state-of-the-art reel-to-reel tape recorders for analysis and, hopefully, deciphering.

Since 1991, the NSA had intercepted encrypted shortwave radio messages for agents "202" and "123," including one on November 26, 1996, from the radio announcer with instructions to study the area of agent 123's "new residence." Previous NSA interceptions of similar Cuban radio transmissions had led to the FBI's 2001 arrest and conviction of Defense Intelligence Agency (DIA) Cuban analyst Ana Montes for spying for the Castro government. When the "Spanish Numbers" transmissions continued after her arrest in 2001, the IC knew there was at least one more high-value Cuban penetration agent operating in the nation's capital.

By the spring of 2007, FBI special agents assigned to the Cuba squad of the Washington Field Office (called WFO for short, pronounced Woof-O) were quietly voicing their frustration over the pace of the investigation. For years, the IC had supplied the FBI with fragmentary intelligence concerning suspected Cuban espionage. As tantalizing as the "Spanish Numbers" were, there simply was not enough identifying data to develop investigative leads, much less identify the penetration agent. The basic facts were extremely sparse—the adversary was Cuba, the target was probably Washington, DC, and the suspect was likely someone working inside one of the US government's foreign affairs or intelligence agencies. It was not much to go on.

However, the IC knew that the CuIS's preferred method of communicating with its penetration agents in the United States was via shortwave radio messages sent in Morse code or relayed by a voice reading a series of numbers. Beyond that sketchy piece of information, the federal investigators could not pinpoint the location of the receiving radio, much less the employer for whom "202" and "123" were working. To those of us working the case, it was a nightmare scenario.

Separately CIA analysts had been assessing defector and field information that strongly suggested the CuIS had managed to place a long-term and presumably high-value penetration agent in one of the US government's foreign affairs or intelligence agencies. The CIA, NSA, and FBI Cuban specialists eventually agreed that the investigation should focus on the official biographies and personal histories of all foreign affairs personnel working in metropolitan Washington, DC. Unfortunately that number could easily exceed one hundred thousand individuals.

The IC had to consider the reality that the Cuban agent could be employed by any of the federal alphabet agencies such as the CIA, DIA, NSA, and NSC. Of course, the State Department would also be high on the list. But perhaps the suspected penetration agent worked for the Department of Commerce, Treasury, or Homeland Security, whose foreign affairs responsibilities might involve access to classified information about the Caribbean island nation.

While the IC compiled its enormous list of potential suspects, the FBI's investigation was floundering. To complicate matters, NSA internal regulations prevented the FBI from sharing certain information gleaned from the "Spanish Numbers" transmissions with other federal investigators, including those assigned to the State Department's Bureau of Diplomatic Security, Office of Counterintelligence (DS/CI).

DS special agents, as well as department employees, do not undergo polygraph examinations as a condition of employment, and as a result, DS/CI personnel were not authorized access to the raw intercepted data nor the IC's analysis of the "Spanish Numbers." The FBI had attempted a preliminary investigation of department employees as potential suspects; however, without DS/CI assistance and expertise, their results were highly limited.

Absent DS guidance, if left on their own to conduct further investigations of department employees, the FBI agents would be like a Humvee charging about in the proverbial china shop. And I say this with the greatest admiration and respect for my FBI colleagues.

The principal State Department building, affectionately known as "Main State," "Mother State," or "Foggy Bottom," is situated in Washington, DC, on a site of land bordered by C Street on the south, D Street on the north, Twenty-First Street on the east, and Twenty-Third Street on the west. Three of the four streets are open to normal vehicular traffic of which two have metered parking. It was officially christened by law in 2000 as the Harry S. Truman building (HST). The primary or "diplomatic" entrance to the facility for employees and visitors is located at 2201 C Street. In 1957, Secretary of State Dulles helped lay the first cornerstone, and the building was completed in 1961. Housing over eight thousand employees in 1.5 million square feet of working space and a large underground parking area, the eight-story-tall building is the third largest federal building in the Washington metropolitan area. The building hosts some of the government's most sensitive information and conversations. A foreign penetration agent with access to the building's secrets would be a catastrophe for the department, the White House, and the IC.

The FBI case languished for five years, constrained by the IC's internal regulations that restricted the dissemination of NSA material to certain elements of the IC. This administrative logjam was creatively overcome in 2007 by Special Agent Kate Alleman, the FBI's liaison officer assigned to DS/CI. SA Alleman was a specialist in counterespionage work, admired by DS/CI special agents and analysts alike. She was also greatly respected for her tireless efforts as a mediator resolving counterintelligence turf disputes among the NSA, CIA, FBI, DS, and others. Privy to all the NSA and CIA Cuba information, she was aware that DS/CI was being fed limited information in order to protect sensitive sources and methods. She was intensely intelligent, attractive, and athletic—she bicycled to work every day, twenty-six miles round trip—and she had an infectious laugh. There was no one in the IC community I trusted more than Kate.

I had retired from the department in 2002. In 2003, I was contacted by the director of the Office of Investigations and Counterintelligence (DS/ICI/CI) and hired as a contractor to work again, three days a week, for DS/CI, where I had served as the deputy director during the six years prior to my retirement. I was appointed as an investigative specialist and provided with a baby-blue, photo-affixed set of credentials, inside a shiny black leather case that was embossed with the gold seal of the Department of State and stated, "This investigative specialist is commended as worthy of trust and confidence. The bearer is authorized to conduct official record reviews and inquiries for this department as directed by the authority of the Bureau of Diplomatic Security, United States Department of State."

This authorization was slightly different from the one in my former special agent credentials, which stated, "This Special Agent is worthy of trust and confidence. The bearer is authorized to carry firearms, make arrests, conduct official investigations for this department, and to protect the Secretary of State, foreign dignitaries, and other persons under the authority of the United States Code."

My new responsibilities allowed me to avoid any involvement in budget, administrative, resource, management, or policy deliberations, which comprised more than 50 percent of my work when I was the office's deputy director. My sole job now was to assist the DS/CI agents and concentrate on the office's counterintelligence and counterespionage investigations. I sat in on interviews, conducted interviews, briefed the IC on the status of inquiries, taught State-specific espionage cases to the IC, searched for old records, provided security briefings to federal employees traveling to sensitive countries overseas, and even edited the final reports of investigations—nothing was too small for me.

At this point in the investigation, I did not know any specifics, only that the FBI was gaining no traction in the "202" case. SA Bill Stowell, DS/CI's liaison officer to the FBI, had provided me some background information in order to help him research old files, but it was nothing of real significance. SA Stowell was a talented and aggressive new addition to the office, and we had worked on several counterintelligence issues. I liked his investigative style, but in this case, he was hamstrung by the IC rules.

One day Kate called Bill and me into her small office in DS/CI, closed the door, and asked us to have a seat. She got right to the point.

"I have a case that you need to be aware of," she said, "but some IC rules prohibit you from seeing specific information."

Bill and I remained quiet, stared at her, and waited for her to continue.

"The FBI is going nowhere fast on a very old case because DS/CI has not been properly brought into the case. You need to look at some code word data that only the two of you can properly analyze and determine if it implicates a department employee," Kate said. "If you agree, I want to bring you over to headquarters where I want you both to sit down, read some papers, and talk with the FBI Cuban analysts. OK?"

"Affirmative," we replied.

Despite our immediate consent, there were significant problems to contend with. At this stage, I was a mere consultant instead of a direct-hire employee (strike one), one who had never submitted to a polygraph exam (strike two), and one who did not plan to take the exam this late in life (strike three). But those things did not dissuade SA Alleman, who had worked with me when I was the deputy chief of DS/CI. At the time, her superb investigative contributions resulted in the arrest and 1998 conviction of East German clandestine intelligence agents James Michael Clark, Kurt Allen Stand, and Theresa Marie Squillacote, American citizens all. Two department Foreign Service Officers (FSOs) were implicated in this case for having provided classified information to Michael Clark but were not brought to trial because the Department of Justice determined that there would be no "jury appeal" in their prosecution. As a direct result of SA Alleman's management of the investigation, I interviewed Michael

Clark and both department employees following Clark's conviction, and I have a very different opinion than that of DOJ.

Off-and-on over the past fifteen years, Kate and I had collaborated in examining hundreds of FBI counterintelligence leads that hinted at a State Department angle. Now after thirty-plus years with the department, I knew where pertinent files and skeletons were kept, had a good understanding of the unique culture of the Foreign Service, and knew who to interview to get answers. Personal relationships and trust still remained critical ties that bound counterintelligence officers. Kate was frustrated with the current situation and ready to move forward.

In the early morning of May 3, 2007, Bill and I were ushered into a windowless office deep in the innards of the J. Edgar Hoover (JEH) building. Completed in 1975 at a cost of $126 million, this eleven-story concrete edifice occupies two city blocks on Pennsylvania Avenue in downtown Washington, DC. The General Services Administration describes it as "dated" and "overcrowded," and indeed it looks more like a Maginot Line bunker than a government building. It is scheduled to be torn down in the near future.

Minutes before we entered the office, we underwent one final scrutiny by a startled FBI supervisor who, at the eleventh hour, still had doubts about the propriety of having a non-cleared department special agent and investigative specialist briefed on code word "top secret" information developed via sensitive technical means. Fortunately the FBI supervisor and I had worked together on several counterintelligence inquiries in the recent past. When he asked Kate if the upcoming meeting was "approved," Kate simply smiled. The FBI supervisor rolled his eyes, looked up at the ceiling, and then at Kate, before glancing back at the papers on his desk. This was one of those "silence gives consent" moments. His trust in Kate and me provided access to the "black" world of ultra-sensitive sources and methods.

Once inside the FBI's sanctum, FBI analysts "Rachel,"* "Donna,"* and "Monk"* smiled and gestured toward empty chairs arranged in a semicircle. We quickly sat and began examining the collected data that had previously been denied us.

Donna took the lead and explained why she had concluded the suspected Cuban penetration agent was probably a State Department officer. She had prepared a short briefing paper for the meeting and handed Bill and me two copies of her notes for a quick review. As we studied the notes, I recognized a unique department acronym on the third page. I immediately blurted out what an incredible clue I thought it was, and after reading further, I loudly announced my interpretations to the group.

Kate, sitting to my left and accustomed to my conference room antics, started to laugh and commented that I had a particularly noisy mind. More reserved, Bill carefully read his copy. At least one of us had to maintain professional decorum, and I was never good at such things.

I finished the last page with many thoughts racing through my head. "If this information is correct," I exclaimed, "and agent '202' is a State Department official, he or she works exclusively or in combination with the department's Foreign Service Institute (FSI), Bureau of Intelligence and Research (INR), or the Cuban desk." The analysts did not say a word, so I pressed on. "Do you have some more clues to share with me?"

---

*In several places, fictional names are used in response to FBI or State Department requirements that the actual names of the persons be redacted.

"Here's our penetration agent matrix," Donna offered, "with nine personal characteristics we have developed from information decrypted from the 'Spanish numbers.'"

I reviewed the document, and we talked for over an hour, slowly analyzing each of the nine characteristics. After some debate, I agreed that seven were probably germane if the Cuban penetration agent was a department employee and added two characteristics of my own based on my interpretation of the data.

As we concluded the meeting, I said, "If this information is correct, we'll identify this guy." It was a gutsy and rather foolish claim.

The team notified us that our Cuban penetration agent had been assigned the codename "Vision Quest" by the FBI. Immediately following our meeting, I was driven to the FBI's WFO, an eight-story postmodern building in Judiciary Square. I was introduced to special agent "Matt," who was responsible for the overall management of the case.

"Welcome to the 'Vision Quest' investigation," Matt said as he shook my hand. He asked for my government classified Secure Internet Protocol Router (SIPR net) e-mail address. "I'll start forwarding you additional information."

My office was located on the nineteenth floor of a modern, steel and glass, twenty-four-story building in Rosslyn, Virginia. Access to my ten-by-eight cubicle was controlled by a reinforced entry door that was activated by a Department of State–issued ID card equipped with an encrypted chip. All visitors required escorts. Cubicle 19106, defined by three six-foot-tall beige panels, was crammed with a black chair and horseshoe desk that supported one push-button telephone and two monitors—one for classified (SIPR net) traffic, the other for unclassified information. The carpet was gray with a trace of green and the occasional Lavazza coffee stain. I plopped into my chair, whose right arm had been "repaired" with black electrical tape, and turned on my unclassified computer. After a cursory examination of certain DS records, I was suddenly not so confident in my parting, boastful prediction to my new FBI colleagues.

The department maintained voluminous files on its current and former employees, but they were stored separately in medical, security, human resources, bureau, and finance offices located throughout the HST, and they were guarded jealously against external review for a variety of administrative, Privacy Act, and internal reasons. If we suddenly started to review hundreds of name-specific files, we would draw unwanted attention to the investigation and effectively announce that a counter-espionage hunt was underway.

However, there was one significant database that could be researched without arousing suspicions or compromising the investigation's confidentiality. The department's Office of Human Resources (HR) annually prepares, in CD format, a list that includes the name and limited personal data of every department employee. Some of the data on this "Alpha list" could be compared against the "Vision Quest" matrix for purposes of elimination.

Great idea, but the immediate technical challenge was how to upload the "Alpha list" onto DS/CI's stand-alone computer system, format the HR data for manipulation, reduce the voluminous information to a spreadsheet, and install profile/matrix filters to the program. The "Alpha list" contained the names of over sixteen thousand individuals and hundreds of thousands of corresponding pieces of data, all of which needed to be electronically crunched for searching. I had zero computer skills besides a typing course forced on me by my beloved mother, Maria, when we lived in Rome, Italy, from1965–1966.

Who was going to convert the "Alpha list" to a user-friendly, hunt-for-the penetration agent computer program? I was now confronted by the same administrative "need-to-know" dictum that had restricted dissemination of the "Vision Quest" matrix for years. I made a tactical decision to consult with a DS/CI agent whose ten-by-eight cubicle was located about fifteen feet from mine.

DS special agent Karin Terry was a young but experienced new arrival in the office. She had previously worked for the FBI and was a well-respected officer known for her outstanding computer skills. A few days after my meeting at FBI headquarters, SA Terry and I walked into the DS/CI office's conference room, where I closed the door and began the conversation just as SA Alleman had done a few days before.

"Karin, I have been read in on a very sensitive case, which I am not allowed to discuss with individuals who have no need to know."

SA Terry looked at me in the same way that SA Stowell and I had reacted to SA Alleman five days earlier.

"But I need your computer skills to go forward with this case," I said. "I was wondering if you would be willing to help, even without knowing the specifics of the cases."

She didn't hesitate. "Of course."

"Well, then, I need you to search surreptitiously through a specific department database called the 'Alpha list' on the unclassified computer system, trying to identify nine personal characteristics."

"When do we start?"

"You can actually access the 'Alpha list' on your unclassified computer because of your clearances, and we can start whenever you're ready."

I followed her into her cubicle, where she patiently tried to explain how she would convert the "Alpha list" to an Excel spreadsheet. I was already lost. She indicated how electronic filters would be attached to the program that would mysteriously identify department personnel matching the nine "Vision Quest" profiles. I had no clue about what she was saying.

"Robert, this may take some time to run preliminary tests and a search program, but I'm confident I can get you the information you are looking for in a couple of work days." The last part I fully understood. I needed to be patient and wait for the results.

When I returned to work the next day, SA Terry leaned her head into my cubicle and beckoned me to follow her to the DS/CI conference room. Once inside, she closed the door.

"Just after you left the office for the day," she said, "I converted the personal information on the 'Alpha list' into an electronic data sheet that I created."

"How did you do that?" I knew there were hundreds of thousands of pieces of data.

"Never mind, it's not complicated. What is important is that the sheer volume of data being crunched caused my server to crash."

Oh, no, I thought. *Caught in the act.*

"The crash caused the information technology folks monitoring such things on the floors below ours to call me immediately and ask what the hell I was doing."

Well, this is bad, I moaned inwardly.

"That was great," she announced gleefully, "because I simply told them I was trying something new and experimental, and the IT specialists volunteered to help me create a special user-friendly program to get your results. I don't think I raised any suspicions because all the information being sorted was unclassified. I should have the information for you soon."

A few days later, she made good on her promise. On May 8, SA Terry poked her head into my cubicle and handed me a list containing the names of twenty-seven State Department employees. "I don't know why you are looking for this person, but if the profile is correct, there's a strong chance your suspect is among this group of names."

Maybe I should have shed my Luddite insecurities earlier in my career and gotten aboard the technology bandwagon. Now I had a list of twenty-seven department employees who had been electronically flagged by the two department-specific and seven FBI-specific characteristics for "Vision Quest." There was only one place in the department that would have the documentation to confirm and narrow down my findings—DS's very own Personnel Security and Suitability (PSS) division. It controlled the security files (referred to as SY Files) of every former and current department employee.

The SY Files were a virtual treasure trove of biographical information: background investigations, security clearance updates, promotions, transfers, overseas postings, commendations, foreign language proficiencies, and disciplinary actions. Access was highly restricted. Over my lengthy tenure, I had reviewed many hundreds of such files, and although I was authorized to see the files in my current capacity as an investigative specialist, I didn't want to draw undue attention. Carelessly requesting files would have been tantamount to announcing that DS/CI was on another quest to identify a run-of-the-mill miscreant or, worse, a spy and traitor. Either speculation would have had department tongues endlessly wagging. Foreign policy and security concerns came in a distant second to juicy office gossip at Mother State.

As luck would have it, Barbara Shields, a senior management officer in PSS, was a dear friend of over twenty-five years with whom I had worked in the 1980s while assigned to the Special Investigations Branch. I trusted her in the same way that SA Kate Alleman had trusted me. We scheduled a quiet sit-down that same day.

"Barbara, I can't give you details about my request," I said, "but here are the names of twenty-seven current department employees. I cannot tell you why I am interested in these good people, but you know what office I work in, and I need complete secrecy about working together on this search."

"Sure, Robert," Barbara said. "What do you need?"

"I need you to request in your name the twenty-seven SY Files to be sent to your office, disguising or hiding any DS/CI interest in these individuals, and then keep the files on this floor for review in one of your PSS unoccupied offices that has a door but no window."

"Sounds easy enough." She laughed. "I thought you might have had something difficult for me."

The following morning I received a phone message announcing that a number of SY Files awaited my review. A large cup of coffee in hand, I greeted a smiling Barbara, who escorted me to a closet-sized office to confront a stack of files over three feet high. I sat at the white table, grabbed the top SY File off the pile, and opened the yellowing outer folder. The papers were over a quarter of a century old. I would need a second cup of coffee and a few solitary walks around the office block to get through just two of the files by the end of the first day.

Each SY File contained upward of three to five hundred sheets of paper that documented the employee's biographic information, the results of the initial and follow-up background investigations, the security adjudicator's summary and decision, oaths of loyalty, and a host of other documents. I spent three to four hours on each file, carefully analyzing every sheet of paper for clues and verifying data regarding the department's and FBI's matrix points. The papers were never in chronological order, and there were always ten copies of everything.

Two files per day, one week later, with only half of the files reviewed, I was getting migraines and feeling dejected. I regretted being so cocky about identifying "202" back at FBI Central. My credibility with my counterintelligence colleagues might be taking a disastrous downturn, which would not bode well for my already dubious reputation or that of DS's within the IC.

A review of the first thirteen SY Files revealed absolutely no person with obvious Cuban connections, no links to INR or FSI, and certainly no one with a background or familiarity with Morse code or high-frequency radio transmissions. Growing worried, I thought that the IC analysts must have developed an erroneous profile. Had I missed something? Where could we go next?

Then, discouraged and exhausted, I flipped open the file for suspect number 14. It was quite thick; the stapled and paper-clipped documents, slightly stained, some discolored or creased at corners, were affixed to both sides of the folder by a metal clip, and I slowly began reading its contents late on the morning of June 7. The file contained information on Walter Kendall Myers Jr., and I soon discovered connections that were too significant to ignore.

I would later confirm what I quickly began to suspect—I had found the Cuban penetration agent.

CHAPTER TWO

Walter Kendall Myers Jr. was born in Washington, DC, on April 15, 1937. The eldest of five children, he preferred his middle name, Kendall, and dropped the "Jr." following his father's death. His mother was the granddaughter of telephone inventor Alexander Graham Bell, and his father was a respected cardiologist. Ironically one of his father's patients was a State Department official named Alger Hiss—Russia's third State Department spy in the 1940s.

Kendall's great-uncle Alphonso Taft co-founded the Skull and Bones Society at Yale, whose future members would include both Presidents Bush and Secretary of State John Kerry.

Living a life of privilege, Kendall left Washington, DC, to complete his high school education at Mercersburg Academy in Pennsylvania, which was established in 1893 and proudly boasted of fifty-four Olympians, seven Rhodes scholars, two Academy Award winners, three Medal of Honor recipients, and one Nobel laureate among its former students. As I sat at the table, flipping through Kendall's folder and skimming his biography, I wondered darkly if the venerable school was about to add "one American traitor" to the distinctions listed on its website.

According to his SY File, Kendall enrolled at Brown University in 1955 and studied European history but left before graduation to join the US Army in 1959. He was assigned to the Army Security Agency where he completed intensive communications training, which would have included a basic course in Morse code, and attended classes to study the Czech language.

He was assigned as a "Voice Interceptor" to a military base in then West Germany where he translated the intercepted radio transmissions of Czech military units.

Familiarity with coded shortwave radio transmissions was one of the FBI's "Vision Quest" characteristics for which I was searching. Other than department communications officers, I had never encountered a department officer who had mastered Morse code. I started breathing a little faster.

Following his honorable discharge as a specialist fifth class on March 17, 1962, Kendall returned to Brown, graduated with a BA in international affairs in June 1963, and commenced graduate studies at Johns Hopkins University's SAIS campus. A division of Johns Hopkins University since 1950, SAIS was and is devoted to the study of international relations and foreign policy. As far as the IC was concerned, it was an environment where foreign intelligence agents under diplomatic, business, journalistic, or academic cover were drawn to assess and dissect our future policymakers and leaders. The campus was also a hotbed of leftist intellectual activity. In short, it was an ideal place for spotting and recruiting future agents. Ana Belen Montes, the DIA's senior Cuban analyst who was arrested in 2001 and eventually convicted of spying for the CuIS, earned her master's degree in 1988 from SAIS. Montes was recruited by the CuIS with the help of fellow SAIS student, State Department Agency for

International Development (USAID) employee and Cuban penetration agent Marta Rita Velazquez. I had worked with the FBI in monitoring Velazquez for many years while she worked for USAID in South America. (Velazquez's DOJ indictment for espionage was unsealed in 2013. She lives in Sweden with her husband, an official with the Ministry of Foreign Affairs, and cannot be extradited to the United States under Swedish law.)

Was history repeating itself? This item was not one of the characteristics we were looking for, but I still wondered if Kendall's long-term studies at SAIS revealed a political orientation that could be of interest to a foreign intelligence service. College campuses of the 1960s were centers of opposition to the US government's policies, and while most students protested peacefully, others such as the Students for a Democratic Society and the Weathermen resorted to violence. Then there were students like Theresa Squillacote, James M. Clark, and Kurt Stand, who were seduced by Marxist ideology, clandestinely recruited by the East German Intelligence Service, and convicted traitors to their country. Had Kendall joined their ranks?

In 1964, Kendall married Maureen Leach, a medical student he had met at Brown. Maureen earned a PhD in microbiology from Georgetown University and became a recognized expert in the treatment of HIV/AIDS patients. The marriage ended in an uncontested divorce in 1977 with Maureen obtaining custody of their two children. Four years later, Kendall was over $3,000 in arrears in his $400 monthly child support, and a $600 lien was placed on his Johns Hopkins SAIS paycheck.

Even more humiliating for the professor, he was ordered by a judge to pay $30,010 for his children's college expenses. This information did not connect with the investigative matrix and was of marginal interest except to understand his lifestyle and, perhaps, his persona. Was the need for money a motivation for Kendall to become a spy? For the FBI and CIA penetration agents, the answer is yes; for department employees, e.g., Irvin Scarbeck, Steven Lalas, and Geneva Jones, the answer is almost always no.

Kendall earned his master's degree and started work on his PhD at SAIS, continuing his passion for international politics with a pronounced interest in all things British. He was an unabashed Anglophile and proud of it. I later learned that Tom Murray, one of Kendall's SAIS students in 1992, disclosed in an article that Myers expressed high regard for the notorious Kim Philby and two other Britons—Donald MacLean and Guy Burgess—who were clandestine SVR agents during the Cold War. According to Murray, Kendall suggested that they were called by their sense of duty to save Europe (rather than the British Empire) and that US and UK policies "turned them into spies." Murray went on to describe how the SAIS student newspaper staff ran a coffee shop in a school basement, named with tongue firmly in cheek as the Alger Hiss Café.

In early 1976, Kendall's colleagues at SAIS were intimately familiar with the State Department's Foreign Service Institute (FSI), where FSOs were trained in area studies and foreign languages in preparation for their overseas careers. Given Kendall's background in European History and teaching skills, his SAIS friends recommended that he seek employment at FSI. He did and was hired as a part-time instructor on a contract basis. That same year Kendall was introduced to Gwendolyn Steingraber, a divorcée with four children who worked in Washington, DC, on US senator James Abourezk's (D-South Dakota) staff. In 1977, Senator Abourezk's distaste for the Cuban economic embargo was well established on the Hill and, in support of this public position, he had taken several trips to Cuba. Gwendolyn's main responsibility was to coordinate with fellow staffers the Senate's vote to extend legislatively the constitutional time limits for states to ratify the Equal Rights Amendment. That failed. What succeeded spectacularly was Kendall and Gwendolyn's relationship. The attraction was mutual, immediate, and forever.

I would learn about Gwendolyn's background later because it was not covered in Kendall's SY File. The department does not investigate the background of spouses.

Gwendolyn was born in 1938 in Sioux City, Iowa. Her early life was characterized by a young marriage that lasted eighteen years and produced four children. Gwendolyn volunteered at her children's schools and was an avid tennis player, competing in city and state tournaments and working with several girls' tennis groups. Apparently bitten by the political bug, Gwendolyn was elected secretary and treasurer of the School of Hope in Aberdeen, South Dakota. In 1971, she was hired by the Brown County Democratic Party, and shortly after that, she volunteered to work as a legislative aide in the Aberdeen joint campaign office of James Abourezk, who was running for a US Senate seat, and George McGovern, the South Dakota senator running for the US presidency. Abourezk's campaign was successful; McGovern's was not.

Gwendolyn moved to Denver in 1974 and remarried; this time it lasted barely two years. Her life took a dramatic turn in 1976 when Senator Abourezk transferred her to his Washington, DC, office to work on special projects and as an assistant to the senator's press assistant. Within months of her arrival, she was introduced to Kendall by one of his roommates. They were soon traveling together on vacations in the United States and destinations overseas. Was Gwendolyn's political indoctrination now in the hands of Kendall Myers? Or was it vice versa?

In March 1979, Kendall resigned his teaching position with FSI to accompany Gwendolyn to South Dakota so she could care for her ailing mother. Political contacts helped Gwendolyn obtain a job there, and Kendall advised his closest friends that he would now have a perfect opportunity to finish his thesis: "When Business Rolled—A Re-Examination of Neville Chamberlain and British Policy in the 1930s." I suspect that in reality Kendall could not bear the possibility of being without the new love of his life following his divorce and years of solitude.

After a year's sojourn in South Dakota, Kendall and Gwendolyn returned to Washington, DC, along with Gwendolyn's mother and children. Kendall resumed his teaching duties at SAIS and local universities, and Gwendolyn was hired by Riggs National Bank, where she would work until 2007. The couple led a quiet life that raised no suspicions among family, friends, or colleagues. To outsiders, they looked like an idyllic Ozzie and Harriet married couple.

Gwendolyn played tennis, and they purchased a used sailboat that they moored on Chesapeake Bay. Gwendolyn would eventually take a home study sailing course offered by the Coast Guard Navigation School in Annapolis and would complete a two-day, onboard sailing class with "Womanship" in 1991.

I later learned that in September 1981, shortly following his return from South Dakota, Kendall applied for a position with the Central Intelligence Agency. This fact was not in Kendall's SY File. In 1982, the CIA declined to offer Kendall a job in large part because he failed the pre-employment background investigation, which includes a personal interview, personal history check, and polygraph examination. He quietly withdrew his application for employment. Kendall, now wise to the world of the IC's pre-employment checks, would never again take a lie detector test. He decided to return to the only agency within the IC that does not administer pre-employment or random polygraph examinations for its employees with code word "top secret" clearances.

Kendall submitted his application for readmission to FSI and on May 8, 1982, after subtle hints from the DS investigators—this was still the 1980s, and "living in sin" was not encouraged—he married Gwendolyn.

That August, Kendall was rehired by FSI as a contract instructor. Any candidate who applied for and was hired by FSI in the 1980s was issued a "secret" level security clearance by DS based on a personal interview and a National Agency Check—all candidates' names were vetted against federal databases to include the CIA. The CIA name check came back with no negative results. How could this be?

Did Kendall fail his CIA personal interview? Impossible, he is too glib and intelligent. Did he fail the CIA personal history check? No, in 1981 there was nothing "disqualifying" about his life that would have caused the CIA to reject his candidacy. Did Kendall fail his 1981 CIA polygraph exam? Kendall told a former student, Brian Lagrotteria, to be careful of trying to gain employment with the CIA because "they will give you a lie-detector test, and they will not accept you if you've done anything wrong." Did Kendall fail the CIA polygraph? Why else would the CIA not hire such a highly qualified candidate? If so, did the CIA alert the State Department to this fact when he applied for a job two years later? His hiring by the State Department is almost conclusive evidence that it did not. The CIA had also failed to notify the State Department that Steven

Lalas, a State Department telecommunications specialist who was convicted in 1993 of espionage against the United States, had failed his polygraph examination when he applied for employment with State after "washing out" from CIA training. Why wouldn't the CIA alert the State Department of Kendall's polygraph failure during the State Department's background investigations? Were there privacy concerns? Did incompetence play a role here?

Unfortunately we will never know.

As a State Department employee, Kendall's "secret" clearance did not authorize him access to classified information except in limited circumstances such as when guest speakers conducted classes at the "confidential" level where Kendall was present. Within a year, FSI offered Kendall a permanent position as the instructor and chairperson of Western European Studies, which upgraded his status to that of a fulltime department employee with a "top secret" clearance. According to State Department regulations, a "top secret" clearance could be issued only upon the successful completion of a non-derogatory full-field background investigation.

For the first time since I started to look at Kendall's official record, I noted a huge anomaly. After FSI forwarded a written application to the State Department's personnel office requesting that Kendall be hired as a fulltime employee, DS opened a full-field background investigation in 1983. The department's investigators were now required to verify his claimed service in the US Armed Forces, his college degrees, his time spent overseas, the circumstances of his divorce, his citizenship, and confirmation of his residences for the past fifteen years. Interviews of references, contacts, friends, neighbors, supervisors, and the like would also be conducted. However, unlike applicable requirements for employment by the FBI, CIA, and DIA, polygraph exams for the State Department were not part of the drill, either then or now.

It took almost ten months to complete the investigation and for the report to be submitted to the DS adjudicators, who would determine whether any uncovered information disqualified him on suitability or loyalty grounds and would preclude the issuance of "top secret" clearance.

Here is the surprising detail I discovered: in 1976, Kendall had been convicted for negligent homicide.

On November 26, 1975, while driving up Forty-Ninth Street in the Spring Valley neighborhood of Washington, DC, Kendall struck and killed Susan Slattery, a sixteen-year-old high school student, and broke the legs of her friend Peter Barlerin, who was crushed against a parked car. Another companion, Bryan Wehrli, suffered a shattered femur.

According to police records, Kendall was driving below the posted speed limit, passed a sobriety test, and answered all questions without any attempts at evasion or concealment. At his first court appearance, he pleaded not guilty and requested a jury trial. Kendall's defense was that at the time of the accident (9:30 p.m.), it was dark when he crossed the intersection of the 3900 block of Forty-Ninth Street, and he saw the teenagers only at the final moment. He stated the victims were carrying dark boxes and were not walking in a designated pedestrian crossing zone. The surviving teenagers explained that they were loading musical equipment in a car parked on the street. This accident appears to be one of those horrible, unforgiving acts of life.

On December 30, 1976, Kendall was convicted by a jury of negligent homicide. The following March, a judge sentenced Kendall to three years of unsupervised probation, with no fine or loss of license. Subsequent to the criminal trial, the Slattery family sued for $1 million in a civil action but ultimately settled out of court for $85,000. Kendall was not associated in any fashion with the State Department on that tragic Thanksgiving Eve.

If I were a State Department adjudicator in the 1980s, I would have reviewed the incident with some concern. I do not know of a single State Department employee who has ever been hired with a conviction of negligent homicide except, now, for Kendall.

Kendall's second encounter with law enforcement was far different. Kendall and Gwendolyn were arrested in September 1979 for possession of marijuana. The facts were outlined in the Supreme Court of South Dakota's decision dated September 17, 1980, ruling on the state's appeal of an order of the circuit court granting Kendall's motion to suppress certain evidence:

> *Acting pursuant to an informant's tip regarding drug-related activity, a search warrant was obtained authorizing a search of a residence at 328 North Grand in Pierre. At approximately 7:30 on the evening of September 17, 1979, several law enforcement officers, led by Hughes County Deputy Sheriff Charles Vollmer, undertook to serve the warrant. The officers positioned themselves at various places around the house.*
>
> *Deputy Sheriff Vollmer opened the screen door without first knocking, whereupon he and the other two officers entered the porch and approached the front door to the living quarters. Finding this door open and observing two occupants in the living room, one in possession of a marijuana pipe and a tray of what appeared to be marijuana, Deputy Vollmer entered the*

> *living room, announcing his purpose to execute the search warrant almost simultaneously with his entry, although he could not recall whether the announcement was made before or after he stepped in the room.*

Kendall's attorneys claimed that Deputy Vollmer's failure to knock at the open door and unannounced intrusion into the house was an unlawful "no knock" entrance that meant all evidence seized during the raid should have been suppressed during the first trial, including multiple bags of leafy substances, water pipes, and a book entitled *Marijuana Grower's Guide*. The leafy substances tested positive for marijuana.

Suddenly the public record involving this case disappeared. I am persuaded that the judge gave Kendall a "suspended imposition of sentence" so that the conviction was eventually expunged from the records. Senator Abourezk wrote a letter to the judge in support of Kendall's request for no jail time. He has always had well-connected friends in high places.

In 1984, almost one year to the day after the investigation was opened, William D'Urso, chief of the Office of Security's Applicant Review Branch, forwarded an unclassified memorandum to the State Department's Office of Recruitment, Examination and Employment (BEX), the department's office responsible for hiring employees.

Kendall was not eligible for a "top secret" clearance. It was simply not possible in 1983 for any US government agency to grant a "top secret" security clearance to an applicant convicted of negligent homicide and marijuana possession and with public financial difficulties in his or her background. DS's decision was communicated to FSI senior management, who shared its contents with Kendall. These so-called "eat dirt and die" letters never suggested the candidate had been denied clearance based on loyalty or suitability factors. They simply stated that a "better qualified applicant" (BQA) had been selected for the job. It was an artifice the department had used for years to avoid unpleasantness—a bureaucratic, face-saving device.

Kendall was devastated with the BQA letter and explained the situation to William, a friend at the Department of Commerce, asking if he knew anything that might reverse the department's decision. Over lunch in a small DC restaurant, William offered to contact a staffer in Senator Sam Nunn's (D-Georgia) office who could be persuaded to forward a letter, on official senatorial letterhead, to the State Department asking for a "status report" on Kendall's employment investigation. William knew the bureaucratic apprehension a letter from a US senator's office would create once received by any department's personnel office. Kendall readily agreed, and within short order, a letter was sent from Senator Nunn's office to the BEX office.

From personal experience, I know exactly what happened when the BEX office received the senator's letter—PANIC. This official correspondence was probably as important as any other factor as to why BEX caved and pressured DS to reconsider the denial of Kendall's security clearance.

Kendall also submitted his own six-page exoneration and explanation letter to BEX. This letter and the senator's written query to BEX were simply too much for the department's hiring specialists, who were also feeling heat from senior officials at FSI management who were asking why such a qualified candidate was not on a fast track to full-time employment. The BEX deputy director sent an unclassified letter to DS's Applicant Review Branch asking DS to review Kendall's letter before the next BEX meeting. While the deputy director may not have personally reviewed all the pertinent documents or even had a personal hand in the request for reversal, his office is responsible for Kendall overcoming a well-defined rejection by security specialists for his access to classified material.

Out of nowhere, DS reconsidered Kendall's request for a "top secret" clearance. A DS memo to BEX attached to the granting of Kendall's clearance, which was signed by the DS director, David Fields, strongly suggested that DS was very unhappy with the pressure put on it to grant Kendall's clearance (memo contents redacted by the State Department). If you believe that DS reigns supreme in such matters, you are mistaken. Senior career State Department employees, dubbed the "Black Dragons" by the rank and file DS special agents, govern the internal security regulations for the department. Kendall's "top secret" clearance was granted in 1985.

And then Kendall's SY File started to unpeel his dark secret. Nothing grabbed my attention more than the revelation that Kendall participated in an FSI-authorized trip to Cuba with two of his FSI colleagues in December 1978. Had I finally uncovered a Cuba connection? I slowly read every single word on the pages that followed.

For years, FSI sponsored a program whereby foreign diplomats assigned to embassies, consulates, and United Nation missions in the United States were invited by FSI, but not necessarily the department, to participate in unclassified lectures that allowed students and professors to engage in candid conversations about diplomatic topics. It was designed as a freewheeling, open forum. One invitee was a first secretary posted to the Cuban delegation at the United Nations in New York City who had lectured at FSI on at least two previous occasions. He was an unremarkable man, average build and height, with short-cropped black hair and a neatly trimmed moustache. In reality, the first secretary was known to the IC as a CuIS clandestine intelligence officer operating inside the United States under diplomatic cover. He would later be identified as co-conspirator "A" in the FBI's Criminal Complaint. Kendall's friends identified him as Carlos Ciano.

FSI had never informed DS that it was inviting Cuban "diplomats" to its campus to engage in "friendly" discussions with federal employees. I had to remind myself that President Jimmy Carter, in 1978, had relaxed the rules of travel that had previously restricted Cuban diplomats to twenty-five miles from the center of the United Nations without prior notification and department approval. This ill-advised White House action would have major counterintelligence repercussions.

At the conclusion of one such FSI academic exchange, Carlos Ciano invited any and all FSI professors and students to visit Cuba. Kendall and two senior FSI colleagues contacted their supervisors to obtain authorization to travel to Cuba, and the permissions were soon granted although Kendall and the other FSI professors had to pay for their travel costs. Kendall and his two coworkers coordinated their itinerary with Ciano, who soon after advised them that their arrival was expected in Cuba. Not surprisingly, the proposed travel of three FSI professors had not been relayed to DS for counterintelligence comment.

Upon arrival in December 1978, Kendall and his two FSI colleagues were greeted by low-level Cuban Foreign Affairs functionaries and taken to the decaying Riviera Hotel, a former American mob establishment in Havana.

A Cuban physician, "Mr. P.," acted as the group's guide during the trip. He was allegedly a Cuban ministry official and would later be posted to the Cuban UN delegation in New York City. Mr. P. was responsible for arranging meetings between the FSI professors and their Cuban counterparts, and he would later be identified as co-conspirator "B" in Justice's indictment. Arriving in Cuba just before the anniversary of the Cuban Revolution, the group met with members of the local, provincial, and national committees for defense of the revolution. In addition to official meetings, the group was allowed in its spare time to roam the streets and engage in spontaneous conversations with Cuban citizens. The trio took occasional trips outside Havana, including a visit to a sugar mill and cane plantation and a trip to the Bay of Pigs, where they visited the museum dedicated to the April 1961 defeat of the United States and its fifteen hundred so-called mercenary lackeys.

Entries in Kendall's December 1978 diary, which were quoted in the FBI's criminal complaint, were revealing:

> *Cuba is so exciting. I have become so bitter these past few months. Watching the [US] evening news is a radicalizing experience. The abuses of our system, the lack of decent medical system, the oil companies and their undisguised indifference to public needs, the complacency about the poor, the utter inability of those who are oppressed to recognize their own condition. . . . Have the Cubans given up their personal freedom to get material security? Nothing I have seen suggests that . . . I can see nothing of value that has been lost by the revolution. . . . [T]he revolution has released enormous potential and liberated the Cuban spirit.*

Kendall continued to gush:

> *Everything one hears about Fidel suggests that he is a brilliant and charismatic leader. He exudes the sense of seriousness and purposefulness that gives the Cuban socialist system its unique character. The revolution is moral without being moralistic. Fidel has lifted the Cuban people out of the degrading and oppressive conditions which characterized pre-revolutionary Cuba. He has helped the Cubans to save their own souls. He is certainly one of the great political leaders of our time.*

Kendall also wrote in his diary that as he stared at the beaches where the CIA-trained Cuban exiles stormed ashore, he "came to witness firsthand the evil face of American imperialism." Kendall's inspired conversion to the cult of Castro was slowly taking hold. Of course, none of this information was in his SY File.

One can only imagine what "co-conspirator B" and his CuIS cohorts would make of those diary entries if they examined his comments left behind in the hotel room while Kendall visited Havana's revolutionary museums. The FBI would later assert that Kendall's trip to Cuba provided the CuIS the opportunity to assess, develop, and eventually recruit Kendall Myers as a spy.

Kendall's final day in Havana, Christmas Eve, was marked by an unusual sequence of events. One of Kendall's two FSI companions had departed on an earlier flight to continue his vacation in Mexico, and when Kendall and his other colleague arrived at the Havana airport, they discovered that their connecting flight to Mexico City and Washington, DC, had been cancelled. Fortunately for them, an American attorney from Atlanta happened to be in the airport obtaining his flight clearance to fly home. He'd flown his private plane to Cuba to participate in the annual Havana regatta. He was quickly introduced to Myers and his FSI colleague by their Cuban hosts. The anonymous attorney was more than happy to have two American guests accompany him, and the two FSI instructors left Cuba via a private flight, a means normally prohibited to ordinary travelers, especially American ones. The identity of the Atlanta lawyer has never been determined.

I would discover two years after reading the Myers SY File that Carlos Ciano, while serving as a CuIS clandestine intelligence officer in New York City under diplomatic cover to the United Nations—the same Carlos Ciano, identified as co-conspirator "A" in the FBI criminal complaint, who invited Myers to visit Cuba—had traveled incognito to Pierre, South Dakota, in 1979 unknown to the FBI or State Department. Excerpts from Kendall's diary certainly influenced and emboldened Ciano to show up unannounced at Kendall's and Gwendolyn's front door. During five days of sightseeing, including witnessing an evening Native American Indian religious ritual, and political discussions, Ciano successfully recruited Kendall to become a traitor to his country. Following Ciano's recruitment pitch, Kendall accepted Ciano's offer to become a penetration agent but only on the condition that Gwendolyn agreed to the scheme.

Once Gwendolyn was briefed on Ciano's true mission, she readily agreed to be Kendall's clandestine partner. The CuIS now had two brand new recruits in its US stable. Kendall was by 1980 a fully committed penetration agent for the CuIS and needed access to government secrecy to achieve his goals. His attempt to join the CIA in 1981 and, following that rejection, his desperate and eventual successful 1985 campaign to overcome DS's initial denial for his "top-secret" clearance made complete sense.

I flipped through the old, flimsy, blue copy and white original papers in Kendall's file until I reached the point in his FSI tenure when he applied for a position as an analyst in the State Department's Bureau of Intelligence and Research (INR). Now my breathing began to slow. INR is the section of the department that sees the most sensitive interagency "top secret" code word information, including communications intercepts and overhead imagery. It also produces some of the best analysis in the intelligence community. My two additions to the "Vision Quest" FBI characteristics hinted that our suspect worked for either FSI, INR, or the department's Cuba desk. While the Cuba desk connection had been eliminated by my initial analysis, I was now looking at one of the twenty-seven finalists who was a male, married with children, had knowledge of Morse code and radio transmissions, actually worked for both the FSI and INR, and had a Cuban connection thanks to a Cuban diplomat of suspicious background.

Kendall was accepted as an analyst in INR on August 25, 1999, and was processed for a "top secret" Sensitive Compartmented Information (SCI) clearance shortly thereafter. Following a review of his SY File and with the concurrence of the CIA, the US government agency that controls the issuance of SCI or "code word" clearances and who had declined to hire him in 1981, Kendall was granted access to "top secret" SCI materials in 1999. He now had his admission ticket to browse America's most sensitive secrets.

I took a quick break and put the file on the desk, turned on the unclassified computer, and searched Kendall's name on Google. Jackpot. Kendall, by 2006 a publicly recognized specialist in British-American relations, became an unwitting public figure and lightning rod on November 28 of that year. At a conference organized by the

American Consortium on European Union Studies in Washington, DC, he spoke at the Center for Transatlantic Relations, a think tank promoting the European Union.

Talking about the "myth of the special relationship" between American presidents and British prime ministers, Kendall stated "there never really has been a special relationship [between the US and the UK] or at least not one we've noticed." During the course of the lecture on the nature of US–UK relations, Kendall said that foreign relations between Washington and London had been "altogether too one-sided for a very long time. The poodle factor did not begin with Tony Blair; it actually began, yes, with Winston Churchill." Kendall concluded that for all Britain's attempts to influence US policy in recent years, "we typically ignore them and take no notice—it's a sad business."

Kendall acknowledged at the end of his talk that he "perhaps ought not to say so much." His comments were prominently reported on November 30 in Britain's *Daily Telegraph* and *The Times*.

The ensuing internal State Department firestorm was all too predictable. Within days, Terry Davidson, the department spokesperson, stated, "The US–UK relationship is indeed a special one. The US and the UK work together, along with our allies in Europe and across the world, on every issue imaginable. The views expressed by Mr. Myers do not represent the views of the US government. He was speaking as an academic, not as a representative of the State Department."

Deputy spokesman Tom Casey later explained that Kendall was called on the carpet by his INR supervisor and given a dressing down. He added, "The comments [by Kendall], frankly, I think could be described as ill-informed, and I think, from our perspective, just plain wrong."

I later learned that as a result of Kendall's academic indiscretions, he was removed from his INR analytical specialty in monitoring English/Irish affairs and shifted to the department's more general European portfolio—one that would unfortunately give him great access to Cuban intelligence data, as both the Vatican and Spain, among other European nations, have interesting diplomatic relations with Castro. His INR-ordered punishment gave him even greater access to classified information of interest to the CuIS.

Toby Harnden, a British journalist, wrote in 2009 that he had a meeting with Kendall in 2003 at Chef Geoff's restaurant in Washington, DC, to talk about the ongoing negotiations between the Sinn Fein/IRA and the hardline Unionist politicians. This was a specialty of Kendall's, but it was unknown if he was authorized to talk to the journalist about such a politically charged topic. Harnden described Kendall: "A tall, imposing figure, I found him to be an erudite and well-read fellow. He was a genial and interesting conversationalist and was much less discreet than most State Department officials. He was clearly no fan of President George W. Bush and seemed to fit the caricature of the pro-European, soft-Left type that is often leveled at the State Department by conservatives."

No mention of Kendall's public faux pas at the American Consortium on European Union Studies was reflected in his SY File. After all, public silliness is not a flogging offense. What did intrigue me even then was the possibility that the file on Kendall was wholly inadequate and incomplete. I came to believe that Kendall had unauthorized meetings not only with foreign journalists and diplomats but also some suspected foreign intelligence officers under diplomatic cover, Carlos Ciano for example.

Would they be in INR's database, I wondered, because INR senior officials must sanction meetings with journalists, diplomats, and foreign intelligence officers in the United States under diplomatic cover? This could be, but INR's database is not shared with DS by the department because they do not want the department security "knuckle draggers," a term Kendall himself used in describing DS agents, looking over their shoulders.

My suspicions were later confirmed when Kendall told me that he had numerous luncheons with European clandestine intelligence officers with diplomatic titles in Washington, DC. A nine-month professional sabbatical to the People's Republic of China, where he had social contact with a French intelligence officer under commercial cover, was not in his SY File.

Kendall was cunning indeed as he carefully avoided DS/CI's counterintelligence radar scope and never submitted a single foreign citizen intelligence officer contact report to DS as required by department regulation.

About four hours into thumbing through Kendall's six-inch-thick file, I was 99.99 percent convinced that if the joint FBI/DS "Vision Quest" espionage matrix were correct, Kendall was our only possible candidate. Although math was never my strong suit, everything seemed to add up.

I walked back to Barbara's office, winked, and said I needed to borrow only one SY File to take back to my office. She smiled and asked if I'd be looking at other SY Files. I said that I would, and she agreed to keep the remaining thirteen for future review.

When I returned to my cubicle, I sent an e-mail on the SIPR net to FBI SA Matt, the case manager, saying, "You need to look at an SY File that I have in my office." He responded hours later indicating that he would come to DS/CI on June 11. I was not in the office later that afternoon when SA Stowell provided Matt the file.

When I returned to the office on June 12 and confirmed that Matt had reviewed the file, I sent him an e-mail that asked, "Did you find the file interesting?"

He replied almost immediately, "Absolutely."

Walter Kendall Myers's twenty-year secret career as a Cuban penetration agent was beginning to unravel—but we still had many threads to tie together.

CHAPTER THREE

Our most immediate concern was that Kendall was working inside INR, an office considered by many to be the crown jewel of the State Department. Staffed by career Foreign Service and Civil Service officers and analysts, INR receives classified information, including highly sensitive technical reports, from throughout the IC and our US embassies. The information, which includes CIA, NSA, and DOD "top secret" and so-called "code word" material, is reviewed and transformed into informational papers designed to assist our diplomatic efforts. And although Kendall's specialty was the US–UK relationship, from personal experience I knew that there was a lot of cross-talk in INR.

We would discover later that through seemingly innocent, random, and casual conversations with fellow INR colleagues, Kendall was able to elicit extremely valuable diplomatic information from the Cuban specialists. As he said during his trial, "I maintained a wide range of contacts in order to obtain information on the US policies toward Cuba."

In 2011, Robert N. Carhart Jr., an analyst and INR colleague of Kendall's, stated, "I know I was one of those sources. Kendall would always say something like, 'How's our friend Fidel today?' Kind of a generic question like that to start a conversation where it was easy to pawn off, or after he expressed his so-called fascination with the island. It was a betrayal . . . basic betrayal to the country and to myself for abusing the relationship."

Thanks to Kendall, whatever human rights, financial, family repatriation, medical, or aid initiatives were being considered, Cuba knew our bottom line in any diplomatic negotiations before they started. Even if we covertly asked Spain or the Vatican, Kendall's area of regional expertise, to work on our behalf on humanitarian issues, Castro was aware of their origins. When Castro closed the Spanish embassy's cultural center in the Palacio Velasco Sara building in 2003, claiming that it was inciting subversion and anti-government sentiments, did he do so because he was informed that perhaps it was being secretly funded by the US government? Does USAID contractor Alan Gross, currently languishing in a Cuban jail since 2009 for "acts against the independence or the territorial independence of the state" by providing an undeclared satellite communications system that allowed Internet access to "pro-democracy groups," owe his situation to Kendall?

Worse, we determined that Kendall perused INR's internal secure SIPR net computer networks to see what informational papers were being prepared about Cuba. Most damning was the fact that when he reported back to Cuba about information gathered by US technical means, those operations were then compromised and shut down. With Kendall deep inside State and Ana Montes deep inside DIA, Castro had an almost complete understanding of our diplomatic and military policies concerning Cuba. No wonder he has outwitted ten US presidents.

As a result of my work, the FBI immediately deployed massive human and electronic resources to monitor Kendall's public and private life. DS/CI made sure that Kendall's every move inside the

HST was documented, and we monitored all of his classified and unclassified computer messages as a matter of course.

Almost immediately, though, disaster struck. Within a few months of ramping up the monitoring, we discovered that Kendall was finalizing his retirement papers with the department's Office of Human Resources. We could not believe our bad luck. After finally identifying our suspect, he was about to leave the information-rich environment that supported his espionage activities.

And he did. He retired before the FBI could obtain evidence that Kendall was taking classified information out of the HST. Kendall would no longer be passing government secrets to his Cuban masters without access to classified information. Ergo—no violation of the espionage statutes unless he had squirreled away some nuts for a rainy day. It really looked like our efforts had been for naught.

I would discover belatedly that Kendall had been alerted to our interest in him due to the bureaucratic stupidity and protocols that force federal investigators to inform the head of any agency whenever the strong possibility exists that one of their own employees is a suspected penetration agent. According to bureaucratic requirements, the secretary of state and her deputy were notified of the FBI/DS's suspicions concerning Kendall—as they should have been. Another senior State Department employee who was similarly nominated by the president of the United States and confirmed by the Senate, and Kendall's ultimate boss from 2006 until his retirement, was Assistant Secretary of State Randall Fort. He was a former corporate officer with Goldman Sachs (director of Global Security) and program director at TRW's space and defense division. He was nominated in June 2006 to serve as assistant secretary of state for INR during President George W. Bush's second term.

In early 2007, the fateful decision was made to inform Fort of the DS and FBI investigation. During his initial briefing meeting with the FBI, he was advised to be careful in future interactions with Kendall so as not to betray any new feelings he might have for Kendall and thereby alert him to the FBI/DS inquiry.

I saw absolutely no value in alerting Kendall's ultimate boss about our suspicions because there would be nothing Fort could offer to assist in the investigation. I had been very vocal in the past in such cases, believing that only those senior officials absolutely necessary should be informed in order to avoid another Felix Bloch leak of information and botched espionage case. Certainly the secretary of state must determine the national security implications of the case and how best to proceed with any investigation inside the State Department. But why the assistant secretary of INR? What's the investigative value?

Kendall would tell us later that in late 2007 he noticed a "chill" in his relations with Randy Fort, who suddenly refused to allow him to sign and forward analysis to department bureaus, something Kendall had done for over a decade. Kendall would reveal later, "I clashed with . . . the assistant secretary of state [Fort] who was my boss."

Kendall initially wondered if it was a result of his impromptu speech at SAIS where he criticized Tony Blair and was admonished by the department. Kendall remarked later, "my boss at INR put me on a 'watch list'" and "thought it would be unwise for us to be going to Mexico for contacts at that point."

Kendall's INR colleagues would begin to ask him in private if there was anything that he had done to Fort to cause such a negative reaction whenever Kendall's name was mentioned. As a result of Fort's sudden change in behavior towards him, Kendall correctly guessed that there was something amiss and decided to plan his retirement immediately. Then Randy Fort made matters worse.

When INR decided to host a retirement party for Kendall inside the HST, a common practice for a twenty-five-year veteran of the department, Fort personally ended all plans for such a ceremony. As a courtesy, Kendall's INR colleagues sought Fort's "blessing" for the farewell party but were stunned when the assistant secretary said, "No way," and then added, "Trust me on this one."

When Kendall's startled and unknowing colleagues relayed Fort's words to Kendall, the CuIS's penetration agent's suspicions were confirmed. To avoid any internal conflict, Kendall's INR colleagues held the retirement party outside the department at the DACOR Bacon House in Washington, DC. Randy Fort was not invited. In 2010, my FBI contacts told me that two senior FBI officials had later held an informal "chat" with Fort to inform him that he had been less than helpful in the investigation.

Kendall retired, and he and Gwendolyn apparently ceased all clandestine activities and focused on learning to pilot their sailboat. The FBI's investigation was at a stand-still, and after eighteen months of futile surveillance, something drastic needed to occur or there would be no possible way to develop an espionage case against them.

Then, in spring 2009, the FBI developed a plan to lure Kendall back into the secret life that he had apparently abandoned. After months of preparation, a bold and risky "false-flag" operation was launched as an undercover agent, codenamed "EK," approached Kendall at the SAIS campus and pretended to be a Cuban intelligence officer. Kendall took the bait, and soon he and Gwendolyn met with the undercover agent at a nearby hotel lounge. Over the course of their conversation, they hinted at their methods, including discussion of receiving messages in Morse code over a shortwave radio, thus confirming that our suspicions had been correct.

Kendall told EK how he and Gwendolyn had already acquired the appropriate sea charts so they could "sail home" to Cuba. There was no indication of when this might happen, but that revelation did not bode well for our investigation. The FBI had to develop overwhelming evidence of espionage against the Myerses before they set sail for Cuba. But what had influenced them to plan to leave the US?

The answer was simple, as Kendall described to EK: "Let me explain something . . . which is important for us and . . . could be important to you. When I left the State Department, one of the reasons . . . I was gonna leave anyway. . . . I was going to leave in 2008 . . . but I clashed with . . . the assistant secretary [Randy Fort] who was my boss."

Kendall stated that, as a result of that clash, he felt "uncomfortable [and] more or less threatened," and he added, "So I've been very cautious about reestablishing contact because I didn't want to, uh implicate you. . . . We have been very cautious, careful with our moves, and, trying to be alert to any surveillance if there was any."

Before departing, they agreed to meet the next day at a different hotel. Most importantly, Kendall and Gwendolyn promised to obtain the information requested by EK and were now prepared to accept espionage taskings. They also insisted that any future meetings begin with the use of a Cuban code word they had employed in the past. That was theatrical to say the least but very much in keeping with their spy personas.

The Myerses would meet again with EK on April 16, April 30, and finally June 4. What had Kendall and Gwendolyn discussed with EK during those hotel meetings? A lot, quite frankly as evidenced by sample statements from their meetings.

Kendall (when EK offered a drink of scotch): "No, no, that's OK . . . while I work, you know." He told EK: "I will get information for you on the next meeting concerning the upcoming Trinidad and Tobago Summit of the Americas meeting."

Even more significantly, Kendall acknowledged that a code name used for him in messages was "202," and Gwendolyn acknowledged that one she used was "123." A match for the intercepted messages. Kendall told EK "to send special greetings . . . and hugs . . . to everybody . . . and all our friends . . . two very old friends" in Cuba. He refused EK's request to identify SAIS students "who could be useful to us," saying, "I don't trust any of them."

At the April 30, 2009, meeting, Kendall said he and Gwendolyn told EK that they were "delighted to have contact again. We really have missed you. And you, speaking collectively, have been a really important part of our lives, and we have felt incomplete. I mean, we really love your country . . . and the people and the team are just important in our lives. So we don't want to fall out of contact again."

Kendall said that he and Gwendolyn "would like to be a reserve army . . . ready when we are needed. I will begin a process of getting back in contact with . . . my old contacts . . . work on new ones . . . to be able to react if the situation gets dangerous or we hear something that makes us worried, that we think you should know. . . . But I think, honestly, we don't want to be back to the regular stuff. . . ."

Gwendolyn was hardly innocent in this matter. Of Fidel Castro, she stated: "He's . . . the most . . . incredible statesman in . . . a hundred years for goodness sakes." She said, "I envy her [Ana Montes] being able to love what she was doing [spying for the CuIS], and say what she was doing and why she was doing that . . . 'cause I can't do it. She was not paranoid enough. . . . But she loved it [spying]; she did what she loved to do."

Gwendolyn confirmed that Cuba was the most comfortable country in which to conduct business, saying, "once you got there . . . we knew we were OK." She stated that her favorite method of passing information to the CuIS inside the United States was by changing shopping carts inside supermarkets because it was "easy enough to do." She said she "would not do it now because they have a camera, but they didn't then."

She reminded EK that Kendall removed secret documents from the State Department and she copied "page-by-page" the documents that Kendall brought home in his briefcase, on a typewriter originally and then a laptop. She added that she never used her own computer to send encrypted e-mails to the CuIS and that they "would go to Internet cafes" to send messages.

And finally, about leaving the United States for Cuba, Gwendolyn said, "we've sailed there. . . . We've always said we'll just come on a boat. . . . We're not taking a train or plane, you know."

They talked about their affinity with Castro, Cuba, and the Cuban people. Kendall and Gwendolyn reminded EK that in January 1995 they had traveled clandestinely to Cuba and spent an evening with Fidel Castro in a small house outside Havana. He awarded them a medal for their service to the Cuban revolution. Nostalgically they discussed their early "brush passes" in New York City and Washington, DC, and how difficult and dangerous they seemed.

Yet despite their voluntary retirement, the Myerses still enjoyed being penetration agents, and the thought of being resurrected on a part-time basis was a joyous prospect. In furtherance of the new relationship, they received and were trained in the use of an encryption device for a laptop computer for the purpose of encoding future e-mail communications with their "new" Cuban handler.

What I really didn't like to hear was how easy it was for Kendall to take classified documents out of the State Department. Kendall had no worries about walking out of Main State with secrets because he put the documents in "official envelopes," and there were no random searches of employees by the Main State security guards. If that method was too risky, Kendall simply memorized key words from documents or took shorthand notes of their contents. When he got home, Gwendolyn transcribed the written notes or recitation for transmittal to Cuba. So simple.

There was no doubt now that Kendall and Gwendolyn were the penetration agents we had been hunting for all these years. But there was one difficult threshold to overcome: Kendall no longer had access to classified material. Any reports or analysis he provided would almost exclusively come from open source materials or sensitive scraps of information elicited from former colleagues. Finding an e-mail message from Kendall to his handlers that might be linked to a specific classified document would be next to impossible.

The Myerses had already made admissions against self-interest about their prior spying activities as well as their willingness to engage in new espionage work on behalf of Cuba, and had accepted clandestine communications equipment to further their endeavors. Was this evidence sufficient to go forward with a prosecution? Damned if I knew!

Working alongside the FBI and DS, the Department of Justice now had to decide whether there was probable cause to arrest the Myerses for espionage or lesser related charges. I attended a number of these meetings where the elements of espionage were debated ad infinitum and ad nauseam. At this point, Senior Trial Attorney Clifford Rones and Assistant US Attorney Michael Harvey decided to go forward with the novel charge of wire fraud, which we could prove beyond a reasonable doubt, because DOJ/FBI/DS were uncertain if the espionage count could stick for lack of specificity on what national security information Kendall and Gwendolyn had compromised. The wire fraud count simply charged that having his US government paycheck sent electronically to his bank while not fully "loyal" to the department was evidence of fraud.

It was a brilliant legal move given our circumstances. Driving the need for quick action were the FBI's discoveries that Kendall and Gwendolyn were planning a couple of significant sailing trips on their $375,000 sailboat and that the GPS compass had been loaded with nautical coordinates for sailing to Cuba. Worse, none of their home calendars or daily planners indicated any scheduled activities in Washington, DC, or anywhere else for that matter, after November 2009.

At one meeting where the FBI, DS, and DOJ prosecution team was assembled in WFO to discuss the ramifications of the Myerses plan for "sailing home," the conversation became tense. We knew that Kendall and Gwendolyn were about to embark on an "over-the-horizon" sailing course to Nova Scotia with a yachting club from their berth in Maryland. What if they suddenly sailed toward the Caribbean? Did DOJ have enough evidence to convince a federal judge to issue an arrest warrant? Could we risk Kendall and Gwendolyn sailing away on a "training exercise"? Could we afford losing them on the high seas while trying to confirm that the threshold for violations of federal law had been tripped? The FBI was uncomfortable with the prospect of the Myerses sailing the

Atlantic Ocean without government surveillance in a vessel capable of a long voyage.

I tried to break the tension. "Can we request that the US Navy have a standby attack submarine ready for use next week?"

"Robert," a DOJ official responded, "are you serious?"

"Well, if they get beyond twelve nautical miles, the US Coast Guard can't intervene, and we need something more robust."

"Like an FBI parachute SWAT team?" an FBI colleague asked.

"There will be no hostile boarding of ships on this investigation," someone replied. Maintaining a sense of humor was the best we could do. We were all tired and anxious.

After the third meeting between EK and the Myerses, DOJ was confident that it had enough evidence to go forward with an arrest and prosecution. It was time to bring Kendall and Gwendolyn in from the cold without so much as a "bon voyage."

A fourth and final meeting with the Myerses and EK was arranged to take place in a hotel located in the 800 block of New Hampshire Avenue. The location was picked because of easy street parking, and the room prices were gentle on the government expense account.

On the morning of June 4 at 6:16 a.m., approximately ten hours before the fourth scheduled meeting, a federal judge signed a sealed warrant for the arrest of Kendall and Gwendolyn Myers for violations of 18 USC 371 (conspiracy to defraud the US government by defeating the State Department's control over its information, acted illegally as an agent of the government of Cuba, and communicated to agents of Cuba information Kendall and Gwendolyn knew to be classified), 18 USC 951(acting as illegal agents of the government of Cuba without prior notice to the Attorney General) and 18 USC 1343 (devising a scheme to defraud the US government and to obtain monies by means of materially false pretenses). On the same date, the FBI established a Command Center located in two large, windowless rooms on the ground floor of WFO. Tables topped with telephones, computer monitors, legal pads, and pens were scattered about. The Command Center was filled with special agents and analysts who had been working the case for years. I was pleased to see that Donna and Rachel were finally smiling. At approximately 3:50 p.m., Kendall and Gwendolyn walked into the hotel lobby and headed to a previously identified room.

At 4:10 p.m., EK and the Myerses were seated comfortably on the beds in the hotel room and began to talk about specific IC technical operations of which Kendall was aware. Kendall's incriminating responses were the final nail in the coffin. By 4:24 p.m., both Gwendolyn and Kendall were in handcuffs and being driven to the FBI's Washington Field Office for initial processing. The Myerses' residence was entered around 5:00 p.m. and methodically searched for any evidence of their espionage activities. There was plenty.

As the scrum of agents and the Myerses entered WFO's first floor for booking, I had my first up-close glimpse of Kendall and was surprised to see just how tall he was. Gwendolyn scowled irritably and snapped at the FBI agents when being fingerprinted. But Kendall was serene throughout. Both had immediately lawyered-up inside the hotel room when they were handcuffed; they were not talking. They were taking the Fifth, something not guaranteed by Cuba's justice system. They would need it and every other constitutional amendment at their disposal to defend themselves.

CHAPTER FOUR

After the FBI's initial processing at WFO, the pair was driven to the District of Columbia's Correctional Treatment Facility, otherwise known as the DC Jail, where Kendall and Gwendolyn became numbers 323487 and 323475.

On June 5, arraignment was held in front of US Magistrate Judge John M. Facciola, the judge who had signed the arrest warrant, in the E. Barrett Prettyman United States Courthouse on Constitution Avenue. The eight-story-tall courthouse is constructed of limestone and studded with aluminum windows. It houses the US District Court for the District of Columbia, the US Court of Appeals for the District of Columbia, and the United States Foreign Intelligence Surveillance Court, the very same courtroom that authorized the electronic surveillance of the Myerses. The courtroom was half filled, with FBI and DS personnel gathered on the left side of the chamber and Myers family members seated on the right. About ten media representatives with notepads and gear were also assembled.

The judge walked into the courtroom, and the audience stood up; he took his seat, and the audience sat down. He began the proceedings. After a review of the charges, the judge asked the Myerses of their guilt or innocence, and they both pleaded not guilty to counts of conspiracy and wire fraud. The most important decision that day for Judge Facciola was whether or not to grant bail. The defense team thundered long and loud that the government's conspiracy case was flimsy. One defense attorney proclaimed that since the conspiracy charge was weak at best and that the wire fraud charges were "somewhat embellished," bail should be granted.

Thomas C. Green, Kendall's and Gwendolyn's attorney, recommended that the court impose a ruling of house arrest for the Myerses and require the indignity of wearing ankle monitoring bracelets. The government advised the court that bail and ankle bracelets were insufficient deterrents in preventing their possible flight from justice. The prosecutors noted that FBI agents found nautical charts in the couple's home and that their Malmo sailboat had a GPS system containing coordinates for sailing to Cuba.

During one of the numerous courtroom breaks, I was approached by FBI supervisory special agent (SSA) "Tony" and asked if I would intervene in a delicate debate between the FBI and DOJ. The Cuban Interests Section, Havana's legal diplomatic mission in Washington, DC., located at 2630 Sixteenth Street, NW, is within two miles of the Myerses' home, and there was discussion between the FBI special agents and the DOJ lawyers concerning the distinct possibility that if Judge Facciola granted bail, Kendall and Gwendolyn might hightail it over to the Cuban diplomatic mission to seek political asylum, and, just like that, the prosecution would end. According to SSA Tony, some of the federal prosecutors were unfazed by that fact and told the FBI that if the Myerses did something as stupid as that, they would have the US Marshals retrieve them. SSA Tony told me that the FBI's attempts to sensitize the prosecution team to the inviolability of diplomatic compounds had failed and asked if

I would inject DS's opinions into the fray at the next break. When the opportunity arose later, I discreetly approached AUSA Harvey outside the courtroom.

"Mike, could I talk to you for a moment in private?"

"Of course. What can I help you with?"

"You know that if Kendall and Gwendolyn flee to the Cuban Interests Section and ask for asylum, this prosecution is over."

"What do you mean?"

"The Cuban mission grounds are inviolate, and the State Department will never authorize any attempts at having Kendall and Gwendolyn forcibly removed from the compound."

I also explained to AUSA Harvey that if the US government were to cut off the water supply or electricity to the Cuban Interests Section in a misguided attempt to force the Cubans to turn over the Myerses, our diplomats in Havana would suffer worse treatment at the hands of Castro. I really didn't have the authority to say that, and while I didn't have a copy of the Vienna Convention in my back pocket, it was true, and I knew it. It was a screwball idea, but how often had US government lawyers confronted such a possibility? The last such imbroglio occurred on November 21, 1985, when Israeli penetration agent Jonathan Jay Pollard tried to hide inside the Israeli embassy in DC before his arrest and eventual conviction for espionage. After a brief stand-off, an Israeli diplomat escorted Pollard off the compound into the waiting arms of the FBI. While the Israelis understood and were influenced by the diplomatic repercussions arising from a failure to cooperate, the Cubans could not care less.

"Mike," I continued, "the State Department does not win many battles against DOJ, but I assure you the White House will back up State one hundred percent in this case, and the only losers here will be us. There will be no physical removal of the Myerses from the Cuba Interests Section. Period."

He looked at me a moment and then nodded. "Thanks."

Back in the courtroom twenty minutes later, as he was summarizing his reasons against granting bail, Harvey emphasized just how close the Cuban Interests Section was to the Myerses' residence. He added that if the Myerses were assigned home detention, and given one slight slip in 24/7 electronic and physical surveillance, the two could sneak undetected into the Cuban mission and seek asylum. To Kendall and Gwendolyn Myers, both in their seventies, a lifetime inside a diplomatic mission would be an option far preferable to that of a federal prison. Life in a jail or life in a protected and privileged diplomatic compound? The choice is easy, as Cardinal Jósef Mindszenty demonstrated from November 1956 to September 1971 when he preferred to live inside the US diplomatic mission in Budapest instead of a communist gulag.

AUSA Harvey concluded by saying that the Myerses would be a "real and present danger to the United States" if they fled to Cuba or Cuban control.

At the conclusion of the prosecution and defense arguments, Judge Facciola said he would issue a written opinion within the week, but until then bail would be denied. Outside the courtroom, members of the press and the Myers family reviewed the thirty-six-page indictment. I recall the Myerses' children leaning against the corridor walls and shaking their heads as they read the charges. I felt some compassion for them but certainly not for Kendall and Gwendolyn. The following week, Judge Facciola denied Kendall and Gwendolyn bail.

The next month, on July 24, 2009, I returned to the E. Barrett Prettyman Courthouse. I arrived at 1:27 p.m., minutes before the start of the next round of legal proceedings. Darting into Judge Reggie B. Walton's Court Room 16, I was surprised to see how much had changed.

There were no crowds, no children, no press, and certainly no Cuban Interests Section personnel. On the left side of the courtroom were two DS and five FBI special agents. On the right were two unknown women and an unidentified female reporter. The courtroom, with six rows of hardwood benches, was largely empty.

A side door next to Judge Walton's bench opened and out popped a smiling Gwendolyn followed by Kendall. Not exactly fashionable, they wore dark blue prison jumpers over white tee shirts. Gwendolyn had her shoulder-length hair pulled back in a lazy ponytail, and Kendall's short and balding hair had a tousled look about it—maybe just a case of prison bed-head. The pair was directed by the US marshals to sit at the defense table located to the judge's left.

Ten minutes later, Judge Walton entered the courtroom, carrying a stack of folders under his right arm that he deposited on the podium before taking his seat. Walton was mid-fifties, with close-cropped hair and a constantly severe expression—like a bird of prey about to pluck up a mouse. He played football in college and in 2005, while driving his car in Washington, DC, spied an individual attacking a cab driver, leapt out of his vehicle, tackled the assailant, and held him until the police arrived. I don't think I ever saw him blink.

On the judge's right, AUSA Harvey addressed the court in his best basso profundo voice, asking the judge for a continuance given the significant number of documents the defense needed to review as part of the discovery process so the trial could go forward. The defense immediately agreed with the motion. Then Judge Walton asked both Kendall and Gwendolyn to stand and face the court.

He briefly discussed a couple of pro forma topics and asked once again if they were still willing to waive their rights to a speedy trial. In clear voices, they both agreed. Both prosecution and defense lawyers agreed to reconvene at 2:00 p.m. on September 25 to continue the hearing. The judge concurred and adjourned the court. Gwendolyn left the courtroom by the same door she entered while Kendall, in ankle shackles, followed behind. The courtroom spectators left by the rear doors.

Outside Court Room 16, FBI and DS special agents conferred with the prosecution lawyers concerning some technical points involving the use of classified documents in the upcoming trial. I spoke with AUSA Harvey about a specific department administrative issue that might require DS intervention, and he readily agreed to call us if he encountered any pushback from the State Department's hopelessly clueless legal office, which so far had been mercifully excluded from any involvement in the investigation and prosecution. SAs Stowell and Alleman and I shook hands and wished each other a good weekend.

Suddenly and without fanfare, Kendall and Gwendolyn's defense team agreed that they would plead guilty to the charges of conspiracy to commit espionage and wire fraud. The DS and FBI SAs were elated because as part of the plea agreement, Kendall agreed to be debriefed by elements of the IC, including DS. His commitment to be interviewed by DS and FBI interrogation teams was a crucial component of the plea bargain agreement, and the level of his cooperation would be taken into consideration when Judge Walton passed his final sentence on Kendall and Gwendolyn.

Fast forward to November 20, 2009. It was a clear yet chilly Friday in Washington, DC, and Judge Walton's afternoon schedule for Courtroom 16 was full, including a closed hearing concerning Guantanamo Bay detainees. I had arrived very early for the scheduled 3:00 p.m. *US v. Myers* proceedings so that I could be sure to find an empty seat. I need not have worried. Four of my fellow DS/CI colleagues accompanied me into the empty courtroom, and we all took seats on the front bench. Over the course of the next twenty minutes, a number of FBI special agents and analysts trickled into the room followed by a small number of journalists and interested members of the public.

As the clock ticked down to 3:00 p.m., AUSA Harvey and Senior Trial Attorney Clifford I. Rones, Counterespionage Section of the Department of Justice's National Security Division, took their places at the left side conference table located in the courtroom well while their defense counterparts, Thomas C. Green, Bradford Berenson, and Judy Gallagher, occupied the jet-black swivel chairs surrounding the conference table on the left side of Judge Walton's podium.

At 3:02 p.m., two beefy US marshals, dressed in a clashing collage of shirts, ties, pants, and jackets, opened a wood-paneled door to the left of the judge's seating area and escorted Kendall and Gwendolyn into the courtroom. As Kendall walked over to the defense counsel's table, he smiled and raised his eyebrows in quiet recognition of those members of the public seated to the right of the courtroom—one of whom looked as if he could be a brother.

Gwendolyn, stoic and wearing an orange prison ID card affixed to her ocean blue jumpsuit, stared straight ahead as she quickly sat across from her lawyers. Her hair was graying, and she looked tired, though serious as always. Once seated, Kendall examined a number of documents arranged in front of him, all the while enjoying a low-key conversation with his wife of over twenty years. After a few minutes, they both leaned across the conference table and talked quietly with Berenson and Gallagher.

At 3:14 p.m., Judge Walton strode into the courtroom and assumed his place on the bench at center stage. His robes were stiffly starched, and he looked ready to throw the gavel at someone. Wasting little time or words, the judge swiftly instructed Kendall and Gwendolyn to stand before him at the podium. He was about to brace them with an extensive list of prepared questions that would be administered under oath.

For the next ninety minutes, Judge Walton conducted his "Rule 11" colloquy with the defendants so that Kendall and Gwendolyn fully understood the consequences of their agreeing to a plea bargain with the US government.

"Do you understand your sentencing options?" Judge Walton asked. "Yes," they both replied.

Staring directly at Kendall, Judge Walton said, "Do you understand that your possible sentence could be life without parole?"

Kendall cleared his throat before answering. "Yes."

Turning to Gwendolyn, Judge Walton said, "Do you realize that in consideration for your cooperation you could still receive a sentence of six to nine years?

"Yes," she replied quietly.

"Do you both understand that by consenting to the plea agreements' provisos you are waiving your constitutional rights to a trial by jury?"

"Yes," Kendall said.

"I do," Gwendolyn said.

"Do you both understand you are waiving your right to confront witnesses?" They did.

"Do you both understand that you must be proven guilty beyond a reasonable doubt?" Again, both said, "Yes."

And the questioning continued.

Rule 11 was the government's ace in the hole should the Myerses ever attempt to appeal their sentence by citing insufficiency of counsel or a lack of understanding of the full implications of the plea agreement. If they chose to pursue either of those options, the Justice Department would simply introduce the Rule 11 colloquy transcripts to demonstrate that the Myerses were fully cognizant of the consequences of their plea deal.

Gwendolyn's stipulation to the facts was sixteen pages long, while Kendall's filled seventeen pages. The judge slowly and in excruciating detail outlined the legal protections and guarantees both were waiving. Throughout the questioning, Gwendolyn and Kendall stood shoulder-to-shoulder and answered the judge with curt "Yes," "No," and "I do" answers. At one point, Gwendolyn quietly complained that standing at attention for so long was uncomfortable.

"Are you pleading guilty to the charge of conspiring to gather and transmit national defense information in violation of 18 USC 793 g. because the government could prove you guilty of the charge?" Judge Walton asked.

"Yes," Gwendolyn said softly.

"Are you pleading guilty because you in fact are guilty?"

"Yes."

Judge Walton turned his attention to Kendall. "Are you pleading guilty to the charge of one count of 18 USC 793 a. and c. espionage charges and two counts of 18 USC 1343 wire fraud because the government could prove you guilty of those charges?"

"Yes," Kendall said.

"Are you pleading guilty because you in fact are guilty?"

"Yes."

At 4:33 p.m., I walked out of the courtroom and hugged FBI analysts "Donna" and "Rachel" and shook the hands of numerous FBI special agents who had worked as a team with SA Stowell and me in identifying, investigating, and successfully prosecuting the Myerses. I had brought five cigars to the proceedings—No. 4 Montecristos, handmade in Havana, of course. In the hallway outside the courtroom, I unwrapped the pale yellow and crimson box and offered a cigar to FBI SSA Tony, one to lead FBI case agent Matt, and one apiece to FBI analysts Donna and Rachel. I then walked over to AUSA Michael Harvey and proffered the final cigar. The look on his face was priceless.

AUSA Harvey lowered his head, grinned expansively, and took the gift. He gingerly put the contraband inside his suit pocket without saying a word. He did not have to. His novel "fraud by wire" charge against Kendall was a precedent worthy of future emulation by the Justice Department whenever US government employees are tempted to spy against their country. In simple terms, Kendall's fraudulent scheme was that he accepted his department salary, sent electronically to his bank, while at the same time he was willingly and knowingly not faithfully discharging his State Department duties. It was a time of celebration, but one thing remained—sentencing.

The three-person DS interview team assigned to debrief Kendall prior to sentencing included SA Stowell, DS/CI analyst Mark Evans, and me. The goal was to question Kendall about his espionage activities and identify department counterintelligence vulnerabilities. Kendall and I hit it off famously, much to the amusement of my FBI colleagues who were witnesses to five sessions that the DS interview team had with Kendall conducted at WFO. The interviews were all professionally videotaped and audio recorded by DS's Training Center staff.

Kendall was fiercely proud of his espionage accomplishments and unrepentant for his culpability in compromising US diplomatic initiatives and the identities of foreign allies, not to mention hundreds of millions of dollars of technical operations. He would explain his motivation during the sentencing proceedings in July 2010. His goal was to protect the Cuban revolultion from adverse interference, manipulation, or pressure emanating from the US government influenced by anti-Castro groups resident in America.

On July 16, 2010, I made my way back to the US District Courthouse once again. This time every seat in Room 16 was occupied by 9:45 a.m. while other spectators waited eagerly in the hallway, and ultimately in vain, in case someone left the courtroom early. Everyone was waiting for Judge Walton to enter and pronounce sentence on Kendall and Gwendolyn for their admitted crimes.

The buzzing courtroom grew fly quiet as Judge Walton entered at 10:14 a.m. The final moments of this three-year drama were about to come to an end. The Deputy Clerk announced, "Criminal Action Number 09-150, United States of America versus Walter Myers and Gwendolyn Myers."

The prosecution was first up, and after sharing the pro forma salutation with Judge Walton, the Myerses' attorney Thomas Green asked for and was granted an eleven-minute recess to address an administrative issue.

When the court reconvened, AUSA Michael Harvey reduced the case to its simplest terms. Starting off with Gwendolyn, he said, "[S]he did it all for thirty years. She feels no remorse about what she did or the harm that she caused to the United States. She, like her husband, is shameless."

Green saw things differently. He said, "If Your Honor please, we have set forth all the factors, which should inform Your Honor in consideration of the sentence to be imposed on Mrs. Myers in our various submissions, and we have discussed those at length, and so I will not belabor the record with a complete recitation of all of that. But there are certain significant things that need to be said."

"With respect to the cooperation that was provided to the United States by Mrs. Myers," he continued, "and for that matter Mr. Myers, when they were apprehended, there was no attempt to deny what they had done, or for that matter to try to avoid the consequences of that....

"They ultimately decided to enter into a plea agreement, save the government the burden of a trial, which in turn, was a process that I think was as protective of National Security as they could be under the circumstances. And what they bargained for basically, the two of them, in return for all of that cooperation, and I should add that that cooperation has been undertaken over hundreds of hours of debriefings with numerous agencies, often at a great personal burden to my clients because of the process associated with bringing them to and from such sessions."

I almost laughed out loud at this point. I was one of the officers involved in some of the debriefings that took place in WFO. Kendall was very happy to get out of the DC Jail general lock-up, where he was held along with murderers and other violent offenders. As Kendall told me at one point, "There are some real bad people in my jail who want to hurt me." I always made sure he had a cup of coffee to start the debriefings and, at his request, I bought him a hot pastrami sandwich and carrot cake for lunch (out of my own pocket) from the Market deli around the corner from WFO. He enjoyed every minute of "his burden," and it is all recorded on video for posterity.

"At this point, I would like to tell you, sir, that Mr. Myers, Kendall Myers, wishes to allocute on behalf of himself and his wife. And I think that before you impose sentence on Mrs. Myers, I would ask that you permit him to provide to the Court those remarks."

Judge Walton asked, "Does she desire to speak?"

Green responded, "She would ask that her husband speak on her behalf and basically on behalf of both of them. But because you're going to sentence her first, perhaps—I'm not sure if you're going to sentence her right now or wait until we move to Kendall. But if you are, I would like you to have the benefit of those remarks."

Judge Walton said, "Very well."

"Can they stand together here before you?" Green asked.

"Yes."

At that point, Judge Walton asked Kendall and Gwendolyn to stand up and approach the bench at the podium, center stage. Kendall appeared chipper as he moved to the lectern as if pleased to be in court with the opportunity to talk. As he stood next to his wife, he faced a stern-looking Judge Walton and spoke for about fifteen minutes.

He commenced by saying: "Good morning, Your Honor. I am Walter Kendall Myers, and this is my wife, Gwendolyn Steingraber Myers. I would like to make a few brief remarks, remarks that will cover our motivation, our relationship, education, and incarceration. First, our motivation. In signing our plea agreement last November, we acknowledged our guilt on the charges brought against us by the government. We wish to add today that we acted as we did for thirty years because of our ideas and beliefs. We did not seek nor receive payment for our work."

His explanation that followed was simple. "We did not act out of anger toward the United States or from any thought of anti-Americanism. We did not intend to hurt any individual American. We share the ideals and dreams of the Cuban revolution. We are equally committed to helping the struggling people of the world."

Listening to Kendall, I had the impression that he was on a self-imposed mission to level the international playing field for Castro against the mighty America. According to Kendall, "The Cuban people feel threatened" by the US, and Castro had "good reason to feel threatened." Kendall continued his statement to the Court. "There are currently people residing in Miami who carried out brutal terrorist acts against Cuba, including the bombing of a Cuban airliner with the loss of seventy-five people. They have maintained an embargo since 1961 to the present. From a Cuban perspective, there is a great deal to fear from the US. On the US side, that's been noted. Cuba and the US have a longstanding relation of hostility, of mutual misunderstanding, of mutual fear of each other. Part of our motivation was to help alleviate some of those fears, to report as accurately and fairly and objectively as I could about what I thought US policy was. But it was also designed to help protect Cuba, to warn Cuba, to try to assess the nature of the threat to Cuba. This is what I was referring to."

Judge Walton interrupted Kendall to ask, "At the expense of your government?"

Standing ram-rod straight, Kendall replied: "I find that hard to answer, Your Honor, only because I believe that anyone who feels as I do that the Cuban people and the Cuban revolution deserve their chance to fail or succeed and should not be threatened, should not be treated to constant bombardment of propaganda and hostile acts—that did require me to act illegally in terms of US law. I'm perfectly prepared to acknowledge, as I have already in signing the plea agreement, that I acted illegally in terms of US law. And I did so, as I've said in my statement, with an overriding objective of helping protect the Cuban people."

At one point, I noticed Judge Walton glance up at the courtroom ceiling for a good fifteen seconds before returning his stare to the two defendants.

The only time Kendall's voice broke during his dissertation was when he talked about his love for Gwendolyn. I knew, on that point, he was absolutely telling the truth. When he was finished, Kendall and Gwendolyn walked back to the defense table and sat down. Their family members, sitting in the front row, had tears in their eyes.

Judge Walton motioned to the prosecution and stated that he was now prepared to hear the government allocution regarding Mr. Myers.

AUSA Harvey walked up to the lectern just vacated by the Myerses and placed papers in front of him before he started his rebuttal. "Thank you, Your Honor. Well, from the government's perspective, Your Honor, there's just no polite way to describe Kendall Myers's crimes against the United States. He's a traitor. He betrayed his colleagues at the State Department, he betrayed the United States government who trusted him with their secrets, with its secrets, and he betrayed our nation. As you just heard, he feels no remorse at all for what he did. He will not even acknowledge the harm that he caused to the United States."

A little later on, AUSA Harvey scored an important point when he noted that after Kendall retired from the State Department, he did not choose to live in the people's paradise of Cuba. As AUSA Harvey explained, "While Kendall may have admired the Cuban revolution, it was always only from a safe, comfortable distance here in the United States."

AUSA Harvey reminded the court, "Certainly the Cuban regime thought the information he provided was very valuable. For their efforts, for their services, both Gwendolyn and Kendall Myers were given medals by the Cuban intelligence service. And in 1995, the CuIS flew the Myerses to Cuba on a clandestine trip for the purpose of having a private audience with Fidel Castro himself. And that's what happened. And they obviously made an impression because when they were arrested, what Fidel Castro said is that the Myerses were deserving of all the honors in the world."

AUSA Harvey said that Kendall had told the FBI undercover agent (EK) that he was thinking of getting back into the spy business because "it would be fun." He continued, "The truth is that Kendall Myers sold out the United States of America every bit as much because he thought it would be thrilling. But today, it's finally time for him to pay the price of his treachery. He should unquestionably be sentenced to life without the possibility of parole."

AUSA Harvey concluded by asking: "I respectfully request the Court impose as part of his sentence a money judgment in the amount of $1,735,054, which reflects every cent of the salary he received from the United States government while he was, in fact, working for the Cuban regime."

With that, AUSA Harvey rested the US government's case. Unfortunately one cannot stand up and cheer in a courtroom.

It was time for Kendall's and Gwendolyn's defense team to speak on behalf of their clients.

Mr. Green commenced: "Your Honor, I stand here with a completely different posture with respect to Mr. Myers. Let me say at the outset that despite Mr. Harvey's description of my clients and the way they led their lives, they actually led a very modest life, not an extravagant life."

Green continued: "I do want to say that despite the profound consequences which he is about to suffer, and which he is, I say again, acutely aware, he did try diligently and with effort of recall in the course of these hundreds of hours of debriefings, all the information that was germane to the questions that were asked, thousands of questions. And he did that, in part, because of the terms of the agreement but also in recognition that it was the appropriate thing to do at that moment and stage in his life."

As quickly as he had stood before Judge Walton, Green returned to the defense table—less than five minutes after starting. When your client pleads guilty, get out of town fast.

It was now time for Judge Walton to announce his sentence but not before he gave a few comments. With his elbows comfortably resting on the bench, and with expressive hand motions, Judge Walton told Kendall that he had a few questions for him that he did not have to answer.

"I am very troubled by this case. The United States is not a perfect nation. I, for one, have seen ancestors who were denied basic rights in this country. A great-grandfather who lived all of his life in slavery, a grandfather who was born into slavery and spent a good portion of his early life as a sharecropper making eight dollars a month and two bushels of corn, and having seen my relatives when I grew up in Western Pennsylvania, who were good workers, who worked in the steel mill, never able to rise above the level of a laborer, including my father. I have very intelligent parents, but because of the times and the attitude about race that existed at that time, the opportunity for them to go to college was not available to them.

"But despite that history, I think the United States has a lot to be proud of, something that I think neither one of you appreciates. America is not the devil that you may believe it is. And that's not to say that America is perfect. I don't find Cuba to be some oasis of freedom and liberty. All you need to do is look in today's *USA Today* and see an article about individuals who had fortunately been released from prison in Cuba.

"So the suggestion that somehow it was pristine on the part of the two of you to harm your own country in order to try and help the Cuban people. . . . I don't see disseminating information to the Cuban government as necessarily helping the Cuban people. I would totally agree with you; I'm sure there are some very good people in Cuba who would like to live a different type of life, but the regime in Cuba does not make that possible. And I just don't see how improving the plight of those good people is in some way enhanced by undermining and betraying your own country. If you believed in the revolution and wanted to do the things that you said, I think the government is correct, you should have defected and you should have gone there and engaged in your life's work in trying to help the Cuban people.

"But to betray your own country and to give over information. . . . And whenever classified information is released, whether you intend to have somebody harmed or not, once you release that information, you never know what the effect will be. And it could, in fact, result in somebody who's involved in the intelligence community having their life taken. And unfortunately, Mr. Myers, and assume since you spoke on behalf of your wife, I see no sense of remorse. None whatsoever. You feel that your conduct was justified for reasons that are beyond my understanding. And I think, as the government says, you're proud of the things that you did. And that's, I think, extremely unfortunate. You are aware, you did have privileges that so many people in this country don't have. And unfortunately you squandered those privileges at the expense of your own government.

"Obviously, in reference to your situation, you have made a decision, and I do give you credit of being honorable in this respect. And that is, that you have accepted the consequences of your behavior, which will result in you being incarcerated for life. And you did that, as I understand, with the hope that at least it would give your wife some opportunity before she departs this world to have the opportunity of being a free person again. And I would agree that there's some level of honorability that comes with having made that sacrifice and choice."

Judge Walton then sentenced Kendall to a period of life in prison without the possibility of ever being released. He also sustained the $1.7 million judgment in the government's favor.

Gwendolyn received an eighty-one-month prison term. Judge Walton did recommend that the two be permitted to serve their sentences in close proximity to each other so that their family would have the opportunity to visit them.

About 11:50 a.m., the doors to Courtroom 16 opened, and the investigators and prosecution exited to shake hands in the hallway one final time. Kate and I hugged and smiled. The Myerses' family and friends remained behind in the front row of the courtroom and talked with the unrepentant defendants and the defense team. I knew that our victory was short lived. I also knew that CuIS clandestine penetration agents still walked undetected in the halls of the State Department.

Gwendolyn was transferred to the Federal Medical Center, Carswell. Located on the grounds of the Naval Air Station Joint Reserve Base in Fort Worth, Texas, this facility houses more than fourteen hundred inmates and is the only medical facility for women in the Federal Bureau of Prisons system. Gwendolyn has a heart condition, so this was the only incarceration site possible. Gwendolyn's fellow inmate is Cuban penetration agent Ana Montes. I wonder what they discuss when seated together for breakfast and dinner.

Kendall is eating his meals alone in "Supermax." Located on thirty-seven barren and sterile acres about one hundred miles from Denver, this five hundred-bed complex was opened in 1971. Officially known as Administrative Maximum Facility Florence (ADX), it was built to house this country's most dangerous criminals. Inmates spend twenty-three hours a day in a cell that consists of an immovable concrete bed, stool, and desk. The shower has a timer attached and the toilet will stop running if attempts are made to block it. A physically secured television screen allows inmates to watch closed-circuit religious, prison, and recreational programs. When an inmate leaves his cell for his five hours—one hour at a time—of private recreation a week, he is escorted by two or three corrections officers. Kendall's fellow foreign intelligence penetration agent inmates include Robert Hanssen (FBI) and Harold Nicholson (CIA), whom he will never meet.

In late 2009, in a modest-sized, windowless room located on the twenty-third floor of DS headquarters, an honors ceremony was hosted by Eric Boswell, the assistant secretary of state for diplomatic security, where individual and group awards for distinguished service over the past six months were proudly announced. Every seat was taken, people leaned against the walls, and the main door was propped open as late arrivers gathered around the doorframe. Late in the program, special agents Bill Stowell and Karin Terry along with PSS supervisor Barbara Shields were called to the podium, draped on one side by the American flag and the other by the State Department flag, to accept a group Superior Honor Award for their roles in the unmasking of "Vision Quest." The citation for the award simply read, *For superior effort working with the FBI to uncover the identity of the suspect of the "Vision Quest" espionage case.*

The initial nomination for the award read,

> *Drawing upon decades of experience, retired DS Special Agent [and now DS/ICI/CI contractor] Robert Booth carefully analyzed the known information and was able to develop a number of indicators or so called "matrix points" which formed a general outline of the yet unknown perpetrator. Remarkably, the dedicated DS team of Robert Booth, Barbara [Shields], Joseph ["Bill"] Stowell and Karin Terry were able to produce his name (Kendall Myers) from the original list of 2,000 potential people within a time frame of 30 days.*

Despite many good efforts by the DS/CI division chief, my name was not included on the award since contractors are ineligible per department regulation. I readily admit that my ego was bruised, but I took strength from an old quip—"no good deed goes unpunished."

In September 2010, Fidel Castro told the *Atlantic*'s Jeffrey Goldberg that "the Cuban model doesn't even work for us anymore," and Raúl Castro announced that the Cuban government would lay off at least 500,000 Cuban government workers by March 2011, hopefully to find jobs created by almost nonexistent bourgeois entrepreneurs. I wondered how Kendall took that bit of news about the maximum leader's explanation of his stewardship of the glorious socialist revolution, something Kendall helped to survive, if he was even allowed to get magazines in his ADX jail.

In 2011, senior State Department analyst Matthew Ouimet, one of Kendall's former colleagues, said, "When a friend of yours turns out to be one of the country's few international spies, that really wakes you up to the reality of counterintelligence matters. What's the worst sin at the bottom of Dante's Inferno? Treachery. It is those who betray a trust."

PART 2

Taiwanese Femme Fatale

Somebody would have to be a complete moron not to know that when you work for the State Department you can't take documents out and give them to anybody.

—US District Judge Harold H. Greene
(During the 1994 sentencing of State Department employee Geneva Jones to 37 months of federal incarceration for her unlawful communication of classified State Department information to a foreign power)

Beware the official, who, to impress women, betrays state secrets.

—Anonymous
(Chinese military journal recovered by Tibetan guerrillas in October 1961)

CHAPTER FIVE

DS special agent Kevin Warrener was livid. His foot stomped on the accelerator of his undercover Crown Vic as he sped away from Washington, DC, down the restricted Dulles Airport access highway. It was a beautiful late afternoon in September, the sun dipping lazily toward the horizon, but SA Warrener had other things on his mind. He was tempted to use the vehicle's blue lights and siren, but he knew his quarry of almost two years had likely already left the airport. He might even have passed him on the opposite side of the road.

SA Warrener raced down the seemingly endless stretch of highway that led to the airport's main terminal where thousands of passengers arrived and departed daily. Its modern, sweeping form finally came into view. Named after the famed secretary of state, Dulles was one of a handful of civilian airports owned and operated by the federal government. Maybe that would make his job a little easier in dealing with the bureaucrats.

He hastily parked in one of the airport's official spaces and hurried into the terminal, heading for the Immigration and Customs Enforcement (ICE) office. As he approached a young ICE officer behind the counter, he displayed the badge and photo credentials that identified him as a special agent with the Diplomatic Security Service.

Warrener knew that another opportunity to turn the corner on a two-year-old FBI–DS counterintelligence investigation was quickly slipping away. He was described by colleagues as "tenacious," "patient," and "gifted" with the perfect mind for counterintelligence operations, and his agents said that he was the kind of supervisor who gives credit when his subordinates do something right but takes the blame when something goes wrong. He was the consummate diplomat when working outside the office. Careful not to reveal too much about his visit, he asked "Chris," the ICE officer, if he could review the 6059B Customs and Immigration forms for passengers recently arrived from Tokyo, Japan, aboard United Airlines Flight #8228.

Chris immediately said "Yes," and the two proceeded to the lower labyrinth of the airport building. After a long march through dimly lit corridors, Chris opened the door to a small, fluorescent lit, windowless room. Inside were approximately fifty cardboard storage boxes containing thousands of customs declarations processed for all passengers arriving at Dulles airport that day—September 7, 2003.

All passengers were required to complete the form, which was distributed in flight, to allow the US Customs Service to protect the United States against the illegal importation of prohibited items and to ensure that all passengers were legally entitled to enter the country. When Chris offered to help search through the boxes containing the 6059B forms, Warrener accepted without hesitation, and they quickly divided the boxes between them.

For the next ninety minutes, the two agents chatted casually to interrupt the boredom of flipping through hundreds of customs forms. Kevin liked his P228 Sig Sauer 9mm semi-automatic pistol; Chris was a fan of his Glock. Both had graduated from the basic criminal investigator's course administered at the Federal Law Enforcement

Training Center in Glynco, Georgia. Both had some friends at the FBI; they were not fans of their respective senior management.

As their conversation and paper-flipping continued, Warrener spotted the customs declaration forms filled out by passengers who had deplaned just hours earlier from UA Flight #8228. Rapidly scanning the blue and white documents, he focused on the first question, calling for the passenger's family name, and in short order had located his suspect's declaration form.

For a frustrating and grueling year of surveillance, DS and FBI special agents had followed every move of Donald Willis Keyser, the department's principal deputy assistant secretary of state for East Asian and Pacific affairs (EAP). He had been involved in a covert relationship with a young, female, Taiwanese clandestine intelligence officer. Had Keyser finally committed his first overt federal crime—lying to his Uncle Sam?

SA Warrener's attention shifted to question eight where the traveler listed the countries he or she had visited while abroad. He noticed that his suspect had printed, in ink, "China and Japan." Glancing at the back of the form, he noticed that his suspect had declared that he had purchased three gifts: one scroll and two wood block prints valued at $150. However, the most important part of the customs form was at the bottom of the page where travelers signed a statement that their declarations were truthful. To Warrener's relief, the suspect had dutifully signed the name Donald W. Keyser and entered the date of September 7, 2003. SA Warrener let out the breath he had been holding. "We got him."

★★★

Born on July 17, 1943, Donald Willis Keyser grew up in Baltimore before enrolling in college in 1961. Between then and 1968, he earned a BA in political science with highest honors from the University of Maryland and pursued postgraduate work at George Washington University at various times. He was married to Beverly Louise Noell in 1963 and had several children in the ensuing years. From 1968 to 1970, he resided in Taipei, Taiwan, and studied the Chinese language through a Stanford University program designed to permit American college students to pursue graduate studies abroad. Keyser was expected to gain insight into Chinese culture and politics by working for local companies, where his immersion with Taiwanese citizens would enhance his Mandarin language skills. One would assume, given the final outcome of his career, that the fervent anti-communist sentiments shared among Taiwan's citizens on the island at that time may have influenced Keyser's pro-Taiwan, anti-Beijing orientation early in his life.

Keyser returned to the United States, where his interests in foreign and Chinese affairs prompted him to seek employment with the State Department. After rigorous exams in December 1970 and May 1971 and a background investigation in September 1971, he was eligible for appointment to the Foreign Service. His first assignment was to the Office of Asian Communist Affairs, where he monitored US–Sino bilateral relations for eight months. From February 1973 to July 1975, he shifted to the Office of East Asia Research in the Bureau of Intelligence and Research, where he prepared reports on the nettlesome question of a China–Taiwan reunification and identified political trends inside the People's Republic of China (PRC), still reeling from the aftermath of the Cultural Revolution. His analytical abilities and reports were of such quality that his work was quickly recognized by senior department China hands, and he was chosen for assignment to the newly opened United States Liaison Office (USLO) in Beijing.

Prior to his arrival in Beijing, Keyser returned to Taiwan in July 1975 for one year, attending FSI's Chinese (Mandarin) Interpreter Training class in Taichung in preparation for his USLO assignment. His final grades of 4/4 (fluent) in Chinese Mandarin and 2/2 (proficient) in Amoy (Taiwanese) were impressive accomplishments.

Keyser arrived in Beijing in June 1976 to join twenty-two fellow State Department colleagues including me who were responsible for reporting on the nascent US–China diplomatic relations that had lain largely dormant since 1949. Brash, arrogant, and extraordinarily competent, Keyser immediately established a reputation within the USLO for befriending diplomats, foreign journalists, and local nationals willing to share information detailing the intrigues and political machinations that characterized the secretive Chinese Communist Party. A number of his sources were foreign diplomats with extensive careers covering Asia.

In late 1976, Stan Brooks and Charles Sylvester, fellow USLO political officers, and Keyser were key Beijing observers reporting back to Washington regarding Mao's death, the purge of Mao's wife and the "Gang of Four," and the ongoing, internecine Communist party infighting. Sylvester was a favorite of the USLO security officers. His father had been a vice admiral who had been assigned to Shanghai before the war, and there a young Charles spent a period of his life. He was a US Navy pilot who eventually joined the Foreign Service in 1961. He was one of the good guys in my book.

Brooks, Sylvester, and Keyser eventually became senior Asia hands for the department and during 1976 kept Washington informed of the succession of power from Mao to Deng Xiaoping. These reports were devoured by the White House and the foreign affairs community because of their candid political commentary—Keyser produced a significant number of humorous, colorful reports that were favorite topics of conversation among the USLO staff. Keyser's skill at eliciting information from foreign diplomats and journalists would be critically important during his future assignments in both Washington and foreign cities.

The embassy cocktail circuits around the world are important venues where diplomats and sometimes journalists meet and share information with their foreign counterparts; this information-sharing concerning a country's political and social developments was the life blood of the profession. However, the potential for misinterpreting the nature of these relationships and reporting requirements was always an issue, so the department promulgated guidelines to ensure that all Foreign Service Officers (FSOs) understood the ground rules. Keyser's failure to abide by these security rules would lead to his downfall.

Following his tour in Beijing, Keyser was assigned as the political-military officer at the American embassy in Tokyo from 1979–1981. The main focus of his work was to monitor the issues arising from the US–Japan Mutual Security Treaty and the Status of Forces agreement. Our professional paths crossed once again when I was assigned to the regional security office in Tokyo from 1978 to 1980. Our contact was very limited as the embassy staff was quite large. The only unusual event concerning Keyser came to my attention in late 1979 when I was approached by a good friend of mine, Patricia, an FSO assigned to Tokyo.

"Robert," she said, "how well do you know Don Keyser?"

"Why do you ask?"

"You knew him in Beijing, right?"

"Yeah," I said. "He's an excellent officer with superb writing skills."

"Fine, but what about him personally?"

This was not what I wanted to discuss, but it was a fair question. "Well, there was some gossip about an extra-marital affair."

She looked me straight in the eye and for a couple of seconds said nothing. Finally she commented "He's quirky around women, and I feel uncomfortable in social settings with him."

"Is there something you want me to do?"

"Not now, but if I do, I'll let you know."

Initially I thought it must have been her imagination. Regrettably I was dismissive of my colleague and her comments, but her keen observations would seem prescient twenty-five years later. To some of his colleagues, Keyser's weakness for attractive, intelligent, and intriguing women was all too obvious. Frankly I did not see that aspect of his life at the time. My friend never brought up the subject again, and I departed Tokyo some eight months later.

Keyser's tour in Tokyo was followed by what is called an "out-of-department" assignment: he was detailed as a special assistant to the governor of Hawaii from May 1981 to June 1982. Upon his return to Main State, his career started to accelerate in terms of responsibility and professional accomplishments. To many of his admirers, he was a golden boy with a Midas touch. Assigned to Beijing in July 1982, he served as the embassy's chief of the Political/Internal Affairs Unit where he was responsible for developing relationships with the country's Ministry for Foreign Affairs, think tank scholars, journalists, and other officials involved in China's political mix.

Following Keyser's highly successful tour in China, the department brought him back to Washington and appointed him the deputy director of the Office of Chinese and Mongolian Affairs. There he supervised a six-person staff that oversaw all aspects of Sino–US bilateral relations, including managing the political and diplomatic agenda for President Reagan's 1984 official visit to mainland China.

After he concluded his two-year tour in Washington, Keyser returned to our embassy in Tokyo and served from 1985 to 1988 as the chief of political/external affairs. Among other responsibilities, he coordinated our Japanese policy, which at the time was primarily focused on not disturbing Sino–US relations.

At the conclusion of a successful tour in Tokyo, Keyser was chosen to be one of the State Department's candidates to attend a ten-month training course at the prestigious National War College located at Fort McNair in Washington. The regimen was designed to bring together military officers from the three branches of service and an equivalent number of senior government officials to study national security issues. Students were required to submit a paper on a foreign affairs topic, and Keyser's analytical report earned him the college's "Certificate for Excellence in Writing."

From August 1989 to July 1992, Keyser served as Minister-Counselor for Political Affairs at our embassy in Beijing, where he headed the section responsible for the conduct of US–China bilateral relations. As such, he was the third highest-ranking member in the embassy, following the ambassador and deputy chief of mission, and was responsible for managing all aspects of Sino–US bilateral relations. His fluency in Mandarin was of such high quality and his contacts with Chinese officials so broad that he was assigned by US ambassador James Lilley to negotiate secretly with the Chinese for the departure of dissident physicist Dr. Fang Lizhi, who had been living inside the embassy compound for seven months as a political refugee.

Ambassador Lilley was the former CIA station chief in Beijing (1973–1975) during a portion of Ambassador George Herbert Walker Bush's tenure in Beijing before the future president's departure from China to become the CIA director. In his book *China Hands*, Ambassador Lilley discusses his 1973–1975 covert assignment to the USLO that was "approved" by the Chinese government as long as the Chinese could have one of their intelligence officers similarly assigned to the Chinese Liaison office in Washington, DC. Lilley hastily left Beijing before I arrived, following an article in the October 30, 1974 edition of the *Washington Post* entitled "CIA Plant," written by columnist Jack Anderson, which publicly exposed Lilley's CIA affiliation while assigned to USLO.

In Beijing, Keyser was promoted to counselor, the department's personal, not diplomatic, rank equivalent to a one-star general. One fascinating aspect of Keyser's tour was that he was the US embassy's principal contact with Zhu en-Tao, who headed the PRC Interpol liaison office in Beijing. As it turned out, Zhu en-Tao was a Chinese MSS intelligence officer who was the handler of Larry Wu-Tai Chin, a CIA employee convicted of espionage in 1986. Keyser knew of Zhu's MSS intelligence affiliation and alerted Dale "Chip" McElhattan, the embassy's RSO, to that fact, just before the two had their first in a series of luncheons with Zhu to discuss matters of mutual interest. Keyser warned Dale to be careful what he revealed to the clandestine intelligence officer. At the luncheon, Zhu advised the two embassy officers that he knew he was persona non grata in the United States and that, during one Canadian trip to Niagara Falls, he had purposefully put one foot inside the United States just to have the satisfaction of "getting one over on the FBI."

Clearly Keyser was aware of foreign intelligence officers hiding behind a multitude of public titles and personas.

Successful as the department's political guru in China, Keyser returned to Washington to assume the directorship of the Office of Chinese and Mongolian Affairs, where he continued to work exclusively on Chinese–American issues, including helping Mongolia emerge into the new geopolitical environment.

Keyser then left the world of China and was assigned for two years as the director of the Office of Asia/Africa/Europe & Multilateral Issues, where he helped coordinate the fight against narcotics and criminal issues. Shortly after his arrival, Keyser was promoted to minister-counselor, the State Department's equivalent of a two-star general. This would be the end of the promotion rainbow for Keyser. He was fifty-three years old and running out of opportunities to serve in more substantive positions in the department.

In 1997, he was seconded to the Office of Inspector General (OIG), where he led policy-based inspections of our embassies located in Russia, southern Africa, Singapore, and Malaysia. During Keyser's tenure with the OIG, he partially revealed his negative attitude regarding DS security practices in an unclassified March 1998 Report of Inspection of our embassy in Moscow. During the inspection, Keyser served as the deputy team leader and finalized the formal Report of Inspection. There were no minority opinions or dissenting comments appended to the findings. On page two of the unclassified report, under the title "Russia Changing: Embassy Mired in the Past," the following excerpt appears:

> *There is a rather striking lack of congruence between, on the one hand, sweeping Russian changes and, on the other, an embassy structure—and mindset—harking back to the days of national struggle with an "Evil Empire." Russian society is unprecedentedly accessible, its political institution and processes open and indeed freewheeling, and its receptivity to foreign ideas and foreign contacts simply unimaginable a decade ago. Yet Embassy Moscow's current security standards and practices, support services and facilities are reflective of an enduring siege mentality more appropriate to Cold War days than the present. They represent a formidable symbolic and practical barrier to our ability to conduct an activist diplomacy suited to the new realities of the bilateral relationship. While security concerns have not dissipated and a need for vigilance surely endures, OIG is convinced that a high priority must be attached to rethinking, and adjusting as necessary, outmoded and counterproductive features of our Cold War regime.*

The statement would have been laughable had the stakes not been so high. Keyser and his like-minded colleagues were the ones who were mired in fanciful diplo-talk. Obviously he still distrusted the department's security apparatus. However, it was not a brave, new Russian world in any respect. As the OIG report was being written, the Kremlin was approving operational plans for the SVR to introduce clandestinely a listening device into the HST and FBI SSA Robert Hanssen, who would be convicted as an SVR penetration agent, was working on the first floor of the building at the same time. While the OIG's Pollyannaish report erroneously waxed favorably about the new Russian society, the Kremlin's intelligence services had not changed its behavior one iota.

In the mid-1990s, the department was forced to remove whole floors from its new chancery under construction in Moscow because the building was infested from top to bottom with listening devices, at the cost of millions of dollars. What had led Keyser and team leader Richard H. Melton to conclude that productive features of the Cold War, such as security rules and regulations, were outmoded? The passing of the Cold War had not diminished the Russians' appetite to target department personnel and American embassies in hopes of gaining access to sensitive information.

Retired SVR Major General Oleg Kalugin, who had served under diplomatic cover as a second secretary and press attaché at the Russian embassy in Washington, DC, in 1965, summed things up much later when he wrote in his book *The First Directorate* that three of the principal targets of the SVR were the White House, the US Congress, and the State Department. Notwithstanding the OIGs fifteen-year-old report, I believe that Vladimir Putin has only quickened the pace of targeting department assets.

Following his assignment in the OIG, Keyser served in 1998 as the State Department's special negotiator in the Office of Special Negotiator for Nagorno-Karabakh and NIS (Newly Independent States), where he toiled away attempting to find peaceful solutions to selected conflicts in parts of the former Soviet Union.

One year later, Keyser transferred to the State Department's Bureau of Intelligence and Research (INR) with the title of deputy assistant secretary of state. INR was, and is, the department's premier analytical component, with access to the most sensitive IC "top secret" technical and human information. Keyser was Kendall Myers's senior supervisor in INR.

During his tenure in INR, Keyser gained unwanted pubic notoriety when, in April 2000, it was reported in the press that DS and FBI special agents were investigating the circumstances surrounding the loss of an INR laptop computer containing "top secret" code word nuclear weapon proliferation information. The agents attempted to determine the circumstances behind its disappearance and the information contained in it from INR's Office of Analysis for Strategic, Proliferation, and Military issues. The investigation uncovered a number of procedural and administrative lapses concerning the purchase and control of the missing computer; however, no individual was identified as being ultimately responsible for its disappearance. The computer was never recovered, and the investigation is still considered an active one despite the lack of leads. Given the public notoriety, sacrificial lambs had to be identified and punished. It turned out there would be only one sizable lamb slaughtered in the whole affair.

Keyser, as the principal deputy assistant secretary of state for INR, was the senior operational officer in the office, and he was chosen as the designated fall guy for the loss. Following the department's recommendation that Keyser be suspended without pay for thirty days, J. Stapleton Roy, one of the State Department's most senior Black Dragons, former Ambassador to China, Singapore, and Indonesia, and Keyser's boss in Beijing, resigned in protest. Keyser was eventually suspended without pay for one week in 2001 and shortly thereafter transferred to the position of deputy assistant secretary of state for East Asia and Pacific affairs (EAP).

Obviously the penalty had no impact on his career—not that it should have since he was not responsible for the disappearance of the laptop. I agree with Ambassador Roy that Keyser was a scapegoat in this lamentable affair. As a result, though, Secretary Albright ordered a review of the department's internal security practices and insisted that individual offices identify officers to be responsible for a revitalized security awareness program. In INR, the person who immediately volunteered and was accepted for the onerous duty was one Walter Kendall Myers—Agent "202" himself. Our Cuban spy had a quirky sense of humor if nothing else.

Keyser and I would cross professional paths over the span of twenty-five years. All encounters were professionally and personally amicable. Don was a good guy in my book. In 2001, when I was the deputy director of counterintelligence and Keyser was the deputy assistant secretary of state for EAP, we were summoned by Assistant Secretary of State James Kelly to discuss a thorny counterintelligence issue concerning the personal "vulnerabilities" of FSOs who were candidates for assignment to countries whose intelligence services had been identified as being particularly aggressive in targeting American diplomats.

My office was, by executive regulation, required to provide either a "yes" or "no" recommendation, on national security grounds, for department officers selected to serve in particularly hostile overseas counterintelligence environments. DS/CI would make a recommendation based on the potentially "disqualifying" information (read: "vulnerabilities") contained in their SY Files. This policy, officially known as the "Pass-Through" program, had its official origins in a National Security Directive Decision (NSDD) signed by President Clinton in 1991. While our "no" recommendation hovered around the 2 percent level, it still caused numerous headaches for the department's personnel office. Our recommendations were a problem in the view of some department staffers who did not understand how foreign intelligence officers target department officers.

Keyser's immediate supervisor, Assistant Secretary of State Kelly, had been persuaded by anonymous department officers that my office's policy of reviewing and making "yes" or "no" recommendations to the director general of the Foreign Service was unfair, capricious, and arbitrary. From 1996 to 2000, the director general of the Foreign Service had upheld our "no" recommendations for proposed assignments 99.8 percent of the time, and that was causing administrative havoc for staffing EAP's embassies. DS/CI was not perfect, but national security must trump any institution's operational needs.

At 2:30 p.m. on August 29, 2001, as I walked into room 4314A in the HST with my senior supervisor, William Armor, I noticed a beat-up wooden conference table in an otherwise nondescript and crowded room. It was likely to be the locus of my drawing and quartering. Professional colleagues Chris LaFleur, a Tokyo colleague from the 1978–80 era, Max Bare, and, to my complete surprise, Keyser, were present. Upon seeing Keyser, my poker face relaxed a bit.

"*Nî hâo*, Robert," Keyser said, saluting me in Mandarin. "It's been some time. How are you doing?"

It is hard not to like Don Keyser. He stuck out his hand, and we shook. Dressed in a three-piece conservative suit, white shirt, and striped tie, he had sparse hair that was now almost completely white.

"How are John, David, and Evan doing?" he asked, inquiring about my fellow Beijing security officers.

"Luckily they've all managed to survive and prosper after our posting to Beijing, and all remain with the department. Of course, of our Beijing colleagues, none has done better than George Bush, no?"

"From ambassador to director of the CIA to vice president to president. Brilliant."

"You know," I said, "we still stay in touch by mail, and when Barbara and George visited Paris in 1994, I was able to arrange for a private little sit-down with my wife and me because Barbara wanted to see my four-year-old daughter, Chloe. George looked relaxed and appeared to be enjoying himself. I even have a photo of the event."

Keyser started to laugh. "George and Barbara had a fondness for you four security guys."

"And I see you've done quite well with yourself in a short period of time."

He put his hand on my shoulder. "One never knows in this business. Now let's sit down and get this pow-wow underway."

The meeting was convened so the participants could better understand how the "Pass-Through" program worked. Armor was happy to let me represent DS's position during the meeting, and I was ecstatic for the opportunity to explain the nuances of the NSDD as interpreted by the State Department. The discussions were generally cordial but sometimes a bit pointed in my direction. By the meeting's conclusion, Keyser and an officer from the Bureau of Human Resources, the two original disbelievers, had apparently been convinced that the program was both transparent and fair. In the end, Keyser asked Assistant Secretary Kelly to give DS the opportunity to explain the Pass-Through program to younger department employees so as to dispel any rumors that DS was running an out-of-control Star Chamber detrimental to their careers. He did, and we did. I am pleased to report the program continues today.

Subsequently Keyser was appointed as the principal deputy assistant secretary of state (PDAS) for EAP, where he was responsible for monitoring, among many challenging issues, major diplomatic and political topics affecting the Beijing-Taiwan–Washington, DC, dynamic.

In his new position, Keyser would be introduced to Chen Nien-tsu, a "junior officer" assigned to the administrative section of the quasi-diplomatic entity of Taiwan operating inside the United States known as the Taipei Economic and Cultural Representative Office (TECRO), located in northwest Washington, DC.

In reality, Chen Nien-tsu, also known as Isabelle Cheng, was a clandestine intelligence officer working for the Taiwanese National Security Bureau (NSB), a foreign intelligence agency. After meeting her, Keyser's future would be forever changed.

CHAPTER SIX

Established in March 1955 and subordinate to Taiwan's National Security Council, the NSB is responsible for collecting and analyzing all intelligence affecting Taiwan's national and strategic interests. Isabelle Cheng was thirty-three years old, a graduate with honors in political science from National Taiwan University. She had worked for Taiwanese legislator Chen Chien-jen before working for the NSB, and he was the current TECRO chief.

When she arrived in Washington, DC, Isabelle Cheng was engaged to correspondent Chris Cockle, a correspondent for the *China Post* in Taiwan who was transferring to Washington. They would marry in July 2004. Cheng's assignment was simply a matter of a Taiwanese clandestine intelligence officer working inside one of its diplomatic missions. By itself, it was pretty much humdrum stuff.

Shorn of all subtleties and eyewash, TECRO employees were nothing more than a bunch of super lobbyists for the Republic of China or the so-called government of Taiwan or, as the department preferred, simply Taiwan. When President Jimmy Carter assumed office in 1977, he discovered that he had inherited a President Ford/ Secretary of State Kissinger diplomatic mess whereby Washington and Beijing maintained quasi-diplomatic liaison offices in each other's capitals while Taiwan and the United States conducted formal relations through their respective embassies. President Carter wanted to end the political charade and formally switch diplomatic recognition from Taipei to Beijing, but others in government circles, including the powerful Taiwanese lobby, insisted that whatever formula the new administration devised could not be achieved at the expense of severing commercial and political ties with Taiwan.

After two years of quiet negotiations between Washington and Beijing, President Carter agreed to "derecognize" Taiwan and accept Beijing as the sole and legitimate government of the Chinese people. Undeterred by President Carter's behind the scenes maneuvering, the Taiwan lobby, heavily supported by Senator Barry Goldwater, was able to convince Congress to pass the Taiwan Relations Act, allowing the United States to continue official business with Taiwan despite formal recognition of the People's Republic of China. Deng Xiaoping, Mao Tse-tung's successor and paramount leader by 1979, was pragmatic enough to accept Washington's special relationship with Taiwan and continue the normalization of relations with the United States.

As a result, the American embassy in Taiwan was decommissioned as was the Taiwan embassy in Washington, DC, and they were replaced by the American Institute in Taiwan (AIT) and TECRO, respectively. State Department officials were authorized to meet with Taiwanese representatives as long as the functions occurred off official US premises. Reaching out to all private and public institutions in the United States, TECRO officials attempted to gain the moral and political high ground for their government in Taiwan.

Covert NSB officers working under TECRO cover conduct business in Washington the same way their diplomatic colleagues in the

SVR, DGSE, Mossad, MSS, and other foreign intelligence services operate in our nation's capital. State Department officers and their foreign embassy counterparts interact by exchanging views on a variety of matters, including strategic and counterterrorism objectives with our allies and, yes, our adversaries. Department officers with oversight for Asian issues meet and develop professional relationships with foreign diplomats and citizenry knowledgeable of that region of the world. Keyser, as EAP PDAS, would have been a prime target for any Asian diplomat assigned to Washington.

As a matter of practice, the FBI conducts surveillance on foreign diplomats accredited by the State Department assigned within the United States who are suspected to be clandestine intelligence officers. At TECRO, Lieutenant General Huang Kuang-hsun, known to his friends as Michael Huang, was the senior NSB officer residing in the United States. His official Taiwanese title, rank, and position within the NSB had been declared to the US government in the same fashion that the senior CIA chief of station's identity is disclosed to senior foreign host government officials. This practical expediency allowed senior US intelligence officers to meet overtly, yet discreetly, with their opposite numbers to resolve various intelligence issues affecting both countries. It was all done on the QT. All other intelligence officers remained clandestine unless liaison circumstances required otherwise. Knowing that Michael Huang was an NSB official, the FBI monitored which TECRO officers would be seen most frequently in his company at social settings or official gatherings outside its official compound. Clearly any newly arriving junior officer assigned to TECRO who associated with General Huang might provide a clue to the officer's true mission. Cheng, who arrived in Washington in 2001 as the newest addition to the TECRO staff, quickly met the FBI's hostile intelligence profile.

What exactly aroused the FBI's suspicion of Cheng? In midsummer 2001, Michael Huang was recorded by FBI surveillance as being fully engaged in his social and semiofficial engagements throughout metropolitan Washington and increasingly accompanied by Cheng. The obvious FBI conclusion was that the senior officer, General Huang, was mentoring his junior subordinate.

In May 2002, Keyser was at a department-sanctioned meeting at the Four Seasons hotel with seven TECRO officials. General Huang and IC officials were also present. Cheng was the official note-taker during the discussions. It was apparent to all in the room that the young officer was Huang's newest protégé. Reportedly Keyser and Cheng did not engage in any discussion during the meeting, nor did they exchange business cards. While this initial meeting did not result in a promise of continuing contact, they were reunited at a subsequent dinner some five months later.

In the fall of 2002, AIT director Gregg Mann hosted a private dinner at his home for TECRO officials, including General Huang and Cheng, certain department officials, and select US and Taiwanese businessmen. According to the attendees, sometime during the soirée Keyser and Cheng moved to Mann's kitchen while the rest of the guests played out a familiar diplomatic waltz in the living and dining rooms. Removed from the general hubbub, the pair spent the next two hours in quiet conversation. Before the evening ended, Cheng and Keyser exchanged office numbers and e-mail addresses.

The next day, Cheng called Keyser at the State Department and suggested that the two rendezvous for a luncheon the following week. Her invitation was immediately accepted. Was the hook baited, and had the prize struck?

Within weeks, Keyser and Cheng were in frequent telephone and e-mail communication, interspaced with midday restaurant meetings in suburban Virginia and Maryland. Occasionally the twosome's rendezvous would include General Huang. The NSB general must have been very pleased with his young colleague's diplomatic success.

In late 2002, after several weeks of monitoring Keyser's meetings with the suspected NSB officer, the FBI quietly approached DS/CI to express its concerns. DS/CI explained to the startled FBI agents that department officers routinely are permitted to meet with foreign diplomats and citizens, including possible intelligence officers, as long as they report their contacts in accordance with department regulations. A department officer simply cannot conduct his or her job effectively without such contacts. The DS/CI deputy chief pointed out that there was no specific DS prohibition against meeting most foreign diplomats without prior authorization from the department. The department's HR office required FSOs to report social relationships, including marriage proposals, with foreign nationals.

The DS/CI deputy chief advised the FBI agents that FSOs have to report contacts to DS per 12 FAM 262 only if a contact (1) asks for classified information, (2) asks the officer to become a spy, or (3) is a citizen of a country designated as being particularly hostile to the US national interests. In these circumstances, the State Department officers also know that, according to internal regulations, there exists a general disclaimer: "The non-reporting of a relationship under this section will not constitute a security violation or result in disciplinary actions, as self-determination is the intent of the criterion." Even more wishy-washy, the foreign affairs manual states that "a security clearance will not be suspended solely because the employee did not report a relationship under this criterion."

On January 18, 2006, during his initial debriefing, Keyser admitted knowing that Cheng was an NSB intelligence officer yet his personal interpretation of the State Department rules did not require him to submit a contact report to DS or HR.

DS/CI maintains an electronic database of all the foreign contact reports submitted by department officers. A quick search of the database revealed that between 2000–2002, Keyser had not submitted a single report concerning any contact with any TECRO official. DS depends on each individual department employee to recognize potential or real counterintelligence threats and alert DS/CI so it can devise appropriate countermeasures as necessary.

Keyser had received several security awareness briefings during his diplomatic career and was cognizant of the modus operandi of Asian intelligence services. The DS/CI agents concluded that while Keyser might be in technical violation of department regulations by not reporting his contacts with two members of a foreign intelligence service, he might have valid foreign policy reasons for meeting with them, and therefore, he decided that he did not have to report to DS/CI.

Keyser maintained a number of professional contacts with other foreign diplomats and clandestine intelligence officers masquerading as diplomats or foreign journalists based in Washington. For example, Keyser had a professional relationship with Bertrand Lortholary, the French embassy's Political Counselor assigned to Washington, DC. In July 2003, among his many duties, Monsieur Lortholary was responsible for monitoring US–Chinese issues and forwarding his analysis to the Ministry of Foreign Affairs in Paris. At the time, Keyser was EAP PDAS, and given his US government influence and knowledge of Asian issues, he would have been a State Department insider the French embassy would want to cultivate.

On July 2, 2003, the French embassy sent a fax requesting a courtesy visit to the department so that Messrs. Lortholary and Keyser could discuss matters of mutual interest. It would be difficult to imagine that the two didn't share some bits of sensitive information during their first meeting. Did Keyser have to submit a contact report to DS following his meeting with Lortholary? Only if Lortholary's behavior at the proposed meeting had triggered DS's mandated reporting requirements for Keyser. Did Keyser have to submit a contact report for his meetings with Cheng? Only if he believed she represented a hostile intelligence threat. According to our counterintelligence database, Keyser did not think so because he had submitted no contact reports.

Like Keyser, Frederick Christopher Hamilton, a young Defense Department employee, had pronounced opinions about what categories of classified US government information could be shared with a foreign government, despite signing a secrecy agreement to the contrary. Hamilton had been assigned as a research technician to the American embassy in Lima, Peru, in the Defense Attaché Office (DAO) from 1989 to 1991. He was a civil service employee working for the DIA. In 1986, prior to his posting to Lima, he wrote a paper entitled an "Analyst's Guide to Foreign Disclosure" in which he advocated the not-so-novel idea that the US government should provide classified information to a foreign government if the United States knew that country "A" was about to attack country "B" and both countries were American allies. His central theme called for reducing military tensions and avoiding diplomatic wrangling by selectively sharing our intelligence with others. Years later, Hamilton would put into practice what he preached.

Hamilton met his foreign military counterparts at social events, and some of his closest contacts included those assigned to the Ecuadorian embassy in Lima. Toward the end of his tour, classified reports began to filter into the DAO's office that the long simmering border dispute between Ecuador and Peru might erupt into a serious conflict. Despite public pronouncements by both sides suggesting that conflict was inevitable, the US military's intelligence indicated that neither side was gearing up for war. Hamilton believed that if his Ecuadorian military contacts in Lima had access to the DAO information and passed that data to their generals in Quito, the cross-border tensions could be reduced.

So, undeterred by his oath of office, Hamilton provided several classified Intelligence and Information Reports (IIRs) on February 13 and May 20, 1991, to the Ecuadorian military attachés. The IIRs detailed the military capabilities of the Peruvian Armed Forces, US intelligence operations, and US sources in the region. The same classified IIRs allowed the Ecuadorian Ministry of Defense to determine if the Peruvian soldiers were truly combat ready or whether the calls to military action were merely saber rattling intended for public consumption. The IIRs concluded that despite pubic rhetoric to the contrary, Peru was not gearing up for a border clash with Ecuador and that any movements by the Peruvian armed forces were defensive in nature.

Hamilton's misdeeds were uncovered the following year, and he eventually pleaded guilty to two counts of unlawful communication of classified information to a foreign country. On April 16, 1993, he was sentenced to thirty-seven months in federal prison.

US diplomats sharing information with foreign diplomats was certainly nothing new; however, the FBI and DS agents needed to determine if Keyser was sharing classified information in an unauthorized fashion with his TECRO contacts. Following months of surveillance, DS/CI and the FBI fully agreed that the developing Keyser–Cheng relationship deserved their closest attention. It was apparent from the beginning that they enjoyed both a professional and social relationship. Quickly the FBI and DS were authorized to conduct both human and technical coverage of Keyser's comings and goings.

At this point, after being informed of the investigation, I decided to alert the FBI and DS special agents of certain aspects of Keyser's background as well as the history of the MSS's targeting of foreign diplomats.

Just prior to Keyser's arrival in Beijing in 1976, Christopher Henry Ballou, USLO's liaison officer, told me the story of how in the early spring of 1965, Keyser explained to his wife Beverly that he needed to leave Baltimore to pursue his graduate studies in Sino-Soviet relations at George Washington University (GWU), a one-hour drive away. Once comfortably situated in Washington, he pursued graduate studies with a focus on Russian affairs and language studies. One unpublicized fact about his move from Baltimore was his undeclared employment with the CIA. While his employment status was not for public consumption, his affections for Virginia Lee May—a young, single, and attractive woman with dark, wavy hair and penetrating eyes he met on the GWU campus—was similarly "close hold" information.

In early 1966, while on a short visit home to Baltimore, Keyser told his wife that he had to travel to California on a secret mission for the CIA for an unspecified period of time. Fully supportive of her husband's career, she wished him great success on his assignment. With his wife's blessing, Keyser moved to San Francisco in July 1966, where he rented an apartment that he shared with May, took Chinese language courses at a local state college, and worked part-time for a maritime agency located on Mission Street.

Not only had Keyser forsaken his wife; he had also abandoned his employment with the CIA, which was unaware of his purported secret California mission. After several months of complete silence, Mrs. Keyser telephoned the CIA through a special number to inquire as to how long her husband would remain incommunicado in California. The CIA's immediate response to Mrs. Keyser was that it was also attempting to locate him.

Mrs. Keyser hired Robert Bruce Tora, a private detective, to find her husband and report back to her. Tora managed to locate the shared apartment. He monitored the activities and eventually provided her with a full report. Mrs. Keyser wasted little time initiating divorce proceedings, and Keyser didn't bother to contest his wife's claims of adultery and desertion. Keyser's first marriage ended in Baltimore County Court on July 15, 1968. Fourteen days following the divorce decree, Donald Willis Keyser and Virginia Lee May married in San Rafael, California.

Keyser's USLO assignment in Beijing was marred by a similar sexual indiscretion. Months after I left Beijing for Geneva in 1977, Brent Jones, my Australian embassy security counterpart and former apartment neighbor, sent me a letter from the PRC telling me that the diplomatic community was all abuzz with gossip that Keyser had been involved in a long-term dalliance with a young female and that US Ambassador Leonard Woodcock had been informed of the affair by Keyser himself.

While extra-marital affairs and sexual indiscretions were not uncommon among the diplomatic community in Beijing during the mid to late 70s, the question on my mind was why Keyser felt compelled to inform the ambassador and apparently his wife of his sexual peccadillo. Fear of getting caught by his wife or colleagues, or something worse?

All foreign diplomats working in Beijing resided in apartments under the strict control of the Chinese government, except the Russians, who lived on an exclusive compound co-located with their embassy. Armed members of the People's Liberation Army controlled entrances and exits to the "diplomatic ghettos," and all USLO officers assumed that the Chinese-operated apartments were equipped with the latest electronic surveillance and bugging gear.

If Keyser had been so indiscreet as to meet his paramour inside one of the diplomatic apartments, or worse, the Beijing Hotel, then the Chinese domestic security service, called the General Investigations Bureau (GIB) was aware of his activities. With film in hand, the GIB would have approached Keyser and attempted to blackmail him. The success of the GIB's blackmail attempt would depend exclusively on Keyser's desire to conceal the alleged affair from his wife and the department. In this scenario, the only way for Keyser to defuse the blackmail time bomb was to confess his sins.

The department was sufficiently alarmed by Keyser's "marital problems" that on June 5, 1978, DASS Victor Dikeos sent SY Channel telegram number 141355 to Ambassador Woodcock outlining counterintelligence concerns about Keyser. If Keyser was worried about the GIB, his fears were not unfounded. Future counterintelligence events in the PRC would reveal that the Chinese intelligence services closely monitor married diplomats.

The Chinese Ministry of State Security (MSS), the GIB's successor, attempted to blackmail Paul Doumitt, a married, forty-five-year-old US embassy communications officer assigned to Beijing in October 1988. While Doumitt's wife remained in France to take care of her ailing mother, he engaged in a long-term intimate affair with a twenty-three-year-old Chinese shopkeeper named Liu "Jane" Jie. As the United Press International (UPI) reported in a dispatch dated November 11, 1988, "An unidentified American who works in the communications section (in Beijing) was the target of a MSS sex entrapment/blackmail attempt." Doumitt was confronted by the MSS in a hotel room across the street from Jane's apartment. He was told that unless he provided the identities of intelligence officers assigned to the embassy, both his wife and the US ambassador would receive graphic evidence of his infidelity. Doumitt declined to provide the MSS with the identity of any actual covert officer, choosing instead to suggest that DS agents assigned to the Beijing embassy as regional security officers (RSOs) "might be" intelligence officers. Returning to the US embassy, Doumitt tearfully told the RSOs of his indiscretions.

After a midnight telephone call to Washington, Ambassador Winston Lord swiftly removed Doumitt from China just ahead of the UPI story. In 1994, Doumitt was assigned to the US embassy in Paris where I was working in the security office. Over time, he provided me with some of the details of the MSS blackmail attempt.

In 2004, the MSS similarly attempted to blackmail a married Japanese diplomat assigned to the Japanese Consulate in Shanghai, whose wife remained in Japan, after he was caught in an adulterous relationship with a Chinese hostess working in a karaoke bar. The MSS demanded that the Japanese diplomat, a communications officer just like Doumitt, provide them with the Japanese diplomatic codes. The conclusion of this MSS blackmail attempt was entirely different from that of Doumitt. The Japanese diplomat returned to his office, wrote letters of apology to his wife and supervisor, and promptly hanged himself inside the consulate. Undeterred, in 2005 the MSS would again attempt to blackmail a married State Department officer traveling outside Beijing after the officer had engaged in sexual relations with a masseuse. Returning home, the officer reported the MSS blackmail attempt to the embassy security officer, and the ambassador ordered his immediate return to the United States. Blackmailing unfaithful married diplomats has been a tool of foreign intelligence services for over a hundred years and, in an attempt to mitigate this vulnerability, DS provides routine and regular security awareness briefings to all FSOs to sensitize them to this danger. Keyser attended many such briefings both in Washington and while serving overseas.

As Keyser was packing up his household effects in preparation for his upcoming assignment to Tokyo, Mrs. Virginia Keyser filed for divorce, charging adultery. Keyser countered with a cross-complaint alleging irreconcilable differences. The presiding judge granted a no-fault divorce on December 13, 1985, on the grounds that they had intentionally lived apart without relations for more than one year. Custody of their twelve-year-old son, Gregory, was given to Mrs. Keyser. On February 22, 1986, Keyser married Margaret "Peggy" Lyons, a reserved, petite, and elegant CIA officer.

★★★

SA Kevin Warrener was the agent identified by DS/CI to be the FBI's go-to person in this investigation, and he was instructed that he was not to discuss the matter further with his colleagues. That would shortly change when Kevin was tasked to travel to Baghdad to conduct a number of counterintelligence inquiries and there was no one left in his division except for a brand new agent by the name of Giovanna Cavalier.

A native New Yorker who in 2003 received a master's degree from Georgetown University's security studies program with a focus on counterintelligence, she graduated from basic agent training shortly before being assigned to DS/CI. Kevin had no choice but to hand over the investigation to her. Just before Kevin's departure for Baghdad, he and Giovanna met with their FBI counterparts to determine the best way to monitor Keyser technically. They wanted to see what information Keyser was communicating to foreign contacts and contrast that with what he might be sharing with Cheng.

Fortunately for the investigating team, Keyser used his office unclassified e-mail system to communicate with Cheng. That allowed the FBI and DS to review his personal messages to his TECRO contact. Whenever an employee logs onto the department's computer system, linked to the Internet, a banner immediately appears advising all users that the system is being monitored by the department's information technology and security staff. The warning is displayed more for reasons of preventing access to porn than finding evidence of espionage. DS agents began monitoring Keyser's e-mail use and discovered that he liked to message Cheng. By the end of September 2004, he was sending her an average of five e-mails a day.

On October 23 and 26, 2002, Keyser sent lengthy e-mails to Cheng detailing his assistance with the translations and conversations between President George Bush and Chinese president Jiang Zemin during the latter's trip to Crawford, Texas. Keyser was able to describe in detail Zemin's views on HIV/AIDS issues, intelligence cooperation, religion, the World Trade Organization, cross-strait relations, and Vice President Hu Jintao's response to Vice President Cheney's invitation to visit the United States. Not only did he report on the meeting, but he also added his critical analysis—a bonus for Cheng and the NSB.

On November 22, 2002, Keyser sent an e-mail to Cheng analyzing press reports that she had sent him regarding the assumption by President Jaing Zemin of additional national security responsibilities. Keyser's analysis benefitted from his access and knowledge of highly sensitive US government information. Keyser knew his prior conversations with Cheng were being reported to the NSB in Taipei and shared with senior Taiwanese officials. Following a luncheon engagement on March 6, 2003, Keyser sent an e-mail to Cheng stating the following:

"Knowing that you are obligated to write up these lunchtime conversations, I tried not to say too much so as to spare you excessive labors. But I hope I didn't say too little and therefore cause you and Mr. Huang to wonder what on earth we were all doing there except exchanging stories and consuming an excellent international meal. I'm sure that NSB will begin to have questions if it appears that good taxpayer money [Taiwanese] is going to excellent meals in nice restaurants that produce nothing of reporting interest."

In this e-mail Keyser acknowledged that Cheng had to prepare contact reports per NSB internal regulations while at the same time he interpreted department regulations to mean that he did not.

On March 16, 2003, Keyser e-mailed Cheng: "[I hope] I haven't inundated you. I think I've sent you the key items, at least as I read the developing news. I'll stop sending now so that you can 'digest' and write whatever you need to write. My yinmou guiji, of course, is to keep you as well informed as possible so that your people in Taipei consider you to be the indispensable officer in Washington. . . ."

Keyser's inadvertent admissions in this e-mail were particularly telling. The "developing news" he'd read, analyzed, and forwarded to his NSB contact could not have been data already available to the NSB. As Keyser correctly pointed out in his March 6 e-mail to Cheng, why would the NSB continue to pay for excellent cuisine only to obtain information of little reporting interest if it wasn't getting something more substantive from Keyser?

Keyser later claimed that the information provided to his NSB contacts was culled from the internet and included data from think tanks and academic institutions—in other words, from public sources. While the information may not have been classified, all Tier-1 foreign intelligence agencies (UK, Israel, Russia, PRC, etc.) spend considerable financial and human resources to locate, review, and analyze public information for inclusion in both their classified and unclassified reports. Most honest analysts will tell you that 95 percent of the data they use to produce classified reports already exists in the public domain and another 4 percent comes from electronic intercepts and what is referred to in the trade as "overhead imagery." The other 1 percent comes from human sources—the least reliable. If Keyser, a respected specialist in Asian issues, identified a specific public document that the NSB should consider, he did so based on his personal expertise and analysis of classified government intercepts and imagery, something not readily available to the NSB. His stamp of approval on certain think tank and academic institution positions was tantamount to certifying their validity. Few other department officials possessed his experience and gravitas when it came to understanding Asian current events.

On March 28, 2003, while Keyser was involved in negotiations with senior South Korean officials, he attended a meeting with the US commander of the Pacific fleet in Korea and shortly reported to Cheng the substance of those discussions. The FBI and DS continued to monitor the relationship closely. It was not difficult to discern that Keyser was sharing information with Cheng. What would be hard to do was link his disclosures to specific identifiable US Government classified documents. It also was a matter of finding something unassailable that would stand up in a court of law. It was a matter of getting lucky too.

One e-mail sent to Cheng caught the attention of DS and FBI when Keyser spelled out his next proposed luncheon: "It is a Spanish/Mediterranean place I mentioned that my Gonfei journalist/MSS [Li Zhebgxin] favors. Perhaps we will see him there. If so, shall I introduce you? And as what?"

Keyser acknowledged that he was meeting and conversing with a foreign clandestine intelligence officer working under journalist cover, a very tricky business at best, even for someone as experienced as Keyser. Even worse, as we discovered by combing through the databases, Keyser had not alerted his EAP supervisors or DS of his conversation with a hostile foreign agent—clearly ignoring IC regulations. While he was willing to acknowledge his professional relationship with a suspected MSS clandestine intelligence officer to a suspected NSB clandestine intelligence officer over the unclassified e-mail system, he did not deign to advise the department's counterintelligence office or submit a contact report.

The FBI and DS couldn't help but shake their collective heads. Truthfully we were getting pretty good at that neck exercise. Besides the technical coverage, the FBI and DS agents followed and filmed Keyser and Cheng sharing many quiet lunches alone.

E-mail communication between Keyser and Cheng in June 2003 indicated that the two were planning a private rendezvous in Taiwan without the knowledge of Keyser's supervisors, office colleagues, or wife. On June 28, Keyser sent an e-mail to Cheng via his office computer in which he cryptically said, "I look forward to hearing from you personally when you take me on the grand Plan A or Plan B around Taipei." Additional e-mail queries revealed that Keyser researched flight information from Tokyo to Taipei and reviewed the availability of hotel rooms in Taiwan for September.

With increasing alarm, the FBI and DS agents reviewed Keyser's e-mail communication with Cheng as they prepared for their Taiwan vacation. On August 30, Keyser informed Cheng that he was "glad that the logistical plan seems OK. I'll try hard for 1830 and I'll let you know if something prevents—also let you know when I'm in striking distance."

The DS agents had already alerted their FBI colleagues that Keyser was scheduled to depart the United States for a scheduled, official trip to Qing Dao in mainland China where he would represent the department at an international forum and that Keyser would be taking a department laptop computer with him on the trip to assist with his presentations. According to department rules, the information on the computer could contain only unclassified data on the hard drive, but given Keyser's apparent disregard for security regulations, anything was possible. Even more disturbing, the FBI confirmed that, along with his department computer, Keyser would be taking his personal laptop to China and probably Taiwan as well. Despite the counterintelligence concerns, there was nothing DS could do to prevent the trip without tipping its hand.

On the afternoon of August 30, as Keyser was preparing to travel to the PRC, Cheng left Dulles Airport for a flight to Taiwan via Los Angeles. On August 31, Keyser flew from Washington to the PRC and arrived in Qing Dao on September 1. That same day he sent a message to Cheng, now relaxing in Taiwan and visiting her supervisors at NSB headquarters: "Since I seemed to have navigated the most [complex] part of the journey successfully, I'm encouraged that the departure plan will work equally smoothly—on Tuesday from Qingdao to Seoul to Tokyo. If all that works, I'll continue on the rest of the journey as planned. If something happens, I'll do my best to let you know by cell phone and internet e-mail." The message was sent via e-mail over an unsecure system from China and handled by one of only three servers in the PRC authorized by the Beijing government to handle e-mail communications. One had to wonder what the MSS may have made of the contents of the message. The MSS's dossier on Keyser, started in 1976, was growing in leaps and bounds.

Contemporaneously with his communication with Cheng, Keyser sent an unclassified e-mail to his immediate superior in Washington, Assistant Secretary of State James Kelly: "Right now, I plan to stay in Japan the remainder of the week, but to be on annual leave. Through brilliant timing, I hit a period when virtually everyone I would have wanted to see has dispersed to the four corners of the globe, from Washington to Seoul to Beijing. As it happens, I have some personal friends in Japan I've wanted to catch up with, including an old friend whose wife passed away in June following a battle with leukemia. Back in the office Monday morning Sept. 8."

Kelly replied that Keyser's annual leave request had been approved. When Assistant Secretary Kelly was subsequently interviewed by the FBI concerning Keyser's clandestine travel to Taiwan, he stated that had Keyser requested permission to travel to Taiwan for either personal or official reasons he would have unhesitatingly denied any such request for a variety of regional political reasons. Without fanfare or official notification, Keyser departed on a flight to Taipei the following day.

Keyser's smokescreen was elaborately constructed. What most disturbed the investigators were the two laptops that Keyser took to both Chinas. In an e-mail on August 30 to one of his department colleagues, he stated that he was bringing "a laptop and accessories" to Qing Dao to help him with his work. What concerned the investigators was the possibility the laptops contained classified information and, if so, that he might share the contents with NSB officials while vacationing in Taiwan with Cheng.

The investigators later discovered their fears at the time were justified. FBI forensic analysts confirmed that a floppy disk found in Keyser's residence held "34 files, nine of which are classified data. All 34 files on the floppy disks show a 'date created' and 'date last modified' of August 29, 2003—two days before the defendant departed the United States for China—indicating that he downloaded all of the files onto the floppy to take with him overseas. Moreover, 9 of the classified files on the floppy disk show a 'date last accessed' of September 1, 2003 and all 9 of those files have corresponding 'link' files on the hard drive of the laptop, indicating that they were accessed from the laptop on September 1, when he was in China."

Given the sensitivities of the case, the FBI decided that none of the US counterintelligence assets in the PRC, Taiwan, or Japan would be alerted to Keyser's presence in Qing Dao as there was probably nothing they could do to further the investigation. Keyser was in the

PRC, headed to Taiwan, and completely outside the reach of DS and FBI investigators.

Keyser was a model diplomat in the PRC, all the while advancing US foreign policy and debating issues with his Chinese counterparts. At the conclusion of his trip to Qing Dao, he returned to Beijing, flew to Korea, and eventually caught a flight to Japan. He had now returned to the DS–FBI's radar scope.

According to subsequent statements provided to the FBI on February 14, 2006, Keyser averred he did not associate with anyone other than Cheng while in Taiwan. However, his subsequent polygraph examination indicated deception on the point. When he was asked if he had illegally provided classified information to any foreign intelligence service while in Taiwan, the needles on the machine also indicated two points of deception. The FBI also questioned Keyser:

Agent: "[W]ho did you meet with when you went to . . . Taiwan?"

Keyser: "Just Isabelle Cheng."

Agent: "[Are] you sure that Isabelle Cheng is the only person you met with?"

Keyser: "I'm certain."

Agent: "The only person you decided to see in Taiwan in 2003 was a known intelligence officer of the NSB. Is that what you're saying to us today?"

Keyser: "The only person I saw when I was there was Isabelle Cheng."

According to his testimony, Keyser only went to Taiwan to spend three days with Cheng. Of course, neither his wife nor supervisor was privy to his visit. He asserted that he and Cheng spent the time in Taiwan sightseeing and that he had contact only with "clerks, shopkeepers" and similar individuals and denied any meetings with Taiwanese officials.

A review of Keyser's credit card transactions for the period of September 3–5, 2003, in Taipei reflected one purchase for $570.01 at the Christian Dior II Taipei and a debit of $333.19 at the Grand Formosa Regent Taipei hotel. Apparently Keyser incurred no other expenses during his three-day stay in Taipei unless he paid for his meals, transportation, and other tourist incidentals with wads of cash that he brought with him from Japan. That scenario seems unlikely.

To further disguise his travel to Taiwan, when Keyser submitted an official travel voucher for repayment for expenses, he stated that he took annual leave because he "found prospective interlocutors to be out of town." There was no claim of any expenses for the Taiwan leg of his travel on his department travel voucher.

Eventually at the direction of DS/CI, the RSO at the American embassy in Tokyo reviewed the Japanese immigration arrival and departure records and confirmed that Keyser arrived in Japan on September 2, departed the following day aboard China Airlines, Taiwan's national carrier, returning to Narita International Airport in Tokyo aboard China Airlines on September 6 before boarding the nonstop United Airlines flight to Dulles International Airport. The Japanese government kept incredibly meticulous records as I had initially discovered when assigned there with Keyser in the late 1970s.

DS agents were taken aback when they belatedly discovered that Keyser did not hide his trip to Taiwan from the US embassy staff in Tokyo. Douglas Morris, assigned to Tokyo in September 2003, told me in July 2007 that everybody at the embassy was aware that Keyser traveled to Taiwan that September. They were all stunned to hear that he had attempted to cover up his trip to Taiwan when he returned to the United States. Maria Malvines, another officer assigned to the US embassy in September 2003, also confirmed in June 2007 that she and other embassy staffers were fully aware of Keyser's trip to Taiwan. She explained to me, following a class I was teaching at FSI, that the trip was not secret within the embassy community and she could not understand why he had lied on his US Customs form. Not surprising, given that they didn't know the true nature of Keyser's interest in traveling to Taipei.

While Keyser would later claim that he was not required to report his 2003 personal travel to Taiwan, one has to wonder why he had previously disclosed personal travel to France in April 2000 and Ireland in 2003 while omitting Taiwan on his official department security forms. Had he simply forgotten about the three-day stopover in Taiwan? Given the elaborate preparations and deceptions preceding the travel, the excuse was not plausible.

Once back in Washington, Keyser's personal and professional relationship with Cheng accelerated. On October 3, 2003, e-mail communications between Keyser and Cheng were monitored as they made arrangements to meet at Les Halles restaurant at 12:30 for lunch. A review by investigators of Keyser's official electronic calendar revealed that he listed a meeting at Les Halles with a "Juergen Probst." The FBI would similarly monitor a luncheon engagement between the two on November 26, 2003, while Keyser's calendar had him dining with a "John Metcalf." Keyser's attempt to disguise Cheng's identity on his official calendar actually started on January 16, 2003, with a luncheon with "Ranade" and would continue until June 3, 2004, when he had a lunch with Cheng that was recorded in his calendar as "Ian Patterson." These luncheon engagements were closely monitored by the FBI.

When Keyser had lunch with General Huang on November 14, 2003, he duly recorded the event. Why conceal private lunches with Cheng but not General Huang? On May 22, 2004, Keyser also listed another meeting with General Huang on his calendar. One of the questions the FBI asked the DS investigators was just how Keyser managed his other duties given that fact that the NSB officials seemed to monopolize his time. There were smiles all around as we speculated that he must have taken a lot of work home with him. The little joke turned out to be on us when we later discovered how much work product he, in fact, kept at home.

The relationship between the senior State Department officer and the young TECRO official began to evolve in a disturbing manner. In December 2003, FBI agents spotted what were described as "physical intimacies" between Keyser and Cheng during a luncheon at a downtown Washington restaurant. Prior to this development, there was nothing recorded or observed that suggested the two were involved in an intimate relationship. But we now feared that Keyser could be induced to engage in pillow talk that was above and beyond public lunch talk. A man supposed to protect secrets was most vulnerable when distracted by the presence of an attractive woman trained in the fine art of eliciting information. We suspected that Cheng had been trained in the fine art of seduction too.

When General Huang, Isabelle Cheng, and Donald Keyser lunched together in early December, Keyser provided sensitive government information about Chinese premier Wen Jiabao as well as Keyser's analysis of the military options being considered by the Beijing government should Taiwan initiate specific international or internal policies. The Justice Department would be able to confirm the contents of what Keyser relayed to General Huang and Cheng when it reviewed a secret NSB telegram written by Cheng and transmitted on December 5, 2003, from TECRO to NSB headquarters in Taipei. The NSB officials in Taiwan deemed the information so sensitive as to require special safeguarding within their own headquarters.

Earlier Keyser was again observed by the FBI at another Washington restaurant on November 14 in the company of Cheng and General Huang. Following a meeting on November 25, Cheng returned to TECRO and composed a secret cable for NSB headquarters in which she listed the main talking points with Keyser. Cheng reported that "Donald Keyser, the Principal Deputy Assistant Secretary of State for East Asia Affairs of the US, continued to explain the recent diplomatic behavior of the PRC." At the time of the luncheons, the federal investigators strongly suspected, but could not know, that following each of the NSB–Keyser meetings, Cheng prepared a written synopsis for NSB headquarters.

On December 19, 2003, FBI agents observed Keyser picking up Cheng from TECRO in his personal vehicle and driving to an out-of-the way restaurant in Maryland. Following a two-hour dinner, Keyser drove Cheng to her apartment in Maryland. According to the FBI logs, Keyser stayed in the residence from 10:58 until 11:45. The following day back in headquarters, the DS and FBI investigative team speculated as to what happened during those forty-seven minutes behind closed doors. They guessed correctly because in 2006 Keyser admitted that while inside the residence Cheng removed her clothes and he touched her all over her naked body but did not engage in any sex act.

Could it get worse? Yes, it did. Possibly most galling to the investigators was the discovery of an e-mail that Keyser had sent to Cheng in which he identified a former department employee as a possible recruitment target for the NSB. In a May 8, 2004, e-mail to Cheng, Keyser said, "This is the kind of person who is ripe for recruitment by careful, methodical, serious intelligence agencies. In the days of the Cold War, Soviet and East German intelligence officers were quite practiced at identifying people like this, people who did not wake up one day and say 'I want to be a traitor' but people whose relatively minor weaknesses and ego gratification needs made them potential targets."

Keyser also added that the former department official was disgruntled and had "spent a career in the foreign service not being taken seriously." While the name of the former department employee was redacted in the court record, his identity was announced in the press. John Tkacik Jr. had previously worked in INR, but he was working for the Heritage Foundation as a senior research fellow at the time of the 2006 court proceedings. When contacted by the press, Tkacik expressed outrage over Keyser's actions and said that he "fervently hope[d] they throw the book at him."

Was Keyser pimping for the NSB? He claimed during the FBI-managed debriefings that he was merely trying to "tell Cheng that officials at the Department of State knew the subject official [Mr. Tkacik] was turning against them [i.e., the State Department]," and he was simply trying to let Cheng know that department officials knew.

Keyser arranged for another get-together on May 22, 2004, so that Cheng, General Huang, and he could sit down and have an in-depth exchange of opinions regarding trilateral relations among the US, China, and Taiwan. In another secret cable that Cheng authored inside TECRO and sent to Taipei, she analyzed the contents of Keyser's luncheon information to include "written materials for

Huang's reference." It appeared that Keyser was not holding anything back from his friends.

The day after his luncheon with the two TECRO NSB agents, Keyser sent an e-mail to Cheng in which he stated, "I'm glad if the background helped. By now you know that, as we say, your wish is my command. All you need to do is ask, and I will do my best to reply quickly, fully and helpfully. No matter the subject, whether official or personal or anything." As the FBI and DS investigators read the May 23 e-mails, there was little doubt in their minds that Keyser was treading in very dangerous waters.

CHAPTER SEVEN

On May 29, 2004, FBI agents observed Keyser and Cheng boarding an Amtrak train at Union Station in Washington, DC. They were destined for New York City, where they spent the day sightseeing, including a cozy hour of drinks together at a New York hotel before returning home.

Keyser sent Cheng an e-mail on his State Department computer the next day in which he said, “Having my arm around your shoulder, your head resting against my shoulder, and then on my chest, your hand in mine for a couple of hours while you were in ‘Dreamland’ was more than ample compensation. . . . Now I’m going to have to think a [sic] particularly cunning plan to induce you to come to Honolulu in the middle of June.” Not surprisingly, never once did the investigators see such romantic messages being forwarded on his department computer to his wife, Margaret.

When the FBI watched Keyser and Cheng walking together in the cavernous White Flint Mall located a few miles outside Washington on June 30, 2004, the agents were alerted to the “mall stroll” from a previous e-mail sent by Keyser to Cheng in which he remarked, “Careful about telling me where you’ll be on Saturday afternoon. . . .

It's been a while since I practiced my 'accidental encounter' methodology at White Flint."

The investigators were amused by Keyser's attempts to impress Cheng with his basic CIA training and pleased to note how he characterized the meeting. Despite future denials, Keyser had defined the clandestine nature of their relationship in writing that day. Then, unexpectedly, Keyser managed to upend the entire direction of the investigation.

Toward the middle of July, he gave the department an official notification of his intention to retire at the end of September 2004. Apparently the department had informed Keyser that he was its top candidate for senior officer at the AIT, the US government's equivalent to TECRO. The only formal requirement for any appointment to the AIT was that the individual cannot be an active department or US government employee. The stipulation was about diplomatic sensibilities and smoke and mirrors and little else. As Keyser had already passed the minimum age for retirement, was a specialist on cross-strait issues, spoke fluent Mandarin, and had spent more than two years in Taiwan previously, there couldn't have been a better candidate. Shortly after considering his options, Keyser announced his retirement in order to prepare for his potential future assignment to Taipei.

The foreign affairs regulations require all department employees to notify the Retirement Office of their pending departure so that the proper paperwork can be completed to ensure a smooth transition to private life. As part of the retirement process, employees are enrolled in a two-month Retirement Planning Seminar offered at the Career Transition Center at the Foreign Service Institute. The conundrum Keyser's impending retirement presented to the investigators was this: while the investigation had confirmed that the department's EAP PDAS was involved in a clandestine relationship with a foreign intelligence officer residing in the United States under diplomatic cover, the special agents had never observed or recorded Keyser physically providing the NSB agent with a genuine classified government document. And now, with his impending departure from the State Department and his access to official secrets coming to an end, the chance of catching him in such an overt act of espionage was vanishing. This was the same investigative conundrum that unexpectedly developed in the Kendall Myers case.

It was time for the Justice Department to decide how the penultimate act of this drama cum comedy would play out. However, until a decision could be made, Keyser and Cheng would continue to meet. Surveillance could be so boring at times for those who watched and waited.

On July 23, 2004, around 8:10 p.m., Keyser once again picked up Cheng at TECRO in his personal vehicle and drove to the Washington Gas utility lot in Rockville, Maryland. During the next twenty minutes, FBI agents observed Keyser in the reclined driver's seat with his head leaning back against the headrest. The agents also observed Cheng in the front passenger seat leaning across the defendant with her back facing upward and head below the line of observation. I wonder if Keyser ever considered for a moment that his evening with Cheng would be described in a Department of Justice court filing.

Neither the FBI nor DS agents were happy when, eight days later, Keyser exited his car with three manila envelopes under his arm and headed in the direction of the Potowmack Landing Restaurant in Alexandria, Virginia, which sits overlooking the Potomac River. Luckily for the investigators, once again, Keyser had clumsily attempted to masquerade the nature of his luncheon and the participants' identities on his department electronic calendar. Once inside, Keyser headed to a table where Cheng and General Huang were seated. Briefly rising out of their seats, they shook hands and got down to work.

The FBI observed Keyser providing one large document to each of the two NSB officers. Cheng put her envelope in her handbag, and General Huang took one document out to scrutinize before putting the paper back inside the envelope. According to the statement of one FBI agent, the envelopes contained documents that appeared to have blue State Department markings on them.

The three talked a great deal over lunch. When Keyser left the restaurant by himself, the FBI agents noted that he was carrying only one manila envelope that was folded up. Whatever was inside those envelopes was now in the hands of the NSB. The FBI would get a better understanding of their contents when they gained possession of the official NSB cables sent to Taiwan by the very participants in those luncheons.

In early August, Keyser forwarded a paper to Cheng via e-mail entitled "PRC weapons." At this point in Taiwan–PRC relations, the Beijing government was again saber rattling, probably for home consumption, that the time was now right for the reunification of China by force.

Regardless of the seriousness of the PRC's intent, the NSB needed to provide its government with quality analysis of the potential Chinese military threat. Given Keyser's experience, his analysis was invaluable to them.

As the Department of Justice attempted to determine exactly what violations of law could hold up in a federal courtroom, Keyser sent an e-mail to Cheng on August 1, 2004, the first day he started his retirement seminar at the Foreign Service Institute. In the e-mail, he further defined their relationship: "After two years of sharing thoughts—and increasingly intimate thoughts—I can no longer imagine how it could be otherwise. . . . I mentioned long ago that you are incredibly easy for me to talk to. . . . And so I continue to say silent prayer (though I am not religious) and make silent wishes that somehow that will be able to endure."

Just a few days after starting his retirement course, Keyser left FSI's Arlington campus and ventured over to Fin, a seafood restaurant located on Nineteenth Street in Washington, DC, with an outdoor café. The FBI agents noted that when Keyser entered the establishment, he held a piece of paper in his hand. Cheng had arrived about fifteen minutes earlier, and he walked directly to her table and placed the document on her menu.

He sat down, and she quietly read the paper before handing it back to him. They enjoyed a casual and decidedly crustaceous lunch, punctuated by animated conversation, before parting some two hours later.

Completely infatuated with Cheng for the past year, Keyser arranged for a meeting with her on August 11, 2004, where the two enjoyed a long luncheon accompanied by fine libations. Afterward FBI agents observed Keyser and Cheng drive off in his car and park on a quiet side street in Washington. The agents observed movement in the car similar to the "rocking motion" noted in their July 23 encounter. For approximately twenty minutes, Cheng's head disappeared from view.

After the parking session was over, Keyser drove Cheng back to her apartment. In a cellular phone call to Cheng only minutes after she returned home, Keyser told her: "The food was good, the wine was good, the champagne was good, and you were good." All told, things must have been good between them. Despite future denials, Keyser's intimate relationship with Cheng had been captured and recorded for posterity.

Six days later, the two-year-old investigation almost collapsed. Once again, Keyser arranged to pick up Cheng from TECRO. Leaving the Taiwan compound in his private vehicle, they eventually parked in a secluded PEPCO power station lot in suburban Maryland. About thirty seconds later, an undercover FBI car glided into position some thirty yards away to record their activities. Unfortunately one energetic FBI agent leaned a little too far outside the car's window with a video camera in hand.

As bad luck would have it, a passerby discovered the Keystone Cops at work. After about a minute, the individual walked over to Keyser's car, knocked on the window, and advised the pair that a white male in a car with DC license plates appeared to be photographing them. Keyser thanked the helpful Samaritan and immediately drove off to Cheng's apartment.

The following day, the FBI tried to prevent an investigative meltdown. In a telephone call recorded that morning, the agents listened as Keyser coached Cheng on how they should react if questioned regarding the PEPCO incident. They discussed a variety of possible explanations and scenarios. Why did innocent people need to coordinate answers when the simple truth should suffice? Keyser was recorded saying: "[W]e just have to think a little bit about . . . explanations and then work out from here. . . . It's obviously . . . not a particularly delightful development. . . . There are probably as many as five different explanations. I don't especially like any of them, but . . .

we just need to think through what each one might mean and then . . . figure out . . . how to address it."

Was Keyser's primary fear that his current wife had become suspicious about his newfound habit of late evenings and hired a private detective to document his infidelity as his first wife had done? Or was Keyser's first concern that he was about to become the victim of a criminal or foreign intelligence blackmail attempt? Maybe he thought that he was wrongfully being watched by federal investigators, for later on in the recorded conversation he told Cheng, "you know and I know that nothing bad has occurred in terms of anything that . . . is contrary to anybody's law or regulations. . . ." Or maybe Keyser made that statement suspecting that the phone call was being intercepted.

The creativity of the FBI knew few bounds. On August 27, 2004, a Fairfax County detective, with permission from his supervisors, knocked on the door of Keyser's residence and stated that he was investigating potential terrorism activity. The detective explained that his police counterparts in Maryland had filmed a vehicle with Virginia license plates registered to Keyser parked near a public utility, which seemed suspicious.

Keyser identified himself as a senior department official, confirming that he was the owner of the car in question and that he was the driver of the car on the night in question. After a few more questions and answers, the Virginia detective said good-bye and left. The calculated gambit paid off handsomely. The specter of terrorism can sometimes be a good thing for those who protect and serve their nation—and their own devious ends.

A few minutes later, Keyser called Cheng and left the following voice mail on her private phone: "I just had an interesting experience . . . but I don't want to share it over the phone. Suffice it to say that the . . . mystery . . . that we experienced a while back has now been resolved. And, actually the outcome is probably the best possible one that we might've imagined. . . . But I'll talk about it later."

Time was running out for the investigative team as Keyser approached his retirement date and no incriminating physical evidence was in hand to go forward with an espionage prosecution by DOJ. In order to determine if Keyser was actually passing classified documents to Cheng, the FBI decided to try to film an entire lunch the next time Keyser met with his NSB colleagues. The investigators had determined that Cheng and Keyser had made reservations for three (General Huang was coming this time) at the Aquarelle restaurant located inside the Watergate hotel.

SA Giovanna Cavalier and her FBI counterpart entered the restaurant twenty minutes before Cheng and Keyser and, with the help of the restaurant staff, were seated at a window with a beautiful view of the Potomac River. Better than the view was the fact that there were no tables or chairs between them and the Keyser party. The surveillance team had a hidden camera that was aimed directly at the Keyser table.

Soon after, the FBI–DS surveillance team watched as Huang, Cheng, and Keyser chatted about their luncheon selections. The investigators couldn't help but marvel at how innocent Keyser's lunches with the NSB agents appeared to the untrained eye. Foreign intelligence services have always taken advantage of the average US citizen's absolute disbelief and disinterest in espionage matters.

At one point during the lunch, the FBI special agent got up to head to the restroom, and just then Keyser pulled out what appeared to be several pages stapled together. As Keyser handed the document to Cheng and General Huang, several diners made their way out of the restaurant, blocking the camera's view. However, SA Cavalier was able to see red underlined writing on the top of the document, which she recognized as being similar to the red "secret/noforn" (no foreign dissemination) label that the department puts on the header of classified documents. She could not, though, discern the exact wording on the document in question.

The next day, the FBI was eager to know about the document and came to DS/CI to discuss exactly what SA Cavalier had seen. While the hidden camera had caught the passing of the document, it was impossible to make out the words. Much to the FBI's dismay, DS/CI could not confirm the marking "secret/noforn," only that the document passed had a heading highlighted in red, like department classification markings. Later Cheng would provide the document to the FBI, and it would show that the words "Talking Points" with a date that had been typed in red and underlined at the top center of the document.

Keyser was within two months of retiring, and the case was not as strong as either the federal investigators or the Justice Department would have liked. The physical evidence to support a conviction of espionage was weak. It was mostly circumstantial fluff and not much more.

Fortunately DS decided with the FBI earlier in the investigation to bolster our prosecution chances by catching Keyser in violation of another federal law. Any federal law would do; we were not particularly picky at this point. Therefore, it wasn't by chance that in early 2004, DS informed him that he needed to submit a security questionnaire, Standard Form (SF) 86, to initiate a routine update investigation to maintain his "top secret" security clearance. According to Executive Order 12986, all individuals with such a clearance were subject to periodic reinvestigations at any time but no later than five years from the date of the previous completed investigation. Keyser was approximately one year shy of the five-year limit, but DS/CI decided to accelerate his reinvestigation.

The SF-86 contains a block in which the employee is instructed: "List any foreign countries you have visited, except on travel under official government orders, working back seven years." Keyser, while indicating that he had taken personal travel to France in April 2000 and Ireland in May 2003, omitted his September 2003 trip to Taiwan. It was not an official trip since he had asked Assistant Secretary Kelly for annual leave for those days. Keyser had simply gone through the ritualistic motions at the time, knowing there would be no problem as long as he did not tell his boss he planned to go to Taipei.

Prior to submitting his completed SF-86 electronically, he printed a page entitled "Certification That My Answers Are True" and signed the block underneath that states, "My statements on this form, and my attachments to it, are true, complete, and correct to the best of my knowledge and belief and are made in good faith. I understand that a knowing and false statement on this form can be punished by fine or imprisonment (18 USC 1001)." On May 3, 2004, Keyser signed the certificate and faxed it along with the required questionnaire to the DS Personnel Security Division in Arlington, Virginia.

When shown the signed certification a few days later, SA Warrener exclaimed even more exuberantly than he did at Dulles International Airport some nine months earlier: "Got him a second time!" Keyser had falsified a federal document in addition to his false sworn statement on his customs form when returning from his trip to Taiwan in 2003. His deceptions were beginning to add up to something meaningful.

The investigators wanted to take advantage of the required clearance update process to see if Keyser would lie a third time to disguise the nature of his relationship with Cheng. Not satisfied with just two counts of 18 USC 1001, we wanted more charges if we could find them. All department update investigations for access to "top secret" material include a personal interview conducted between the employee and a security investigator. If done properly, the interviews can elicit information that otherwise wouldn't be disclosed during an investigation. It could be a great investigative tool in the right hands.

On August 9, 2004, a DS special agent met with Keyser at FSI to conduct the required update interview. Every special agent of the Diplomatic Security Service was responsible at one time or another in his or her career for conducting update investigations both in the US and abroad. I cannot remember how many hundreds of update inquiries I had managed over my twenty-eight years, but I never forgot the critical step of reminding the interviewee of the necessity to be candid and truthful. To emphasize that point, employees were reminded that any falsification of fact could result in a loss of security clearance and possible criminal sanctions. The agent interviewing Keyser had been briefed beforehand regarding our interests.

Keyser was advised of the importance of being absolutely honest and candid during the interview and was specifically told that it was a crime under Title 18, United States Code, specifically section 1001, to knowingly falsify or conceal material facts related to the background investigation. He was untruthful when he denied being involved in a reportable relationship during direct questioning. Moreover he had fibbed on his signed SF-86 about his relationship with a foreign national, his vulnerable personal behavior, and his foreign travel. After the meeting, the interviewer thanked Keyser for his time, closed his notebook, and returned to his office. When informed of the results of the interview, SA Warrener exclaimed "Strike three!"

David H. Laufman, the assistant United States attorney (AUSA) and senior Department of Justice official assisting with the investigation, decided it was time to confront Keyser given his impending retirement. In late August 2004, he directed the FBI to interview Keyser under circumstances that would underscore the seriousness of the chat. Maybe they would get lucky and find evidence of a crime of espionage or, better yet, an admission of guilt.

Running out of time, and with AUSA Laufman's blessing, the FBI decided to intercept the next document Keyser passed to Cheng or General Huang regardless of circumstances. Once again, the team was able to determine that the trio had made reservations for the afternoon of September 4. The FBI and DS SAs spent all day on September 3 practicing for the intercept and possible arrest and search. SA Warrener had just returned from his temporary tour of duty in Baghdad and readily volunteered to be part of the team that would search Keyser's residence. SA Cavalier was a member of the team that would detain and question the two NSB agents.

On September 4, Keyser strolled into the Potowmack Landing restaurant in Alexandria, Virginia, and joined Cheng and General Huang for lunch. At the cozy and casual setting, the surveillance team noted that Keyser passed a legal-sized manila folder to Cheng, who put it away on her person. As on every other occasion, Cheng picked up the tab for the meal. She must have had deep pockets and an open expense account. After finishing dessert, the trio stood up, and the two NSB officers left the restaurant separately from Keyser. FBI special agents detained Cheng and General Huang as they walked to their car while a separate FBI team stopped and questioned Keyser.

Both TECRO officials immediately told the FBI of their identity and did not attempt to conceal the fact that they were also NSB officers. Cheng quickly surrendered the manila folder, in which the FBI special agents found six pages of typewritten notes, one of which contained the caption "Talking Points." As the agents thumbed through the pages, they did not find any security classifications or other government markings. The absence of such indicators was not a good sign.

SA Cavalier quickly made copies of the six typewritten pages on a copy machine made available by the restaurant's management. Diligent as ever, she then ran a blank sheet through "at least twenty-five times," as she later told me, in order to remove the images from the photo machine's memory.

While the FBI was interviewing Cheng and Keyser, SA Cavalier returned to her office and logged onto her classified telegram program. Due to her position in CI, she had the ability to access almost all department cables processed and transmitted through the classified system. She ran search terms that matched up phrases, dates, and topics in the "Talking Points" document that Keyser had just passed to the two NSB agents. She quickly determined that several exact phrases and statements from the Keyser document matched wording from both confidential and secret/noforn department cables. The phrases were so exact that had Keyser been writing the "Talking Points" for a college research paper, he would have been expelled for plagiarism.

SA Cavalier quickly notified her superiors and the FBI of her findings. Her discovery was essential for a federal judge to authorize a search of Keyser's residence. A department analyst would later conclude that whole sentences and paragraphs contained on the pages created by Keyser were lifted from official US State Department documents classified at the confidential level.

Back to the Potowmack restaurant. What to do with two TECRO officials and a senior department officer suspected of conspiracy to commit espionage? There was not any incriminating evidence such as spy paraphernalia on their persons. The FBI's solution was simple. Separate General Huang from his protégé and question them individually. Divide and conquer and hope for the best outcome.

One block from the restaurant, two FBI agents stopped Keyser, identified themselves, and asked if he would be willing to answer some questions. Keyser agreed, and all three returned to the Potowmack restaurant and quietly occupied an inside table. Declining the option to use the restroom or order food, Keyser requested a glass of water—the only sustenance he would have during the following four-hour "talk" with the FBI agents.

He readily identified himself as the principal deputy assistant secretary of state for EAP and confirmed that his luncheon partners were TECRO officials. The FBI agents advised Keyser he was not under arrest and free to leave at any time. Initially Keyser was very talkative and told the agents he had just finished lunch with two "liaison officials." He also admitted providing them with a manila envelope that had six documents inside. He commented that he had known General Huang since 2001 and had been introduced to Cheng by Gregg Mann at a private reception for Henry Tsai held at Mann's home in 2002.

Getting quickly to the point, the FBI agents asked Keyser if he was passing restricted, sensitive, or classified information to unauthorized persons. Keyser's response was to raise his eyebrows. He remarked that he was authorized by his position to pass "classified but releasable" State Department information to his TECRO contacts. He said a principal deputy assistant secretary of state has the independent authority to release classified information to foreign officials. He added that he was also passing such information to TECRO ambassador David Lee.

One quickly had to question how many TECRO officials were using Keyser as their favorite source. Or maybe Keyser was passing one set of "classified but releasable" information to the TECRO NSB agents and another set of "classified but releasable" data to a TECRO Ministry of Foreign Affairs official. Why the need for three different contacts? Only later during the interview would Keyser admit that Cheng and General Huang were NSB agents and not Ministry of Foreign Affairs officials. To justify his practice of passing classified information to TECRO officials, Keyser advised the FBI that National Security Council member David Wilkins was similarly providing TECRO senior official David Lee with "classified but releasable" data. With Keyser's unexpected NSC revelation, it was clear that the government of Taiwan had excellent sources available to it in Washington.

Shifting gears, the FBI agents asked Keyser if he provided the NSB agents with information that was classified government data. He replied he'd prepared "talking points" taken from open source information that included scholarly papers, newspapers, and Council on Foreign Affairs publications and had reduced the salient points on sheets of paper that he provided General Huang and Cheng. What Keyser was unable or unwilling to recall was whether his "oral talking points" may have included classified but not releasable information.

In response to FBI questions, Keyser commented that he wasn't required to report his contacts with legitimate diplomats and foreign intelligence officers to the Diplomatic Security Service or anyone else. The two agents had one last question before allowing him to go about his business. They asked if he thought "top secret" or classified documents would be found during the ongoing search of his home. This was Keyser's first inkling that his talk with the FBI was part of a much larger investigation. He replied that he would be "astonished" at such a possibility. The last FBI question served to alert him that the ongoing conversation was not just a casual interview. At the very moment he was talking to the two FBI agents in Alexandria, FBI and DS agents were executing a search warrant at his home to determine if he had violated federal law by unlawfully removing classified US secrets to his residence.

The two agents thanked Keyser for his cooperation and left him sitting alone at the table. Unfortunately for him, the FBI interviews of his luncheon partners had not been completed. Actually they were just about to start, and they would be appetizing.

Separated from General Huang and uncertain of her legal status or professional future, Cheng had been convinced by the FBI to return to TECRO and turn over the classified NSB telegrams she had transmitted to the NSB headquarters in which she summarized the conversational details of her luncheon engagements with Keyser over the past two years. An interesting diplomatic privilege was in play at this point. TECRO officials did not enjoy the same diplomatic immunities enjoyed by fully accredited diplomats to other diplomatic missions. They were protected from searches and arrests only while inside the TECRO building or in their cars. Cheng was being detained at this point and could have been arrested by the FBI. Maybe this was the motivation for her to cooperate? The TECRO cables would be critical in confirming the nature of her relationship with Keyser.

David Laufman, the federal prosecutor in the case, would eventually reveal that Cheng "voluntarily retrieved" all the classified cables she transmitted to NSB headquarters along with Keyser's e-mails. No NSA skullduggery here. . . . Cheng just gave the DOJ critical evidence in support of a prosecution. And what did the TECRO cables reveal?

For example, on September 23, 2003, Cheng transmitted a cable to NSB headquarters detailing Keyser's written analysis of Chinese foreign minister Li Zhaoxing's speech in Washington and private conversation with Secretary of State Colin Powell. A few weeks later, Cheng sent a secret cable to NSB headquarters describing Keyser's analysis of Taiwanese president Chen's controversial visit to New York that had Beijing fuming with anger. Cheng ended her cable by stating, "Mr. Keyser's talk is very sensitive. It involves his e-mail communications with others. In order to keep this mutually beneficial and trusted relationship, please conceal the intelligence source of this report if this report is cited."

And again in a secret cable to NSB headquarters on November 25, 2003, Cheng concluded her report by saying, "The sources . . . of Keyser's information is/are unclear. Please do not use this intelligence to avoid exposing of intelligence sources." Regardless of future claims by Keyser, the NSB unhesitatingly desired to keep his identity secret—the hallmark of a clandestine relationship.

While Keyser was being interviewed inside the Potowmack restaurant, an FBI/DS team drove up to the Keyser residence at 9500 Quail Pointe Lane in the suburb of McLean, Virginia. Located on one-third acre, this five-bedroom, $750,000 home was similar to its neighbors on this quiet cul-de-sac. Quiet, that is, until now. Opening the door, the third Mrs. Keyser, Margaret, was handed a copy of a search warrant.

The agents subsequently discovered more than 3,600 classified documents, including more than twenty-five "top secret" papers, neatly catalogued and arranged throughout the house. Documents were found in closets, the basement, and the couple's den. So many classified papers and computer files were discovered that a call went out for more FBI and DS agents to assist with the search. One DS agent showed up wearing blue jeans and a sweatshirt; an FBI agent arrived in a black evening dress and pearls. They all spent hours scouring the house. Of particular interest to the team were a Sony VAIO laptop computer and unlabeled computer disks.

During the search, SA Warrener noticed a magnet affixed to the kitchen refrigerator with the following message: "Beware of Female Spies. Women are being employed by the enemy to secure information from Navy men on the theory that they are less liable to be suspected than male spies. Beware of inquisitive women as well as prying men."

SA Warrener took a photograph of the magnet and added it to his DS/CI Keyser file, titled "Dogpatch." And then SA Warrener was confronted by unpleasant fallout from the search. He and his FBI colleague had to search the bedroom belonging to Keyser's young teenage daughter.

"Do you have to go through her room and her stuff?" Margaret asked.

After glancing over to his FBI counterpart, Kevin said, "Yes, we do."

"Can I be inside while you do your job?" she pleaded.

The immediate answer was "No." As a father, SA Warrener was conflicted about what he had to do. When they finished their search of the young teenager's room, the SAs removed a laptop and advised

Margaret that they would have to seize the computer. The young teenager protested and said that her schoolwork was on the laptop and she needed it for her projects. She was a student at the Thomas Jefferson High School for Science and Technology, a magnet school operated in Fairfax County for academically gifted students. The SAs had no option, and the laptop was seized.

Subsequent examinations by forensic specialists revealed that the disks for Keyser's computer contained thousands of pages of classified information. None were found on the young teenager's laptop.

Midway through the search, following his four-hour chit-chat with FBI agents, Keyser arrived home. SA Kevin Warrener and I later had a conversation about what happened after Keyser entered the house.

"Robert," Kevin told me, "he looked absolutely miserable."

"What happened when he arrived?"

"He came in the front door and did not call out to his wife or children. He just walked over to the living room couch and sat down."

"Did he say anything to the special agents walking around the house?"

"No, he just sat there on the couch with his head in his hands."

As the federal agents were literally tearing up his house, he sat alone and spoke to no one. His family was elsewhere in the house. I asked Kevin if any neighbors came over.

"As far as I can remember, the only people loitering outside were agents and technicians."

"So it was all peaceful while the search went on?"

"Sure was," Kevin said, "but I am not so sure how peaceful it was inside the house when we left."

After several hours, the agents concluded their search and prepared an inventory of the seized items, including classified materials and the laptop computer. As the government van drove off, Keyser was seen closing the front door. Presumably he went to explain to his family what had just happened.

While Keyser's home was being "tossed"—as they say—SA Cavalier was authorized to drive immediately to Annapolis and interview Keyser's boss, Assistant Secretary of State James Kelly, to inform him of Keyser's activities, including the unauthorized trip to Taiwan. Kelly was attending a reunion with his fellow graduates from the US Naval Academy (BS 1959) and was clearly having a lovely time with his wife and friends when SA Cavalier and a fellow DS special agent pulled up outside the reception. Approaching Kelly, they identified themselves and asked if they could have a quiet moment in an empty room.

Scotch in one hand, cigar in the other, a puzzled Kelly followed the two SAs to a secluded anteroom. Kelly was clearly upset at being interrupted, and when they explained why they were there, he had even more reason to be upset. He had been left out of the loop regarding possible espionage activities of his right-hand man.

There was nothing that the FBI or DS could have done to avoid this omission; Kelly was too close to Keyser, and the decision was made by senior department and FBI officials not to inform him of the investigation prior to Keyser's initial interview by the FBI. SA Cavalier had a copy of the "Talking Points" paper which she wanted Kelly to review and comment on their sensitivity and level of classification. Perhaps Kelly should have been told about the FBI's and DS's interest in Keyser after the reunion was over, or had the news broken to him in pieces, waiting to have him review the document until after he had calmed down a little.

Kelly's interpretation of the information passed by Keyser to the NSB agents was very different from that of DS and the FBI. Upon reviewing the "Talking Points" document and seeing that some of the phrases and statements matched those found in classified department cables, Kelly stated that was not why he had classified the department cables.

As classifying authority, he had just kicked off a chain of events that could allow Keyser to avoid being prosecuted for passing classified information to a foreign clandestine intelligence officer.

CHAPTER EIGHT

The classifying authority in the State Department has the independent, autonomous right to state whether or not something that he, she, or they classified is still classified or was misclassified in the first place. When SA Cavalier asked Assistant Secretary Kelly to explain why he had classified those department cables, he reminded her that he signed off on hundreds of classified documents a month and could not give her an immediate answer.

Just as quickly, Kelly offered justification for Keyser's meetings with Cheng and General Huang despite the fact that Keyser had been doing so behind his back. When told about the unauthorized trip that Keyser took to Taiwan, Kelly appeared a bit more upset, but he refused to say anything suggesting that Keyser had acted badly. He expressed his disapproval only of not being informed of the DOJ inquiry. The interview was a disaster for the investigation.

Once back in the office, SA Cavalier called SA Warrener, still at Keyser's residence with the search team, to advise him of the results of the interview. SA Warrener told her about the thousands of classified documents found in Keyser's basement. SA Cavalier badly wanted to travel and join the search team, but her branch chief ordered her home to sleep.

Justice Department officials reviewed all the materials removed from Keyser's home and concluded there was irrefutable evidence of a crime. But was it espionage or something else? On September 15, 2004, Magistrate Barry R. Poertz issued an arrest warrant, number 1:04M803, authorizing the FBI to arrest Keyser—not for espionage, but for lying, or more technically, "in a matter within the jurisdiction of the executive branch of the government of the United States, [Keyser did] knowingly and willfully falsify, conceal and cover-up by trick, scheme and device a material fact, and make a materially false, fictitious and fraudulent statement and representation."

At this stage of the investigation, DOJ decided to arrest Keyser for a lesser crime, 18 USC 1001, for making false statements. Senior government lawyers concluded that the available evidence would not support the test for a charge of espionage; it was assumed that a contrite Keyser would be asked to assist the US government in its formal damage assessment and assist the FBI in unraveling the true nature of his relationship with Cheng.

For a few days following the FBI interview and DS/FBI search of his house, Keyser probably convinced himself that the unfortunate episode was a simple misunderstanding and everything would be all right. With an arrest warrant in hand, on September 15, 2004, SA Cavalier and her FBI counterpart drove to FSI and arrested Keyser while he was working in a computer lab. He was led away to an awaiting government vehicle, all the while vigorously protesting his innocence. Out of respect and so as not to embarrass Keyser in front of his colleagues, he was not patted down or handcuffed until he was in the parking lot.

Keyser underwent a perfunctory medical check at the Alexandria detention center. He refused to be fingerprinted, revealing a petulant and combative character that was amusing to the law enforcement folks present. They were all too aware of his history of asserting his constitutional rights during legal situations. During Keyser's 1985 divorce proceedings in Alexandria circuit court with his second wife, Virginia, he cited his Fifth Amendment rights under the US Constitution in declining to provide the court with the address of his residence or to provide details of the degree of his involvement with a female friend.

This time his refusal meant that he spent several hours in custody before submitting to the fingerprinting. He was eventually released on a $500,000 bond cosigned by his wife. He also surrendered both his diplomatic and "tourist" passports and was forced to wear a monitor ankle bracelet for approximately the next nine months

On September 16, 2004, the *New York Times* and the *Washington Post* reported on their front pages that Mr. Donald Keyser, a senior member of the State Department, had been arrested for "concealing a trip to Taiwan" and is "suspected of improperly passing documents to Taiwanese intelligence agents."

What did General Huang's and Cheng's TECRO nominal boss Chen Chien-jen have to say about all this? Nothing much. He left Washington, DC, shortly thereafter. However, on September 24, 2004, the sixty-five-year-old diplomat was interviewed about the Cheng/Keyser case in his new position as Taiwan's representative to the European Union. He said that Cheng was a rare civil servant, who was outstanding, and he respected her job, and he urged reporters not to make up stories about her. Most significantly, Chen, who was head of TECRO when Keyser took the side visit to Taiwan, declined to say whether he had been informed beforehand or afterward of Keyser's September 2003 visit to Taiwan.

In a question and answer session before the Taiwanese legislature on September 23, 2004, Taiwanese premier Yu Shyi-kun said that it was hard to judge whether Keyser had passed discussion topics or classified information to the Taiwanese agents. He also stated that "according to one of Keyser's close friends, Keyser had a habit of preparing talking points for people he meets with, and usually puts discussion topics in envelopes." Vice Minister of Foreign Affairs Michael Kau stated before the same legislative session that his ministry had no knowledge of the Keyser/Cheng relationship. He would get the NSB's transcripts of the communications sent by General Huang from TECRO without attribution.

A year later, in December 2005, senior TECRO official David Lee would advise American officials that Taiwan would not condone clandestine intelligence activities against the United States. This reaction was similar to the Israeli government's public reaction following Jonathan Jay Pollard's 1985 arrest for espionage. Cheng and Pollard were rogue operations who were certainly not known to, much less authorized by, senior government officials who depend on the generosity of the White House in all things international.

Months before Keyser's arrest, Cheng married Chris Cockle, a Washington, DC–based correspondent for the *China Post* newspaper. Cockle was responsible for monitoring and reporting on the State Department's relationship between the two Chinas. The DS and FBI investigators found the relationship between the journalist and the NSB agent intriguing.

On August 1, 2003, Philip T. Reeker, deputy spokesman for the Department of State, was taking questions from reporters gathered at a Foreign Press Center briefing in Washington, DC. Seated in the audience was Chris Cockle, representing his paper. Toward the end of the question and answer session, Cockle took the floor and asked, "About ten days ago, there was a senior Taiwan official who was in Washington for various meetings. However, we [the press] were never able to find out exactly why he was here or who he met with. I wonder whether you can give us some details as to who he met with and what was the outcome of those meetings, and whether the issue of the referendums [independence v. unification and Taiwan's fourth nuclear power plant] was discussed?"

Reeker responded, "I really can't. As you know, from time to time, in keeping with our One China Policy and our unofficial relationship with the people of Taiwan, we have had particular meetings, but I do not have any details to refer to you."

Cheng should have known what the Taiwanese official was doing in Washington, but maybe she did not brief Cockle or else she did and Cockle needed a second source for his next article. Keyser definitely would have known all the details of the Taiwanese official's activities while in the United States, but the two never met to my knowledge.

Shortly after Keyser's arrest, Cockle sent a letter to his Washington-based Taiwanese correspondents urging them to verify facts before writing stories linking his wife to any counterintelligence activities involving Keyser, all the while imploring his colleagues to consider the implications of their stories. One wonders if the new Mrs. Cockle had been as candid with her husband as she was with the FBI that September afternoon in 2004.

Following his September 4 encounter with the FBI and DS agents, Keyser retained Robert S. Litt, partner at the powerhouse Washington, DC firm of Arnold & Porter. Litt counted former president Clinton among his clients. Between September 2004 and December 2005, Keyser and DOJ lawyers jockeyed for position on the outlines of a plea agreement, during which the court granted several extensions of time for the indictment of Keyser. During that time, Justice Department lawyers debated how to prosecute Keyser. Had, as Keyser claimed, the FBI and DS stumbled onto an intimate but nonsexual relationship? One in which he shared pre-cleared sensitive information with a known clandestine foreign intelligence officer as part of a department backchannel initiative with Taiwan? Or was Keyser a witting pawn and spy extraordinaire in the department?

Complicating matters was the question whether the government would go forward with an espionage prosecution and risk disclosing classified information concerning the US's relationships with Taiwan and the PRC. Some of this classified information was simply too sensitive to reveal/authenticate in open court. The Justice Department had similarly refused to divulge similar sensitive information in the 2003 "Parlor Maid" case involving a married FBI agent, James J. Smith, who was intimately involved with Katrina Leung, an FBI counterintelligence asset and approved FBI double agent working against the MSS. Unfortunately the MSS "doubled back" Leung on the FBI, and DOJ was unwilling to reveal classified information during the ensuing trials. No espionage trial ensued. Leung eventually pleaded guilty to one count of lying to the FBI and one count of filing a false federal tax return, and Smith pleaded guilty to the charge of falsely concealing his alleged affair with Leung from the FBI and was sentenced to three months of home confinement.

DOJ attorneys approached a number of US government employees for their assistance in the prosecution. Many of the potential government experts declined or were unable to authenticate the classified nature of the information recovered from Keyser's e-mails to

Cheng. Their apparent unwillingness, and at times outright refusal, to assist created tension between DS and senior members of the Foreign Service.

Would the federal prosecutors settle for a safe plea agreement to the lesser charges of perjury and unauthorized retention of classified material in order to secure a conviction?

In late November/early December 2005, the lawyers reached an agreement whereby Keyser consented to plead guilty to a three count Criminal Information: one count of unlawful removal of classified documents and two counts of false statements. A plea arrangement between the government and a defendant constitutes a contract between two parties in which each receives the benefit of a legally enforceable bargain. DOJ offered Keyser a reduction in sentencing that potentially carried a maximum of thirteen years in a federal penitentiary in exchange for his agreement to "cooperate fully, truthfully, and completely with the United States, and provide all information known to the defendant [Keyser] regarding any criminal activity and intelligence activity by himself and/or others." It was a straight-up *quid pro quo* deal.

On December 12, 2005, Keyser was seated in room 900 of the United States District Court for the Eastern District of Virginia. It is housed in a modern, ten-story, brick and stone structure, which some referred to as a twenty-first-century fortress, at 401 Courthouse Square in Alexandria. The courtroom was split in two with the courtroom well containing the judge's dais separated from the counsel's lectern and supporting tables for the judge's staff, which consisted of the law clerk, the courtroom deputy clerk, and the court reporter. The other half of the room was occupied by seven rows of church-style pews. I was seated on one of the left side benches.

Keyser, thumbs pressed into his cheeks, sat on a hard wooden bench while his lawyer conversed with the DOJ attorneys. I noted with some surprise that only thirteen people were present before the start of the proceedings. Maybe it was too early in the morning for some, or perhaps a plea agreement was simply a teaser for things to come. For the FBI and DS team in the courtroom that morning, it was an ecstatic experience despite disappointment on the espionage charge.

As Litt and his defense team huddled with their client, Keyser talked, smiled, and laughed yet never once acknowledged the presence of his family seated behind him. Dressed in a light-grey and white pinstripe suit, Keyser appeared quite dapper and relaxed as he engaged his legal experts in a conversation unheard by the court spectators.

At 10:10 a.m., Judge Thomas Selby Ellis III entered the courtroom. Judge Ellis flew jet fighters with the Navy from 1961–1966 and then left military service to obtain his JD from Harvard University in 1969. He was nominated to the post as federal judge by President Reagan in 1987 and has been known to tell defendants, "life is about making choices and living with the consequences."

Everyone stood up at the court clerk's direction, wished his honor a good morning, and sat down after the judge installed himself in a massive leather chair behind his equally imposing desk.

"Good morning, Your Honor," Keyser replied in response to the judge's salutation as he left the defense attorneys' table and moved to the podium. The court clerk administered the oath and Keyser said, "Good morning again, Your Honor," in a calm and detached voice. But five minutes later, Keyser's voice started to crack when he explained to the judge and the assembled audience that he knowingly and voluntarily waived his rights and would plead guilty to three violations of federal law. Keyser had concluded his preliminary statements, and it was time for Judge Ellis to review the government's case against him.

As the judge recited the three counts against the defendant—willfully and unlawfully removing classified information from his place of work from 1992 to 2004, a violation of 18 USC 2071; making a false statement on his US Customs form on September 7, 2003, a violation of 18 USC 1001; and making a material false statement to a Diplomatic Security special agent on or about August 9, 2003, a violation of 18 USC 1001—Keyser gripped the sides of the lectern and listened impassively.

When the reading was concluded, Judge Ellis asked Keyser, "Do you understand the charges?"

Keyser put his hands in front of him, elbows resting on the lectern, and said quietly, "I understand, Your Honor."

Judge Ellis listed the potential consequences of pleading guilty to each charge, indicating that the first charge could result in three years in jail without parole plus a fine of $250,000. The other two charges of false statement carried a maximum penalty of five years of federal incarceration without possibility of parole on each count and an additional fine of $250,000 for both counts. He noted that while the government and Keyser were bound by the sentencing portions of the plea agreement, the court was not similarly bound. He also advised Keyser that there would be no leniency in any future sentencing concerning Keyser's expected cooperation with the FBI because cooperating with the debriefing was already a condition of the plea agreement.

Judge Ellis noted that Keyser's attorney would be allowed to attend the debriefings administered by the FBI and State Department.

In a decision that would come back to haunt Keyser, his defense team agreed to allow the results of any polygraph examination to be admitted in future court hearings if the government decided to contest Keyser's plea. Judge Ellis reminded Keyser that in a trial the burden would be on the government to establish guilt beyond a reasonable doubt and to the unanimous satisfaction of all twelve jurors. Keyser stated that he understood.

The judge continued by asking if Keyser was offering to plead guilty because he believed that he was guilty. At 11:43 Judge Ellis directly asked Keyser, regarding Count One, "Are you in fact guilty?"

The defendant responded, "I am, Your Honor."

The judge then asked him to explain in his own words what had led him to be brought before the court.

In response to charge one, for the count of unauthorized retention of classified material, Keyser explained that he had worked for the federal government for thirty-two years and it was common practice for department personnel to have their office materials packed up in boxes at the conclusion of an assignment and forwarded to their next posting. Employees can forward classified materials under secure methods to their next assignment under certain circumstances and with prior approval from their bosses, but not to their homes.

He further explained that he was "insufficiently attentive" when his personal materials from his last assignment in the Bureau of Intelligence and Research were collected at the conclusion of that assignment and boxed up. Keyser insisted it was a temporary secretary assigned to his office, whose name he could not recall, who was responsible for stuffing thousands of highly sensitive documents into empty cardboard boxes that eventually ended up in his house.

As I listened to Keyser's explanation, a vision danced in my head of an employee "inadvertently" packing thousands of classified documents into many dozens of cardboard boxes for shipment out of a restricted area in full view of INR workers who never objected or questioned.

Keyser continued his explanation. "I transported the boxes home, . . . and I came to learn they were in the basement." Of course private homes or basements don't ordinarily qualify as a SCIF in any US government's security rules. He had earlier explained that he and some of his office colleagues "very infrequently" brought classified material to his house from his office so that he could work on time-sensitive issues. However, Keyser acknowledged that this practice was contrary to department security regulations.

At this point, a member of the prosecution team interrupted Keyser.

"Your Honor," Mr. Laufman, the AUSA, exclaimed, "the classified material was neatly arranged on shelves in the basement. Could you please have Mr. Keyser explain how he had come to understand there was classified material in his home?"

Judge Ellis asked Keyser to explain. Speaking directly to the judge and without glancing over his shoulder to his third wife, Margaret Lyons, who sat in the first row of the public gallery, Keyser said, "My wife told me."

All the government agents in the courtroom dropped their jaws at his assertion. Not only had the prosecutors not revealed in court that Margaret Lyons was a senior official at the Central Intelligence Agency, then on loan to John Negroponte, the director of National Intelligence; they had also attempted to downplay the fact. When FBI and DS special agents executed a search warrant on the Keyser residence, they discovered a number of CIA "top secret" materials intermingled with department documents. Now in federal court and under oath, Keyser was acknowledging that not only was his spouse in potential violation of internal CIA regulations for not returning the documents but that she may have knowingly participated in the federal violation of the unauthorized retention of classified information.

I recall looking over at Margaret Lyons, elegantly coiffed and conservatively dressed, seated between her daughter and an unidentified middle-aged gentleman as Keyser answered the judge's questions. She betrayed no emotion as she stared directly ahead.

Keyser's statement before Judge Ellis rolled on as he asserted that he had tarnished his professional reputation because he knew that Cheng was an intelligence officer and he had developed a personal relationship with the NSB agent that he hid from his wife and the department. When he concluded his statement, Judge Ellis asked him to be seated. As he rejoined his defense team at 12:05 p.m., he did not appear as jovial as he had been at the beginning of the hearing. Never once had he glanced over to acknowledge his wife or daughter who quietly and painfully watched the proceedings.

At 12:15 p.m., Judge Ellis accepted Keyser's informed plea and for all practical purposes the case of the *United States of America v. Donald Willis Keyser* appeared to be over. But nothing could have been further from the truth.

Before the court would pronounce sentence, Keyser would have to tell all and cooperate with the DOJ investigation. Many FBI and DS special agents involved in the two-year investigation were displeased with the terms of the plea agreement but were powerless to influence the outcome. They were convinced that Keyser was guilty of passing classified material to a foreign intelligence agency—espionage. By agreeing to cooperate with a damage assessment team and discussing in detail his two-year association with an admitted NSB intelligence officer, he avoided being charged with espionage. So the Keyser legal defense team and the Justice Department hammered out an acceptable exit strategy to end a two-year legal conundrum. I do not think that either Keyser or the federal investigators were happy with their respective lawyers' agreement.

The primary question that DOJ and State wanted answered concerned the identity or content of the documents that Keyser had disclosed. The government was willing to forego more serious charges against Keyser as long as he cooperated in reconstructing specific information he had provided to Huang, Cheng, or others so the intelligence community could evaluate the damages to US security. Fortunately for DOJ, Cheng had been persuaded by the FBI to turn over the originals of her reports on Keyser along with his observations and critiques following her detention outside the Alexandria, Virginia restaurant.

Other questions arose as well. Did Cheng provide the FBI with authentic classified TECRO cables, and could their introduction in court damage Keyser's claims of innocence? Many of Keyser's defenders questioned the TECRO cables' authenticity; however, that question was answered in August 2006 when the government of Taiwan overplayed its hand and hired American attorney Thomas Corcoran Jr., of Berliner, Corcoran and Rowe, LLP, to file an emergency motion (TECRO Memo of Support to Minimize any Potential Adverse Impact Interest on US or Keyser) with the US District Court for the District of Columbia. The motion (Case 1: 06MS00369) attempted to compel the United States government to return the TECRO documents that Cheng had turned over to the FBI. Moreover, in a separate written motion to the court, the Taiwan government requested the motion itself be sealed and kept secret from the American and Taiwanese public. This appeared to be at variance with an official statement from the Ministry of Foreign Affairs in early September 2004 that declared Taiwan had nothing to hide and would fully cooperate with US authorities.

The federal prosecutors responded to the motion by filing a reply indicating that Cheng "voluntarily retrieved" the TECRO cables from her office before turning them over to the FBI. On August 11, 2006, Federal Judge Paul Friedman not only quashed the TECRO-initiated motion during a five-minute court hearing but also ruled that the request itself would now be part of the public record. One can safely assume that Judge Friedman could see nothing but legal mischief in belatedly assuming jurisdiction over one component of the Keyser case that had already been adjudicated in a Virginia federal court. More importantly, he could see no legal merit in sealing the motion itself. Taipei's attempt to complicate matters in the federal prosecution of Keyser for mishandling classified information had been thwarted thanks to Judge Friedman. Was this how the Taiwanese government intended to cooperate? Did its end-run reveal Keyser's culpability in the unauthorized transmittal of classified US information to a foreign power? On September 20, 2006, the TECRO case was consolidated in the Virginia court with the Keyser case. TECRO renewed its motion in this court, and Keyser filed a similar motion. Both motions were terminated without hearing in January 2007 upon the final disposition of the case.

The Taipei government was in all likelihood anxious to recover a TECRO secret electronic telegram forwarded to Taipei on November 25, 2003, in which Cheng states, "Donald Keyser, the Principle Deputy Assistant Secretary of State for East Asia Affairs of the US, continued to explain the recent diplomatic behavior of the PRC." Neither the November 25 cable nor secret TECRO cable dated May 22, 2004, in which Cheng reported that Keyser provided "an in-depth exchange of opinions regarding trilateral relations between the US, China, and Taiwan," would help Keyser's claim that he didn't pass sensitive information to the Taiwanese.

While the IC was concerned with the nature of the information passed to the NSB, the question the investigators most wanted answered was the one Keyser did not know: was Cheng's presence at the private dinner party in September 2002 contrived or not? Did General Huang bring Cheng to Mann's house to dangle her before Keyser in hopes they would begin some form of relationship?

To the investigators, it was obvious that Taiwan already had Keyser as a source through General Huang. They were already professionally acquainted and could contact each other at will, and, importantly, no department regulations prohibited such an association. Why would the Taiwanese government bother to have two intelligence officers working the same source? While wholly speculative, many of us believed that Cheng might be a more appealing confidant than General Huang. Perhaps the NSB knew something of Keyser's personal history. If so, that may have led the agency to conclude that an intelligent, young, and attractive woman who shared Keyser's interest in Sino–US relations would be more successful in eliciting useful information from Keyser. As Keyser himself said in court in December 2005, "However, I understand that my personal relationship with her [Cheng] might have made me vulnerable to attempted exploitation or pressure."

One additional piece of the investigative puzzle stuck in the craw of the investigating team. To combat any potential espionage charges,

Keyser was arguing that he did not know he was supposed to report contacts with suspected foreign intelligence officers. Shortly after Keyser's arrest, SAs Warrener and Cavalier were instructed to proceed to the EAP's Human Resources office to obtain Keyser's personnel file, which would have contained signed forms acknowledging his contact reporting requirements. To the amazement of the two agents, Keyser's folder had mysteriously disappeared from the Human Resources files. In its place was a file that contained a few sheets of paper less than two weeks old. Sad to admit, but the "misplaced" file might have contained documents supporting Keyser's assertions.

Despite interviewing a significant number of Human Resources employees responsible for maintaining the office's records, the file was never located.

SA Cavalier was told that she would be a member of the first team to debrief Keyser, scheduled for January 18, 2006. As a relatively young member of DS, she was extremely nervous. She had studied the man for almost a year, and she had also studied Cheng. She tried to put herself in their heads.

When I talked to SA Cavalier about the interview and how she prepared herself for the encounter, she had an interesting observation.

"It all came to attraction and ego for Don," she said. "Physical attraction and his oversized opinion of himself."

"And how does Isabelle fit in?" I asked.

"Cheng played the role of the curious schoolgirl to perfection," Cavalier explained. "Her attempts to obtain information were often disguised as pure curiosity—the bright and inquisitive yet naïve and slightly inexperienced schoolgirl looking to her mentor to impart his vast knowledge upon her. Not only did she stroke his ego in a way that was incredibly appealing to him, but he had such an ego that it allowed him to feel that the relationship was not subject to any security rules." To SA Cavalier, it was clear that he thought he knew better than any of the DS agents regarding what the rules should be and which applied to him.

One of the obstacles that the debriefing team had to overcome was Keyser's claim that Cheng was a benign entity and that his meetings with her constituted a diplomat fulfilling his EAP duties. Some of the main issues at play here included whether, at his level, he would have been meeting with a relatively junior diplomat as well as whether any meetings he had with diplomats would have been "give and take"—i.e., he would have both provided information and received valuable information to report back to the department. Keyser did not submit one single report of his meetings with Cheng, General Huang, or MSS clandestine agent/journalist Li Zhebgxin for that matter. In Keyser's office calendar, he had disguised his meetings with Cheng and General Huang by using code names—something he never did for any other meeting with foreign diplomats in America.

The investigators needed to prove that Keyser was aware Cheng was in fact a hostile intelligence officer, and SA Cavalier was up to the task. She made the risky decision to emulate Cheng in the debriefing. She studied Cheng's style, the way she dressed (videos and stills), and how she conversed with Keyser (FBI recordings). Cheng was conservative, not overtly sexual. She came across both as an intelligent woman and a bright-eyed schoolgirl in awe of Keyser's genius. She wore styles that were respectable while remaining young and feminine.

When the interview day came, SA Cavalier wore a button-down shirt and a skirt. She wore her hair exactly as Cheng did, long and neatly combed with a side part. She looked like someone that a seasoned diplomat might want to impress; now she had to figure out how to press the right buttons.

When SA Cavalier walked into the debriefing room on January 18, 2006, people lined the walls—representatives from the Department of Justice, National Counterintelligence Executive, DS, the FBI, and individuals from those IC agencies that had an interest in the case. A rectangular table occupied the center of the room. SA Cavalier was teamed up with an FBI agent who told her that she could go first and ask the DS questions before the FBI would ask theirs.

The DS questions were simple enough: did Keyser treat Cheng as an intelligence officer, did he take his laptop to Taiwan, and how did the three thousand-plus classified documents end up in the basement of his home? SA Cavalier and her FBI counterpart sat on one side of the table, and Keyser and his lawyer, Jeffrey Smith, sat on the other.

SA Cavalier started the interview by introducing herself and complimenting him on his career with the department. She told him that everyone with whom she had spoken about this case had nothing but wonderful things to say about him. Keyser's demeanor changed and his posture became more relaxed. He might have even puffed up a bit, sitting up a touch straighter in his chair. The door was open.

SA Cavalier told Keyser that she had some questions for him and apologized for taking up his time. He said that was what he was there for. She asked him to tell her about his job, and he did. She asked him what Cheng did for TECRO, and he commented that she was a political officer.

Leaning forward ever so slightly, just as she had witnessed Cheng do on several occasions while Cheng and Keyser shared lunch, she said that she was a bit confused about the difference between a diplomatic political officer and a covert intelligence officer assigned to a diplomatic mission. She expanded by adding that, as a mere DS agent who had never served overseas, she did not understand the broader context of these roles for our State Department and for the various Ministries of Foreign Affairs. Concluding the broad question, SA Cavalier asked Keyser to explain the day to day functions of a political officer.

In great detail, Keyser explained the role of a diplomatic political officer—having served as one himself, that was easy. She then asked him to describe what an intelligence officer does. With skilled prose he defined the intelligence collection and reporting process. Just as easily, SA Cavalier asked him to describe Cheng's duties at TECRO and whether they were more in line with the duties of an intelligence officer.

At this point, Keyser became visibly upset when he realized that he had been trapped by his own clear explanation of the two very different functions. Keyser said, "Yes," that Cheng did perform the duties of an intelligence officer and he was aware of her (NSB) position.

SA Cavalier would have liked to keep up the act longer as the eager, confused girl in awe of Keyser, but he was on to her at that point. When asked why he never reported the relationship with Cheng, Keyser replied that it was because of embarrassment. Asked why he met one-on-one with her, he responded it was because he was enjoying her company. Finally he was asked what Cheng told him her position was at the NSB, and he replied that she said, "Assistant to [General] Huang."

Keyser did not like the questioning at all. He shot a glance over to his lawyer, leaned back in the chair, crossed his arms, and returned his stare to SA Cavalier as if there was no one else in the room.

Keyser was asked if he was aware of the Asian intelligence practice of throwing attractive young women at older men. He said he was. When asked why he did not think she would be recruiting him, Keyser said that it was because he was sixty years old, because they knew he was going to be retiring, and because since 1964 Taiwan had not attempted to engage US diplomats in clandestine relationships. Keyser said that he had been embarrassed to talk about his relationship with Cheng to the department because he thought it would be seen as a personal relationship.

Keyser said that he did not think the Taiwanese were attempting to recruit him. He denied having physical intimacies with Cheng. (The FBI had videos of their car encounters.) He said he did not require department approval to travel to Taiwan. (The FBI had his e-mails to Cheng and others regarding his travel restrictions.) He added that he used "bad judgment" when he did not tell his colleagues about his clandestine trip to Taiwan but it was not a "lie." He said he was unaware of IC regulations (known as DCIDs) mandating that he report contact of any kind with a foreign intelligence officer. (DS had obtained several acknowledgement forms he signed that specifically outlined his reporting requirements when having any kind of relationship with a known foreign intelligence officer.) He blamed an unidentified "temporary secretary" in the department for inadvertently packing up the thousands of classified documents from his last office and sending them to his home. The remaining answers to her questions concerning the laptop and basement documents were answered with "Yes," "No," or, most frequently, "I don't recall/don't remember."

SA Cavalier had one final question for Keyser.

"Mr. Keyser," she asked, "when you were in Taiwan, where did you leave your laptop [containing classified information] when you left the hotel to sight-see with Cheng?"

"I locked it up in my suitcase."

According to SA Cavalier, the resulting gasps of the counterintelligence audience caused a good deal of the oxygen to escape the interview room. The NSB technical team must have had a field day.

At the end of the interview, and after Keyser and his lawyer left the room, everyone chimed in and judged Keyser to be significantly deceptive on all the substantive questions. Over the course of several interviews, he never wavered from his positions.

After four debriefings (January 18, January 27, February 21, and March 28) and two polygraph examinations (February 14 and April 5), DOJ concluded that Keyser had failed to cooperate with the investigation as promised on December 12, 2005, and was prepared to jumpstart the prosecution. On June 29, 2006, the government filed a motion to find Keyser in material breach of its plea agreement and to release the government from its obligations under the plea agreement. According to the government's July 5 memorandum in support of the motion,

> *. . . the defendant [Mr. Keyser] failed to fulfill his cooperation obligations under the Plea Agreement. Instead of volunteering information about matters that he knows are of interest to the government, he has addressed issues of importance only when directly asked. Even then, his answers frequently have been evasive and incredible. Throughout his debriefings, the defendant has sought to conceal the facts regarding his relationship with Taiwanese intelligence officer Isabelle Cheng, his activities while in Taiwan in September 2003, and his knowledge of the classified materials at his house. On several occasions, moreover, he has acquiesced to the truth (and sometimes incompletely) only after being confronted with incontrovertible forensic evidence*

> *by the interviewing agents. The defendant's lack of cooperation has been particularly egregious with respect to the nature of his relationship with Cheng and Taiwan's National Security Bureau, the stockpile of classified material found throughout the defendant's residence, and his taking a laptop computer and classified material to China, Japan, and Taiwan in 2003.*

DOJ was thoroughly frustrated and wanted out of the plea agreement and went back to court in an attempt to dissolve it. That would allow the government attorneys to pursue Keyser's possible violations of other federal statutes. On July 21, 2006, the Justice attorneys appeared before Judge Ellis in room 900 at the Alexandria federal courthouse and formally requested the court to dissolve the previous December 12, 2005, plea agreement so the government could bring additional charges against Keyser. The DOJ lawyers maintained that Keyser had not been cooperative during the court-mandated debriefing sessions with the FBI and that his polygraph examinations indicated deception when he was asked if he had passed classified information to a foreign intelligence service. Courtroom spectators numbered less than half of those at the previous hearing. Besides the author, the individuals in the room that day were a correspondent for the *China Times*, one representative from the FBI, and an unknown middle-aged gentleman in the back row.

Judge Ellis quickly entertained the government's petition but reminded the federal lawyers that should they proceed with a criminal case, classified information could be cited as evidence. Therefore the legal rules governing such circumstances as outlined in the cumbersome Classified Information Procedures Act would make prosecution difficult in the District Court for the Eastern District of Virginia. There were smiles all around at the defense table. Then Judge Ellis, known for his no nonsense courtroom demeanor, made it clear that he wouldn't tolerate any "judge shopping" on the part of Keyser's defense team should the case go forward. There were smiles all around at the prosecutor's table. Judge Ellis ruled on a number of substantive legal issues and set August 25 for a status conference. As quickly as the proceedings started, Judge Ellis concluded the day's hearing.

As I walked out of the courtroom, I was pleased that the US government was now going to have its day in court and a jury could rule on Keyser's assertions of innocence. Once again, I couldn't have been more wrong!

As expected, Keyser denied that he had violated the plea agreement. His principal argument, in a nutshell, was that he had declared from Day 1 that he was not engaged in espionage.

By mid-December 2006, the government had thrown in the towel and abandoned its attempt to void its plea bargain agreement. The DS and FBI special agents were appalled. At this point in the legal odyssey, was the Department of Justice simply not prepared to risk a court trial in which Keyser would be charged with violations of the espionage laws and sensitive US government information might be disclosed in open court to prove that Keyser had actually passed honest-to-goodness classified data to the NSB? DOJ finally decided to let Keyser's guilty plea to two counts of false statement and one count of unauthorized retention of classified material be the last word in this case. Judge Ellis selected a day in January for the sentencing.

On January 22, 2007, I was once again in room 900 awaiting Judge Ellis's appearance. On the right side of the courtroom were approximately fifteen active and retired Foreign Service officers who were present to offer their visible support for Keyser. Seated among Keyser's State Department colleagues was his wife Margaret. Sprinkled among them were several members of the American and international press including representatives of the Taiwanese news agencies. On the right side, I sat with representatives of the DS and FBI counterintelligence sections.

Litt had grown a goatee since his last court appearance and was wearing a dark gray pinstriped suit set off with a red and white tie. Keyser's support group was dressed in a sea of dark colors, and Keyser wore a conservative gray suit and subdued tie. At 10:17 that morning, Judge Ellis strode into the courtroom as we all stood up, and then we promptly sat down while he began the day's hearing. Judge Ellis set the tone for the morning's session by advising everyone that he had read a "mountain of material and did not need it regurgitated orally" during the forthcoming proceeding.

The next few hours were taken up by both sides reviewing the same federal Rule 11 soliloquy recited to Kendall and Gwendolyn Myers and how it might influence Judge Ellis's sentencing. Following discussion of other matters, a lunch break was ordered. When the court reconvened at 1:05 p.m., Keyser was stone-faced and stared straight ahead as he walked into the courtroom holding his wife's hand. If he recognized me, he made no effort to acknowledge my presence.

It became clear that Judge Ellis was not accepting Keyser's version of the events surrounding his clandestine relationship with Cheng. Nor did he seem to be swayed by Litt's pitches for leniency.

During Keyser's oral statement to the judge, he said he had been "unforgivingly careless" and "took risks with a foreign intelligence agency's employee." He went on to remark, "I can't imagine what I was thinking when meeting an attractive and interesting Ms. Cheng in 2002." He acknowledged that he compounded his mistake by not reporting his relationship to the appropriate department authorities, and he apologized to "Your Honor for lying."

Judge Ellis was not persuaded by Keyser's excuses. When Keyser told the judge, "I want to stress the fact that I was not an agent of the NSB," Judge Ellis quickly interrupted and asked, "Were you duped?"

Keyser answered "No, I was not." The left side of the courtroom could not have disagreed more with Keyser's statement.

Following Judge Ellis's questioning of Keyser, it was time for his lawyer to take up the cause. Speaking directly to the judge, Litt recommended a sentence of probation and characterized the case as "the classic Greek tragedy of a great man brought down by his tragic flaws."

Litt claimed that Keyser's judgment was clouded by an emotional attraction to a younger woman. He tried to pull the court's heartstrings, in hopes of avoiding jail time for his client, by noting that Keyser had a high school-aged daughter and that he was married.

Judge Ellis interrupted Litt's speech. "Many, many criminals have school-age daughters and spouses," he said, further noting that Litt might find "more traction" if he tried another approach.

Litt veered off-point once again, claiming that the information that Keyser provided to Cheng was "generally useless stuff," but he was simply not finding traction with Judge Ellis. He was similarly unsuccessful in persuading Judge Ellis to be lenient with Keyser by sentencing him to probation, time served, or home detention.

At 4:40 p.m., Judge Ellis asked the court if there was any reason why he shouldn't pronounce sentence. Without objection, he continued and announced that Keyser was "guilty of three serious criminal offenses" and that as far as he was concerned the case was "a big deal." He then commented that he had received a letter of support for Keyser signed by Sharon Papp, the American Foreign Service Association's (AFSA) senior legal counsel, in which she attempted to minimize Keyser's actions and blamed overzealous DS investigators for his legal dilemma. A number of DS special agents were insulted by the tenor of the letter. (AFSA was and is the union for many Foreign Service employees.) AFSA's appeal proved to be unpersuasive to the court.

Former ambassador and supreme Black Dragon J. Stapleton Roy, who had resigned in protest for Keyser's punishment in the missing INR laptop incident, submitted a letter to the court pleading that Keyser be spared jail time as did ambassadors William Itoh, Jeffery Bader, Winston Lord, and Philip de Heer, secretary general of the Netherlands Ministry of Foreign Affairs.

Judge Ellis continued, stating that Keyser's suggestion that his backdoor relationship with Cheng was a venue by which to promote America's foreign policy objectives was not, in his opinion, "the way to advance foreign policy." In the end, the judge sentenced Keyser to one year and one day in the federal penitentiary system.

In October 2007, Cheng ended her silence in this affair when she was interviewed in Taiwan, where she was pursuing a doctoral degree and seeking government funding to study abroad. Tearfully she told the *China Times* she was seeking "a second life" and that Keyser was "a very patriotic person and he is even stripped of his pension." (Contrary to Ms. Cheng's statement, Keyser did not lose his pension.) However, she declined to answer any questions about the relationship with her former confidant, citing her confidentiality agreement with the NSB. As a result of her educational petition to the Taiwan government, Cheng was provided funds to continue her studies in England, where she obtained a PhD from the School of Oriental and African Studies at the University of London. She currently serves as a lecturer in East Asian studies at the University of

Portsmouth. Reportedly she has "retired" from the NSB and is enjoying her married life with Chris Cockle.

In 2005, Taipei proposed to the Israeli government that General Huang assume the position of director at the Taipei Economic and Cultural Office in Tel Aviv. Located on the twenty-first floor of the Round Building, it serves in a similar quasi-diplomatic capacity to the TECRO office in Washington, DC. Diplomatic protocol mandates that a sending country must discreetly propose a candidate for an ambassadorial appointment (or equivalent in this instance) to the receiving country for approval. In General Huang's case, Tel Aviv demurred. Maybe it was done in deference to the United States, or perhaps Israel did not want yet another spy operating under diplomatic cover in Tel Aviv and working the same small number of foreign diplomats as its Mossad officers. A similar request by Taipei to the Australian government for a diplomatic posting for General Huang was also declined. It appears that General Huang was considered unsellable, damaged goods in Taiwan's tiny and ever-shrinking overseas diplomatic representation community. He was rewarded with a senior position in NSB headquarters.

Robert S. Litt remained a partner at Arnold & Porter until appointed to President Obama's team at the Justice Department, where one of his duties included monitoring Foreign Intelligence Surveillance Act applications. In 2009, he was appointed as the general counsel of the Office of the Director of National Intelligence.

SA Kevin Warrener was awarded the State Department's highest medal for valor—the Award for Heroism—in December 2012 for his "decisive leadership, unwavering commitment, concern for his colleagues, and bravery during the September 14, 2012, attack on US Embassy Tunis and the subsequent repair and rebuilding."

In March 2014, Benjamin Pierce Bishop, a fifty-nine-year-old civilian contractor for the US Pacific Command in Hawaii, pleaded guilty to one count of transmitting national defense information to a twenty-seven-year-old female Chinese national residing in the US on a student visa. They initially met during a public conference. One year earlier, according to a March 18, 2013 District of Hawaii US Attorney's Office press release, although Bishop had received numerous counterintelligence briefings, he had transmitted classified information concerning nuclear weapons, missile defense, and war plans to her via e-mail. He lied on his official government forms about traveling to London with her on a vacation. Bishop's lawyer, Birney Bervar, characterized their relationship as "two who were in love," not espionage.

Keyser served one year and one day of federal incarceration and was released in January 2008. He underwent three years of supervised release. Shortly after leaving prison, he provided presentations at the Shorenstein Asia-Pacific Research Center at Stanford University. His listed research interests, among others, are US policy toward China and "Cross-strait," otherwise known as China–Taiwan, relations. I was told that Keyser's third wife served him with divorce papers the day he entered prison.

On December 10, 2013, the China Policy Institute blog (University of Nottingham, U.K.) listed the following contributors, among others: Isabelle Cheng (Portsmouth University) and Don Keyser (retired US State Department).

PART 3

Leaks and Losses

Secrecy is the first essential in affairs of State.

—Cardinal de Richelieu

It is much to be wished that our printers were more discreet in many of their own publications.

—General George Washington

I was amazed—and Moscow was very appreciative—at how many times I found very sensitive information in American newspapers. In my view, Americans tend to care more about scooping their competition than about national security, which made my job easier.

—GRU Colonel Stanislav Lunev

CHAPTER NINE

On May 27, 2010, Bradley Manning, a young US Army private assigned as an intelligence analyst to a top-secret communications center in Iraq, was arrested by army investigators and charged with the unauthorized transmission of classified US government information to the WikiLeaks website. Included among the purloined documents were over 250,000 State Department cables dating from December 1966 to February 2010.

Ten months after Manning's arrest, Carlos Pascual, the US ambassador to Mexico, was forced to depart Mexico City after WikiLeaks revealed several classified diplomatic cables sent from the American embassy that were critical of Mexican president Felipe Calderon and his government's war on drugs. When asked by the US press if the leaked cables harmed US–Mexican relations, President Calderon replied that they caused "severe damage."

One month following Ambassador Pascual's resignation, Ecuadorian Foreign Minister Ricardo Patino advised US Ambassador Heather Hodges that President Rafael Correa had demanded her permanent expulsion following the WikiLeaks publication of a 2009 classified diplomatic cable critical of a senior Ecuadorian police official.

Some suggest that the State Department cables leaked by Private Manning influenced events surrounding the beginning of the Middle East's "Arab Spring."

Leaked cables do matter.

When in 2013 Edward Snowden provided *Guardian* columnist Glen Greenwald with thousands of pages of information concerning the NSA's domestic and foreign surveillance programs, he revealed, among many other technical US government collection efforts, that the NSA was eavesdropping on the private cell phone conversations of German chancellor Angela Merkel and Brazilian President Dilma Rouseff, both of whom expressed outrage about these activities. Within months, President Rouseff cancelled a state visit to the United States.

Chancellor Merkel's tepid support for President Obama's foreign policy efforts following the Snowden disclosures, especially with respect to President Putin's annexation of the Crimea in March 2014, may well have been influenced by the *Guardian* articles.

In July 2013, French President François Hollande exclaimed, "We cannot accept this kind of behavior between partners and allies. We ask that this immediately stop." Leaks that have sovereign heads of state angry at the United States are serious indeed. To date, no State Department secrets have been compromised by Edward Snowden. Yet our diplomatic relations with allies have been severely damaged.

In April 2014 the *Guardian* and the *Washington Post* were awarded the 2014 Pulitzer Prize for Public Service for publishing US government secrets. Unauthorized disclosures of classified information to the press have serious consequences. From my first days as an investigator, I was assigned the undesirable task of identifying State

Department leakers, and during my twenty-eight-plus-year career in DS, I investigated a number of cases where secrets had been leaked to the press or lost on planes, trains, and automobiles.

★★★

A little historical background is necessary to understand just how common unauthorized disclosures are and the national security ramifications they entail. Leaking of sensitive information by State Department employees to foreign diplomats and domestic journalists is not a recent phenomenon. In practice, the press always reads gentlemen's mail every chance it gets.

The origins of the United States Department of State are found in an act of Congress that created the "Department of Foreign Affairs" on January 10, 1781. In July 1789, President George Washington signed legislation that created "the secretary to the Department of Foreign Affairs." These titles were changed in September to the Department of State with a secretary of state at its head. Shortly thereafter President Washington would have to deal with a secretary of state who was unable to keep sensitive information confidential.

Former attorney general Edmund Randolph replaced our nation's first secretary of state, Thomas Jefferson, when he resigned in 1793. In August 1795, Secretary Randolph was summoned to President Washington's residence without explanation. Standing before the president and several members of his cabinet, Secretary Randolph was handed a paper that he was instructed to read and explain. Apparently members of the British navy who boarded a vessel sailing to Europe intercepted a dispatch sent from Joseph Fauchet, the

French minister assigned to the United States, to his superiors at the French Foreign Ministry in Paris. In it, the French diplomat analyzed private discussions between Washington and his cabinet in which Washington arguably was expressing an anti-French tilt. The French dispatch cited Secretary Randolph as the "source" of the French minister's analysis of the so-called "privileged" information. President Washington invited Oliver Wolcott, the new treasury secretary, and Secretary of War Timothy Pickering to interrogate the secretary of state about his indiscretions. Ultimately Randolph submitted his resignation, which Washington accepted.

Secrets are created every day in Washington, DC, by the federal government—when personnel at the National Security Agency create codes, when CIA case officers talk to their foreign agents, when FBI agents debrief their sources, when the Joint Chiefs of Staff discuss troop movements. When these secrets are revealed to the press, they become media or news leaks. While the correct technical term is "unauthorized disclosure," the terms are often used interchangeably. But not all leaks are created equal. Just as the motives for leaking differ, so do their intended and unintended consequences.

The first kind of leak is the approved or authorized leak. Truthfully most news leaks are orchestrated by the White House and its administration using an anonymous, ubiquitous "senior government official" to communicate specific policy views without having to go publicly on the record. Leaking is a method for advancing the US government's political agendas and positions without attribution and blowback on the administration and its officials. Leaks serve to air potentially contentious policy issues beforehand in order to gauge reactions in the US and abroad. It's simply a matter of discreetly floating trial balloons and testing political waters.

The second category of leaks is the unapproved or unauthorized disclosure of government information. These leaks occur when a government employee, without prior supervisory or administrative approval, releases information to the press or other unauthorized recipients. These disclosures are investigated by federal agents of the US government. The least damaging are those involving sensitive, but unclassified, information that is administratively controlled against unauthorized release for a variety of legitimate reasons dealing with the internal workings of the applicable department. This category of information is usually marked as "For Official Use Only" by many executive branch agencies, but in the case of the State Department, up until the mid-2000s the data was stamped "Limited Official Use." It is now marked as "Sensitive But Unclassified." The nature of the information does not meet the criteria to be classified as national security information and, while sometimes embarrassing or unsettling to government officials, does not jeopardize our national security interests. Although these types of leaks are treated as an administrative inquiry rather than a criminal investigation, they are not without consequence—the leakers are subject to disciplinary actions as specified by department regulation.

The really damaging leaks involve the release of truly classified government information to unauthorized recipients, most often the press. When the unauthorized recipient of classified information is a clandestine foreign intelligence officer, the "leak" is called espionage. At the outset, these leaks are typically treated as potential criminal violations and investigated accordingly. For reasons of administrative or political expediency and the difficulty of prosecuting such cases, they rarely end up in a court of law. Instead the leaker, if identified, typically receives department disciplinary action, up to and including dismissal.

Before State Department personnel gain access to national security information, they must successfully undergo a federal background investigation and take an oath affirming their responsibility to safeguard sensitive information. The oath taking is neither a novel nor new concept. On November 9, 1775, members of the Second Continental Congress signed an oath of secrecy to protect the cause of liberty and their lives. Today, the yellowed and faded "secrecy" document rests in a hermetically sealed case in the National Archives, just to the left of the Constitution.

★★★

To understand why State Department personnel "leak" classified foreign policy information to the media without prior authorization, one does not have to look any further than the September 21, 2008, edition of the *Washington Post* where a headline blared "U.S. Backed U.N. General Despite Evidence of Abuses." The column detailed how the White House came to support the candidacy of Rwanda's major general Emmanuel Karenzi Karake as the UN's deputy force commander for the ten thousand soldiers conducting peace-keeping operations in Darfur despite previous allegations that Karenzi had been involved in 1990s human rights abuses in Rwanda. General Karenzi was a junior officer in the Rwandan Patriotic Front that in 1994 helped overthrow the Hutu-dominated Rwandan government, which was responsible for the death of over eight hundred thousand Tutsis. The article, purportedly based on one classified department telegram and a classified INR report, stated that Karenzi commanded the 408th Battalion that was involved in reprisal killings and civilian deaths. Written by *Washington Post* staff writer Colum Lynch, the article also quoted extensively from a September 2007 "confidential" memo written by Kristen Silverberg, who is identified as the "head of the international organization bureau." It detailed the internal State Department squabble that pitted one bureau against another over the official US government position on General Karenzi's appointment.

The article quoted from the "confidential" memo by saying that "IO [International Organizations] is aware of the political complications that would ensure [*sic*] from US and/or UN rejection of [Karenzi] and that he is not among the worst human rights abusers from Rwanda." Opposing IO's position within the State Department was the Bureau of Democracy, Human Rights and Labor (DRL), which reportedly had "credible evidence" of human rights abuses that "occurred under his [Karenzi's] command" and stated "it's impossible for the department to support his candidacy for policy reasons and in light of legal considerations."

To be clear, the department had prepared a position paper on the Karenzi appointment. Initially a classified draft version of the "Silverberg memorandum" quoted in the newspaper had been circulated to many offices in the department, including the US Mission to the United Nations in New York City, for review, editing, and approval. State Department officers who were interviewed by DS agents during the preliminary unauthorized disclosure investigation pointed out that the quotes published in the *Washington Post* derived from a circulating draft of the classified memo. This is important to understand because it helped the agents identify a potential timeframe for the leaked information and the two offices that had access to the draft during that period.

Lynch revealed that the *Washington Post* staff had obtained State Department documents from "an anonymous source that was critical of US support for Karenzi." The newspaper was proud to reveal that it had a document, confirming that it had a draft copy. The *Washington Post* was pleased to report that the authenticity of the document "was confirmed by US officials familiar with the internal debate." The sad fact is that if you believe this staff writer, there were a number of government officials willing to discuss "secret" information and the internal workings of the department with the press. But what most distressed a number of department officials was that their dirty laundry was being aired in public.

The internal debate was between IO and DRL, both of which submitted their views to Assistant Secretary of State for African Affairs Jendayi E. Frazer, a former student of Secretary of State Condoleezza Rice at Stanford University, who would make the final decision regarding the matter. According to additionally leaked classified documents, Frazer had assured African Union Darfur mission leaders on September 7, 2007, that the White House would interpose no objection to General Karenzi's continued position as deputy force commander. It turned out that UN secretary general Ban Ki-moon would eventually agree to an extension of Karenzi's tenure with the UN Mission.

To DS agents, the identity of the leaker was clear. The investigation disclosed that the leaker had access to the classified documents, had intimate knowledge of internal department workings, and was able to see the gist of the "Silverberg memorandum" during the early August preliminary "draft" stage. The investigation disclosed that the wording quoted in the *Washington Post* derived from a draft version and not the final copy. The leaker was a department employee dissatisfied with an official State Department position who had hoped to derail the administration's position on General Karenzi and expose the role of a rather inexperienced political appointee named Jendayi Frazer in rejecting the considered judgment of much more senior department officials. While the evidence was insufficient for a prosecution, investigators were fully confident of where the leak originated and who leaked it. DOJ declined to prosecute the department suspect, citing lack of "jury appeal."

★★★

On April 10, 1986, while serving as the acting chief of the Office of Special Investigations (SIB), I realized one of my worst fears when summoned by telephone to report immediately to Clark Dittmer, the director of investigations. Director Dittmer had been the assistant special agent in charge of DS's Washington Field Office when I first joined the State Department in 1974, and he was not an individual to be trifled with; if possible, he was one to be professionally avoided at all costs. Towering well over six feet tall, solidly built, with a flat-top style hairdo and no hint of humor, he had been nicknamed "Darth Dittmer" by some office punster due to his reputation for not suffering fools or subordinates lightly. There was not one agent in our organization who looked forward to an audience with him.

My apprehension that morning was no different from other visits—I was panicky. I was ushered into his sterile inner sanctum, bare of any personal mementos or pictures but prominently featuring his manual Remington typewriter, and the office door closed behind me. I was trapped.

Director Dittmer, resplendent in his usual solid brown suit, motioned me to remain standing while he rattled off the latest problem dumped in his lap by the department seniors.

"Robert, this case is going to require your fullest attention," he barked.

"Yes, sir."

"While you may feel as though you did a good job on the *Washington Post*, *Los Angeles Times*, and Lorton Reformatory leaks, those were easy cases—anybody could have solved them. This new one is different."

Thanks, I thought. *I needed that.*

According to Director Dittmer, the secretary of state was furious to discover that Assistant Secretary of State (A/S) Elliot Abrams had been contacted on April 7 by Rowland Evans, a syndicated columnist for the *Washington Post*, requesting A/S Abrams to confirm the existence of a classified telegram sent from our embassy in Buenos Aires.

Director Dittmer continued, "On April 8, Robert Novak, another syndicated columnist, also contacted A/S Abrams by telephone asking him to confirm the existence of a classified State Department cable identified as 'Buenos Aires 2888.'" In 1986, both Messrs. Evans and Novak were writing articles for the *Washington Post*. In 1991 A/S Abrams would be convicted of two misdemeanors for unlawfully withholding information from the Senate Intelligence Committee regarding the Iran-Contra affair, for which he would be pardoned by President George H. W. Bush in 1992.

"Yes, sir," I said. "I understand."

State Department telegrams from diplomatic posts overseas are commonly identified by the post of origin. In this case, our embassy in Buenos Aires used sequenced numbering starting with the number 0001—the first cable sent after midnight on January 1, 1986. The ambassador had sent a "secret" message to the department in April 1986. This telegram was Buenos Aires 2888.

According to Director Dittmer, later on the afternoon of April 8, William Kritzberg of the *Washington Times* had also attempted to contact A/S Abrams at his office. Unsuccessful, he contacted Deputy Assistant Secretary (DAS) William Walker and asked him to verify the authenticity of certain sentences that Kritzberg claimed were parts of Buenos Aires 2888.

Apparently everybody in Washington has seen this "classified" cable, I thought.

Walker refused to discuss BA 2888 with Kritzberg and promptly notified A/S Abrams's office, which immediately alerted the secretary of state's office of the leak. After confirming that information contained in a classified department telegram was now in the hands of the press, DS was notified later that evening.

"This is no laughing matter," Director Dittmer said. "The secretary's office is absolutely livid about this leak to the press."

"Yes, sir."

"They are demanding that we identify those who were responsible for the leak immediately."

"I will get on it right away," I said. "Who will be helping me on the case?"

Director Dittmer gave me a quizzical look and scowled as he reached for something on his desk, saying nothing. *Oh boy, here I go solo again*, I thought. *We have only two other agents in the office and both are swamped with investigations.*

At this point, Director Dittmer handed me a copy of that morning's *Washington Post* and asked me to scan the front page, which contained an article with sentences underlined in red.

Under the heading "Ambassador Assails O'Neill Delegation," *Washington Post* staff writer Patrick E. Tyler described a recent Congressional delegation (CODEL) visit to Buenos Aires and liberally quoted from a classified department cable identified as BA 2888. The opening sentence of the article stated, "The U.S. Ambassador to Argentina, Frank V. Ortiz Jr., in a strongly worded cable to Washington has criticized House Speaker Thomas P. (Tip) O'Neill Jr. (D-Mass) and other members of a traveling congressional delegation for allegedly pressuring political leaders in Buenos Aires to condemn Reagan administration policies in Central America."

The article described how Ambassador Ortiz, who accompanied the fourteen House members to meetings with President Alfonsín and other government members, cited boorish congressional solicitations of condemnations from Argentine officials of President Reagan's foreign policy initiatives in Latin America as the worst he had witnessed in his Foreign Service career. "When I saw the speaker off at the airport, I frankly told him in my 35 years of service I had never seen such a performance. . . .To me it seemed to come close to raising constitutional issues of the legislative branch intruding far into the prerogatives of the executive branch." An unsmiling Director Dittmer now handed me a copy of BA 2888, classified "secret," and drew my attention to specific sentences highlighted in the Tyler article.

Specifically in paragraph four of the *Washington Post* article, the sentence beginning with the words "Congressman Russo (Rep. Marty Russo [D-Ill.]) exceeded all bounds in his attacks on the president . . . with Russo stating that [the] president [is] seeking armed confrontation with Nicaragua" was a word-for-word quote from paragraph three in BA 2888. Later in the article, a sentence beginning with the words "Throughout the visit, Russo and Stark (Rep. Fortney H. [Pete] Stark [D-Calif.]) joined Speaker O'Neil in attempting to obtain official Argentine condemnation of administration policies" was a word-for-word quote from the final sentence of paragraph three of BA 2888.

Instinctively I knew that I was about to be launched on another unauthorized disclosure investigation in an attempt to identify a department employee who had provided a copy of a classified document to the news media.

"Now, Robert," Director Dittmer said, "I realize your chances of identifying the culprit are slim as probably one hundred people saw the telegram within the first twenty-four hours of it getting here—any one of whom could have deliberately or inadvertently leaked it."

"Yes, sir."

"Do your best, and we will report back to the secretary our preliminary results as quickly as possible. At least the seventh floor will know that we are doing something."

Ahhh, I thought, *the seventh floor, where the secretary of state and the Black Dragons have their offices. I need to tread carefully here.*

Left unsaid was the certainty that the Black Dragons were breathing fire over the fact that confidential comments of a respected colleague had been provided to the media. I laughed inwardly as I reviewed the sentences circled in the *Washington Post* article. The article did not compromise any national security information; however, it reported the candid views of an American ambassador, and the department was now embarrassed to see its laundry hanging out in full view of Congress and the rest of the world.

What Director Dittmer would not point out to the Black Dragons was the fact that all of one agent would be spared to do the job—me. I guess that made me a very special agent in a perverse sense.

"Now drop all of your other investigations and concentrate on this one," Director Dittmer ordered.

I was dismissed from his office before I could get a straight answer as to whether we would pursue prosecution in the unlikely event that we found the culprit. I returned to my office and opened up case SB12-0846-100-0042 entitled "Unauthorized Disclosure / Washington Post." News leaks were so common that we did not bother coming up with fancy names for the investigations like "Blue Moon" or "Operation Pampas Tippling." No matter, the first order of business in any leak investigation was to contact those department employees who initially had access to the telegram. Perhaps not surprisingly, everyone I called said that he had been expecting my call. Maybe this time I would not be treated like a leper seeking shelter from the plague.

Pen in hand, copies of the *Washington Post* article and BA 2888 in my briefcase, I sought out Elijah Kelly Jr., a special assistant in the department's Information Management Section. He was like a traffic cop responsible for routing and distributing telegrams received from overseas missions. Sitting in his small office, Kelly patiently studied a copy of my underlined telegram and advised me that Buenos Aires 2888 had been received in the State Department at 1:52 a.m. on April 3 (Thursday). His examination revealed that the cable was properly marked "secret" with the added "NODIS" caption (No Distribution outside the department and limited distribution inside the department to specific addressees). Unfortunately NODIS in this case meant that at least nine offices in the building (SW, S/S, S/S-S, SS/I, D, P, INR, S/P, and CATB) had received copies!

In addition, I was told that per the instructions of Brunson McKinley, a senior manager in the secretary's executive office, a copy was sent to Phillip Habib, the undersecretary for political affairs. Kelly's log sheet indicated that a copy had been sent to the National Security Council at the White House; however, it was unclear who had instructed the secretary's executive office to do so.

My initial fears were confirmed. By 8:00 a.m. on April 3, 1986, less than seven hours after BA 2888 was processed inside the State Department, at least nine offices, encompassing as many as one hundred employees, not including the NSC staff, were in possession of the cable. So much for NODIS! It was time to start interviewing those department employees who had been the initial recipients of BA 2888. The lyrics to "Don't Cry for Me Argentina" ran through my befuddled mind.

On a related note, I still keep a copy of an unclassified July 17, 1991, memorandum from Acting Secretary of State Lawrence Eagleburger to Assistant Secretary of State Bernard Aronson summing up my investigation into the leak of State Department classified cable Mexico 7966 to *Proceso*, a Mexican weekly newspaper: "Unfortunately, DS was unable to identify the individual responsible for the unauthorized disclosure. The Bureau of Diplomatic Security noted that ARA/MEX's undocumented processing and distribution of the cable, which was revealed during the inquiry, precluded a successful resolution. One of the lessons learned from this sorry episode is that we all need to hold more closely sensitive cables and memoranda."

Despite numerous unauthorized disclosures of State Department cables, they are not managed inside the department in a manner to prevent leaks—or worse—for the investigators, to identify the perpetrators.

On April 1, I interviewed William Walker, deputy assistant secretary of state; James Michel, principal deputy assistant secretary of state; Robert Kagan, special assistant for policy; and Bob Loftis, staff assistant to the assistant secretary of state. Walker informed me that he had spoken to Ambassador Ortiz on April 1, 1986, just after the CODEL had a "wheels-up" from Argentina. After hearing Ambassador Ortiz's stinging comments concerning the conduct of the CODEL, Walker recommended that a candid assessment of the trip, with NODIS caveat, be sent to the seventh floor immediately. Of course, Ortiz did so.

Walker related how surprised he was to receive an early morning telephone call on April 8 from William Kritzberg, a reporter from the *Washington Times*, inquiring specifically about BA 2888 barely four working days after the cable was sent to Washington.

"Funny," Walker said to me, "Kritzberg specifically asked me to confirm the existence of BA 2888 in the early afternoon, and later on that same day Rowland Evans asked me to authenticate some paragraphs from the same cable."

"What did you tell them?" I asked.

"I told them both that I had not seen all telegrams for the past few days, so I could not confirm or deny the authenticity of BA 2888."

"Seems like it was compromised, no?"

"Special Agent Booth," he said, "I am under no illusion but that BA 2888 was most likely in the hands of numerous Washington, DC-based reporters by April 5."

This comment would later lead me to conclude that whoever leaked the document did so before the weekend of the April 5–6, less than sixteen working hours after BA 2888 was received in Washington. I asked Walker what the possible motive might be for leaking the cable, and he said two possibilities came to mind: to harm President Reagan's foreign policy objectives or to embarrass CODEL members—or maybe both.

Special Assistant Kagan told me that Kritzberg had called him on April 9 and quoted to him from the last paragraph of BA 2888, asking Kagan if he wanted to comment on the substance of the cable. Kagan acknowledged that he had previous professional discussions with Kritzberg and would have welcomed an opportunity to put a positive spin on any forthcoming story involving his region of responsibility. But he said that he declined to discuss BA 2888 with the reporter. Kritzberg told Kagan that he obtained the document from a department source. Kagan suggested it was quite possible that the same person leaked the cable to all three media sources. I was not the least bit surprised by his comment since multitasking abilities were not unheard of in department circles.

James Michel, a young department South American specialist with whom I spoke, was unaware of the leak until an official meeting on April 10 and had not received any telephone calls from the press asking about BA 2888. Still he provided me with insight into the cable's political fallout when he said, "The leak would harm President Reagan's success on the upcoming Contra Aid vote and discourage President Alfonsín from being candid in forthcoming discussions with our ambassador."

"What about the Speaker?"

"Embarrassment, for sure."

Imagine that—an administration official going after House Speaker Thomas Phillip "Tip" O'Neill Jr., the man who once exclaimed that President Reagan was "the most ignorant man ever to occupy the White House."

On April 17, I was ushered into the plush offices of A/S Abrams. After I introduced myself as investigating the unauthorized disclosure of BA 2888, he told me that he was aware of the ongoing inquiry.

"I was in Haiti on April 3, 1986," he said, "and I cannot recall with any precision when I may have read BA 2888 before returning to Washington, DC."

By consulting his daily planner, he told me with certainty that he had spoken with Evans at 3:50 p.m. on April 7. He pointed out a handwritten note from this day where he had written the name "Evans" and what appeared to be "BA 2888."

"During the telephone conversation, Evans read me a portion of BA 2888," Abrams said, "and then had the audacity to ask for a copy so that he could write a column about it."

I asked why Evans felt comfortable placing the call and making the request.

"I am a professional friend of Rowland Evans, and while we have appeared together on his weekend television program, we do not socialize. And I told him I would certainly not provide him with a copy of BA 2888."

Abrams then added that Robert Novak contacted him on April 8 and also attempted to obtain a copy of BA 2888, with the same results. Novak told Abrams that he could really help the administration's position in Latin America if he could have a copy of the cable. After Abrams declined, Novak asked him to think it over. Abrams reviewed his telephone log sheets and noted that William Kritzberg had attempted to call him at 2:40 p.m. on April 8, but Abrams did not return his call.

Immediately after hanging up the phone with Evans on April 7, Abrams called Nicholas Platt, special assistant to Secretary of State

George Shultz, telling him to alert his boss to the possibility of a forthcoming media leak. Platt later advised Abrams he had informed the secretary, who was none too pleased with the news.

"Special Agent Booth," Abrams said, "I am sorry that I cannot offer any further assistance, but I hope you identify the leaker." He stood up from behind his desk and did not offer his hand or tell me to call him if I had further questions, but I suspected his remark was genuine, for whatever that was worth.

I interviewed Nicholas Platt, Deputy Executive Secretary Brunson McKinley—with whom I would serve as his RSO while he was the US ambassador in Haiti later that year—and Kenneth Quinn, another deputy executive secretary. All the officers said that while the leak was a breach of security procedures, it was not particularly damaging or sensitive in terms of national security. Then why, I asked, was it classified at the "secret" level? To a man, they claimed that ambassadors must be candid in preparing reports on congressional visits to foreign countries and that public disclosure would harm the department's relations with the Hill and, in this case, Argentina. Nicholas Platt commented that he had contacted Rod McDaniel at the National Security Council and was told that BA 2888 was kept within the NSC offices and was not passed to the West Wing of the White House.

In theory, an investigator should interview any and all persons who had access to the leaked information. But in practice, secretaries, low-level administrators, and the like were rarely interviewed because they simply were not stakeholders in the drama. By and large, they did not have any special interest in the subject matter. I could not recall a single instance when such department employees were suspected of leaking information to the press.

There is a standard litany of thirteen questions for unauthorized disclosure investigations, including asking the employee whether he or she leaked information or who might be responsible for the disclosure. So far, all of the interviewees denied being the source of the leak, but several of them had firm beliefs as to where I should concentrate my efforts. Every person to whom I spoke was a career FSO who, as he explained, would never wish to hurt or embarrass Ambassador Ortiz or harm the department's relations with Congress by leaking the cable. That would be unseemly conduct and professionally counterproductive. To them, it made absolutely no sense that a career colleague would be a viable suspect.

With precious few leads, I accepted their insight and went back to check the notes from my interview with Elijah Kelly in which he explained where and how the cable was initially distributed within the building. If the old Foreign Service hands' suspicions were correct, then the leaker could be a non-career department employee. I needed to focus on an office that received BA 2888 and was staffed with younger, perhaps indiscreet, Foreign Service officers, political appointees, and civil servant employees. To me, that would be the department's Policy Planning Staff (S/P), an office responsible for formulating diplomatic policy initiatives, which works directly for the deputy secretary of state.

I had previously interviewed S/P Director Richard H. Solomon on April 11 and now revisited my notes. According to Solomon, he had not personally reviewed BA 2888 before he was informed of the leak during an April 10 senior staff meeting. He did advise that it was standard practice in his office for sensitive cables such as BA 2888 to remain in a safe where staffers could review them at their leisure.

While Solomon's comments were helpful, it was Lloyd Richardson, a staff assistant in S/P, who provided traction for my investigation. During our interview on April 15, he explained that his office was responsible for preparing an internal distribution cover sheet for BA 2888.

Richardson said, "Although NODIS cables weren't intended to have wide distribution, it's S/P practice to keep such cables in the S/P 'read file' maintained in a safe in room 7311."

"What are the rules regarding your read file?"

"The read file is a folder containing classified documents and telegrams that are thought to be of interest to all S/P staffers."

"Do readers have to sign a sheet indicating they have read documents in the read file?"

"No, we use the honor system. It allows S/P personnel to peruse the file as they wish, and though they don't have to sign any form when they read documents or cables, no documents can be taken out of the office space."

"Mr. Richardson," I asked, "just how many individuals assigned to S/P would have access to the read file that had a copy of BA 2888?"

"Fifteen," he answered immediately.

If my only clue was correct, I had just fifteen possible suspects. That was a more manageable number. I asked Richardson if he would walk me over to room 7311 and allow me to remove S/P's copy of BA 2888 out of view from the office workers. From the front of the safe, and with Richardson's assistance, I removed BA 2888 with my thumb and forefinger, gently clasping a corner of the 2-page stapled document, and eased the telegram into a manila envelope.

Thanking Richardson for his assistance, I returned to my office and had SA Michael Posillico personally deliver S/P's telegram to the

FBI Laboratory, Identification Division, Latent Fingerprint Section for analysis. I then gathered up all the official and security files for the fifteen suspects. The folders, just like Kendall Myers's SY File, contained all the personnel, security, and administrative records of the employees from the time they applied for employment with the department. I was looking for someone who might give me some insights into the personalities and inner workings of S/P. I wanted to identify a cooperative source who could point me in the right direction. Within two hours of reviewing the SY Files, it was clear who that would be.

One file contained information about a young employee whom I identified as "Confidential Source A," or simply CSA, who had previously worked with both print and electronic media before joining the department. I believed it likely that in one way or another CSA traveled in the same after-hours social circles that included reporters such as William Kritzberg of the *Washington Times*. Sometimes you have to be very lucky to be successful. My gut instinct, based on the SY File contents, was that CSA was not my suspect, but CSA knew the identity of the leaker. It was now time to close this case before memories started to fade. At my request, Richard Solomon arranged for me to have a private room, close to the S/P executive offices, in which to interview CSA inconspicuously.

On April 15, at my instruction, a very young CSA was escorted by a senior S/P officer into a tiny office containing two chairs and a desk. After the pro forma introductions, only CSA and I remained in the cramped quarters.

Sitting across from CSA, I displayed my department credentials. "Good morning, I am Special Agent Robert Booth in the Special Investigations Branch, and I am currently conducting an unauthorized disclosure investigation."

CSA displayed no emotion as he stared back at me.

"I am attempting to determine how a State Department NODIS cable, which I think is BA 2888, may have been compromised to correspondents Robert Novak and William Kritzberg in less than seventy-two hours of having been processed inside the State Department."

Without any hesitation, CSA advised that he had a prior professional relationship with William Kritzberg when they both worked in New York City. "When I started work in Washington, DC," he continued, "Kritzberg had transferred down to Washington, and as a professional courtesy, I wanted to help him expand his contacts in S/P."

I could not believe what I was hearing. I might actually be onto something here. As we talked, CSA identified two of Kritzberg's contacts in S/P, one of whom I had already interviewed and a new individual—"Mr. Penn."

"Have you ever read or seen BA 2888?" I asked.

"I have never seen S/P's read file copy of BA 2888."

"I need to remind you that you must be entirely truthful during the course of an official investigation, that any false statement during the course of this interview could be used against you in either an administrative or judicial hearing."

To bolster my admonishment, I advised CSA that I had asked for all the department telephone records for individual S/P office phones. Those telephone records, normally reserved for administrative and budgetary reasons, would give me the numbers of every single incoming and outgoing department telephone call. They had been a gold mine for me in the past, and I knew they were an incredible investigative resource. Many department employees had given me dagger eyes when I pushed these records across the interview table after they had already answered—incorrectly—one of my questions about a specific telephone number received or dialed by their office telephone.

"You need to know," I told CSA, "I have both William Kritzberg's private home and office telephone numbers. All I have to do is run our State telephone logs to see if those two numbers were called from a State phone or vice versa during the time frame in question."

After a quiet pause, CSA said that he received a telephone call in his office from Kritzberg on April 7 asking him to confirm the existence of BA 2888. When CSA said that he had no idea of what BA 2888 was about, Kritzberg quoted from the cable and said that "it was a State Department source" who had provided him with the document. CSA related that he felt uncomfortable discussing BA 2888 any further with Kritzberg and ended the telephone conversation quickly but amicably.

"And that was it?" I asked. "No more calls from Kritzberg to S/P staff?" I continued to probe gently about times and telephone calls. Finally my patience was rewarded.

"I do remember that during the first week of April, I heard that Kritzberg had left a message for Mr. Penn to call back urgently," CSA said. "I am not revealing any secrets here, but it is well known in the office that Mr. Penn is in full support of the White House's stance in Latin America and that if Mr. Penn leaked the telegram it would have been to bolster the administration's position and embarrass Speaker O'Neill."

I could not believe it. Talk about good luck. If CSA's comments and opinions were even half correct, my universe of suspects had just dropped to one!

"One final question, if I may," I inquired. "Is there anybody else in S/P that you think may be able to assist me with this investigation?"

After about a minute CSA said, "I would be happy to introduce you to a colleague of mine who might be able to help."

Ten minutes later "Confidential Source B" (CSB) entered the tiny, windowless office, and we started to talk across a small wooden table.

CSB confirmed that Mr. Penn would have had access to BA 2888 by April 4 and that he (CSB) had always had some concerns about Mr. Penn's contacts with the press. On one occasion, during an after-hours social event hosted at a private residence in Washington, DC, he had witnessed Mr. Penn and an Australian journalist, Peter Samuels, engaged in deep conversation during dinner in which CSB overheard Mr. Penn say, "Well, if you read the traffic [cables] between Washington and Europe. . . ." CSB had been present at similar social functions with Mr. Penn and believed Mr. Penn was very indiscreet in his discussions with private citizens.

As a final comment, CSB said, "I believe there is an ideological affinity between Mr. Penn, Kritzberg, and the *Washington Times*."

"Thank you for your insight and candor," I said.

Mr. Penn was a GS-13, "Schedule C" official assigned to the Office of the Secretary, Policy Planning Staff (S/P) as a speechwriter since February 15, 1985. The moniker "Schedule C" comes from the US government's personnel regulations identifying non-career personnel working for the department at the pleasure of the administration, or in more colloquial terms, a political appointee. Given his rank and title, I knew he would not have any Black Dragons protecting him. Without that shield, Mr. Penn would have to submit to a confrontational interview under my control. I had always been a firm believer in Sir William Blackstone's overarching premise that truth can be determined through the cross-examination of witnesses. I was so proud of myself that I could not wait to inform my boss of the status of the investigation.

Later that evening, I was ushered into Director Dittmer's office. I could barely contain my excitement. After years of investigating unauthorized disclosures, I had finally gotten to the point of requesting authority from Director Dittmer to conduct a confrontational interview.

"Director Dittmer," I announced, "I am confident I know who leaked BA 2888!"

Imagine my dismay when Director Dittmer appeared aghast. It took me a few seconds to guess why. First, he probably thought I was exaggerating (strike one). Second, if my assertion was true, the result must have been due to "unnecessarily aggressive" interviews on my part that would have to be justified up the bureaucratic Black Dragon line (strike two). Third, and worst of all, if I was right and had actually fingered a department official, like a Black Dragon, he or she would now have to be punished, and DS would have hell to pay for actually having done its job (strike three). In the world of leaks, no one is ever caught, and if caught, rarely punished.

Relief immediately spread across Director Dittmer's face when I said, "My suspect is a Schedule 'C' political appointee."

"Robert, schedule the confrontational interview as quickly as possible."

I told him I would wait for the FBI's fingerprint analysis results from the original S/P copy of BA 2888 before scheduling the interview. Director Dittmer readily agreed.

The FBI gave me my answer five days later—Mr. Penn's fingerprints were all over it.

CHAPTER TEN

Days before my talk with Mr. Penn, I sat down with Special Agent Mark McMahan, a former Arlington County police officer who had joined DS as a SA in 1984, to discuss how best to frame and conduct the interview. Agents must consider various factors such as the age, department position and title, rank, gender, education, and employment history of the interviewee—all contained in the SY File—to determine the order and structure of the questions. I have always been of the opinion that, within the first few minutes of an interview, it is important to ask a question or two that you are confident the suspect will lie about so that, when appropriate later on, he can be confronted and have his confidence shaken. Lying to federal investigators is simply a reflexive, self-preserving act for those who leak classified information to the press. And, as Vice President Dick Cheney's aide "Scooter" Libby discovered in 2007, lying, as opposed to leaking, is the act that most often gets an individual in trouble unless, of course, you have a presidential intervention to spare you jail time.

Mark and I finally decided to avoid any "Mutt and Jeff" or good guy–bad guy routine and employ the old Joe Friday scenario, asking many questions requiring simple "yes" or "no" answers. Confident of our approach, I called Mr. Penn on April 23, identified myself, and advised him that I was conducting an official investigation involving official State Department matters. I asked if he could be available for an interview, and he answered that he could be available in about one hour. He did not ask for a lawyer to be present.

I alerted Mark to prepare for the interview. The Special Investigations interview room was a tiny, interior office space, painted "puke" green and crammed with an oak conference table along with eight solid oak chairs. The only other item gracing this room was a solitary bookcase, stocked with pathetic looking pamphlets and worn out telephone books. Upon entering the space, Mr. Penn would be seated with his back to the door facing the two of us. There were no visual distractions and nothing on the table except two legal notepads. Not exactly Gestapo central but dreary enough for our purposes.

Mr. Penn arrived around 2:15 and told the secretary that he was looking for agent Booth or McMahan. Once alerted, I sent Mark into the interview room and went out to introduce myself. Standing about 5′6″, in conservative clothes, clean shaven, hair neatly combed back, Mr. Penn would go unnoticed in a crowd of two. I introduced myself and quickly guided him over to the interview room.

Inside Mark shook Mr. Penn's hand and directed him to his prearranged seat. Before we started the interview, I provided him with a standard "Warning and Assurance to Employee Required to Provide Information" form, which he read and signed. The form explains to employees they are being interviewed concerning job-related issues and are required to respond to questions unless their answers would tend to incriminate them.

He started the interview by explaining that he had been employed in S/P as a speechwriter since February 15, 1985.

"What are your general responsibilities in the office?" I asked.

"My primary duties are to draft speeches for department officials and 'remarks' for other public functions."

"So it is a good job?"

"Yes," he said. "I enjoy my position at the department, and I have good professional relationships with my colleagues, even spending social evening hours with many."

I paused for a few seconds after his answer, opened a file on the table, and perused the contents for about thirty seconds. Looking up, I closed the file folder and glanced over my right shoulder to Mark before looking directly at Mr. Penn.

"Any recent problems or commotion in the office?"

"None that I am aware of," he replied quickly. To this point, Mr. Penn was genial and forthcoming.

"Any recent leaks in the press that caused problems in S/P?"

"None that I can think of." It was lie number one.

I produced the April 10 edition of the *Washington Post* and pointed out the article entitled, "Ambassador Assails O'Neill Delegation." I asked him if he remembered reading that article. He said "Yes" and added that he read the *Post* daily and thought he had read that article the day it was published. I asked whether he recalled that segments of a State Department cable were quoted in the article, and he said "Yes."

Mark next asked our suspect if he had been able to read S/P's copy of the cable. Mr. Penn answered that he probably had read BA 2888. To the question whether he had discussed the cable with anybody, he replied that he "did not disclose it to anyone." Chalk up lie number two.

At this point in the interview, I noticed that our suspect started shifting uncomfortably in his chair and that his hands, which had rested comfortably on the table since the beginning of the interview, were now clasping his cheeks. It was time for the first trap question.

"Mr. Penn, do you know William Kritzberg of the *Washington Times*?"

"Yes."

"Give me some background, please."

He acknowledged that someone working in S/P first introduced him to William Kritzberg, but he could not recall who made the first introduction or where it occurred.

"Mr. Penn, are you currently in contact with Mr. Kritzberg?"

"Yes."

"Mr. Penn, how do you maintain the relationship?"

He remarked that he normally talked to Kritzberg by phone, that he had conversations with Kritzberg several times prior to April 10, 1986, and that the purpose of the phone calls was to schedule and then cancel appointments to have lunch together.

I casually passed a knowing glance at Mark. We had a department employee sitting in front of us who acknowledged reading BA 2888 the first week in April and who knew William Kritzberg, the first individual to ask senior department employees to confirm the contents of BA 2888. The trap question had been to get him either to admit that he knew Kritzberg (good for us) or lie and say he didn't (also good for us).

Mark asked, "You would not have disclosed portions of BA 2888 to Kritzberg or other unauthorized persons, would you?"

"No." It was lie number three.

Our suspect commented, to direct questioning, that Kritzberg never made any reference to him about BA 2888 and that he did not have any contact with him during the first two weeks of April. Well, that was lie number four.

Now it was time to see just how truthful Mr. Penn was going to be with me. I knew that Kritzberg had called the S/P office before April 5 and left a message with one of the S/P officers for our suspect to contact Kritzberg "urgently." A standard practice for leaving colleagues a message then was to use a small, yellow "memorandum of call" form that indicated who called and at what time. Previously an S/P employee had allowed me to see the form from "Kritzberg" to Mr. Penn, dated April 4, which had the word "urgent" underlined and capitalized in the message block.

"Mr. Penn," I asked, "do you remember getting any telephonic messages in the office from Kritzberg around the time of the leak?"

"No." That was lie number five—maybe.

Four and a half lies later and our suspect was beginning to fidget visibly. I knew by reviewing department telephone records that his office telephone had been used to call Kritzberg's office phone on the morning of April 7 and that, according to time and attendance records, our suspect had reported for work that day. While it was possible that another employee used his telephone to call Kritzberg, the probability was about as likely as Chicago Mayor Rahm "Rahmbo" Emanuel going through a day without using the word "mother."

"Have you ever discussed BA 2888 with anyone?"

He answered slowly this time. "To the best of my recollection, I have not talked about that cable with anyone inside the building."

I thought, *What is this "anyone inside the building" disclaimer about?*

"Have you talked to anyone outside the building about BA 2888?"

"I am certain that I did not."

It was lie number six. Time to ratchet up the interrogation.

"Would you be willing to undergo a polygraph examination in which the only issue would be whether you had disclosed the contents of BA 2888 to any unauthorized person?"

After thirty seconds of quiet deliberation, Mr. Penn said, "I'd have to think about it." He was now squirming so much in his seat that I thought he would fall off. His hands moved all around his head, and he had a tough time looking either one of us straight in the eyes.

There was nothing left to do but ask our suspect if he would immediately prepare and sign a sworn statement denying that he disclosed the contents of BA 2888 to anybody not authorized to see it. He agreed, wrote a one-paragraph denial, and signed the document, by which he acknowledged that any false statement on the document is a violation of federal law—the exact same proviso that had Don Keyser incarcerated as a felon in 2007. Mr. Penn's physical agitation during the final questions was so extreme that I planned to have his chair equipped with a seat belt at our next meeting.

I told him that we would probably call him back to set up another short, clarifying interview in the near future. We all stood up and shook hands, and Mark escorted our suspect out to the main corridor.

The next morning I reported to Director Dittmer that I was confident that Mr. Penn was responsible for disclosing BA 2888 to the media and that he had just executed a false sworn statement of denial. I told Director Dittmer that we would be calling our suspect in for a second interview shortly in order to clarify some of his answers.

Director Dittmer was visibly surprised. I think this was the first time that a department leak investigation was relatively successful, so we were sailing uncharted waters. He gave me approval to continue the investigation.

I called Mr. Penn that afternoon and arranged the next interview for the following day as I was scheduled to leave on April 25 for a four-day vacation in Bermuda with my future wife. He said he would check his schedule and get back to me. He called back when I was out of the office and left a message. My secretary wrote down that he "said he could wait until you get back from vacation." Boy, I bet he could have waited until Hell (or Bermuda) froze over to see me again.

When I returned from vacation on April 30, I reported to Director Dittmer's office, where I was informed that during my absence Mr. Penn hired a lawyer who had contacted the department to advise DS that in any future interview Mr. Penn would have his lawyer present.

What was the takeaway message? Mr. Penn had knowledge of the circumstances surrounding the unauthorized disclosure but was willing to confess only with the assistance of legal counsel.

In fact, one Gordon Diddlemeyer called my office at 4:00 that very afternoon and left a message that he wished to arrange a second interview with Mr. Penn. Before I could return the call, I was summoned to Director Dittmer's office and told that the department's legal advisor's office, known simply as "L," directed that I was not to contact the Department of Justice to discuss the potential prosecution of a suspected leaker nor was I to talk to Mr. Penn's legal representative without L's approval. L had never conducted or prosecuted criminal investigations and had not contacted me or seen my report of the investigation. L was simply the legal mouthpiece for the department. What the hell was going on here?

Maybe the surprised look on Director Dittmer's face back on April 10 was in some sense prophetic. I had done my job, closed the SIB's unauthorized disclosure case involving the *Washington Post* and BA 2888, and moved to other investigations. And there matters rested until mid-May.

On May 16, 1986, at 12:35 p.m., the Department of State held a televised press briefing as it does every day in the Press Briefing Room, room 2209 of the HST, before the assembled accredited State Department Press Corps. The department's spokesman, Charles E. Redman, read the following from a prepared brief:

"The Department is dismissing a mid-level employee because he made an unauthorized disclosure of classified information to the news media. We regret that because of this transgression the Department is losing an otherwise productive and trustworthy employee. But we believe that leaking classified information is a serious breach of discipline required of all public servants. It is essential that the public be informed concerning the activities of government. However, we must recognize that the national interest often requires that information concerning national and foreign relations be protected against unauthorized disclosure.

"Officials who leak do not serve the larger national interest by disclosing information but instead may well be undermining the process of making foreign policy and protecting national defense. Leaks can betray confidences and embarrass other governments, making them less willing to confide in us. Leaks can undermine the confidentiality needed in a decision-making process to ensure a full and candid airing of all points of view. Leaks can also threaten the security of our nation or friendly nations, or the safety of individuals, of our sources of vital information.

"Because of the potentially serious consequences of unauthorized disclosures of classified information, the Department will continue to deal strictly with any of its employees who have made unauthorized disclosures of classified information."

The assembled journalists went berserk.

Q: "Copy?" (This was a journalist asking if he could get a photocopy of the just-released statement.)

CR: "Yes."

Q: "Who was the man? First of all—second of all, was he given a polygraph test?"

CR: "What was your first of all?"

Q: "That we can get a copy of that."

CR: "Yes."

Q: "Second of all—"

Q: "Just a copy or just the text?"

CR: "Yes, you may have a copy."

Q: "Was he discovered by a polygraph?"

CR: "No, the employee did not take a polygraph test."

Q: "And who is he?"

CR: "I'm not going to discuss the name of the individual involved. The important point is that the Department has dealt strictly with an individual who has made an unauthorized disclosure of classified information. The specific name of the individual involved is not material to that point. I can tell you that he was a GS-15 non-career employee."

Q: "What was the story about?"

CR: "I can't give you that."

Q: "Is he in violation of any law, and can he be prosecuted for what he did?"

CR: "The Department is dismissing the employee who leaked the classified information. In the particular circumstances of this case, the Justice Department has declined to prosecute the employee for this unauthorized disclosure, but criminal prosecution will be undertaken in future cases if appropriate. Concerning the nature of the information, let me say, as I did, that I wouldn't comment on the substance of it, that it would be inappropriate to confirm or deny that a specific story involved classified information. I can tell you that the unauthorized disclosure involved matters to our diplomatic relations. It did not involve defense secrets."

Q: "Chuck, when someone leaks a name this afternoon—"

CR: "No. The reason I won't give you his name is because it's not my intent, nor the Department's intent, to publicly embarrass the individual in that sense. He has been dismissed from the department. He has paid that price for his transgression. The point to be made is that he made an unauthorized disclosure of classified information, and the Department intends to deal strictly with those kinds of unauthorized disclosures."

Q: "Did he make it to a publication?"

Q: "Did he admit to the charges on which he was accused?"

CR: "The individual has apologized to the Secretary for his actions."

Q: "So he's not contesting his dismissal, or is he?"

CR: "I said he has apologized to the Secretary."

Q: "All right, a separate question, then. Is the individual contesting—are there any bureaucratic procedures underway now in which there is a contest of this action?"

CR: "He has been dismissed. It has been done, Ralph."

Q: "Is there a way he can—"

CR: "It's over. That's right, it's over."

Q: "Can you identify the law that he would be in violation of or that in future cases people would be prosecuted for doing what he did? What is the nature of that law? And does it also apply to the news agencies that publish leaked material when they know that it's classified information?"

CR: "I'm not in a position to give you that legal reading."

Q: "Can you tell us when all this occurred? When he was dismissed, when the leaks occurred?"

CR: "He was dismissed today."

Q: "He was dismissed today?"

CR: "That's right."

Q: "How long had the investigation gone on before—or was there any investigation?"

CR: "There certainly was an investigation, but it's [*sic*] duration I can't give you any details of."

Q: "Did he have a meeting with the Secretary of State?"

CR: "I can't go into the details of how he did it, suffice it to say he has apologized."

Q: "Did the Secretary dismiss him himself?"

CR: "The Secretary dismisses his employees; that's right."

Q: "Himself? He did it himself?"

CR: "If you're implying does he have to be in person to do it, I don't want to lead you to believe that. But he has been dismissed by the Department. The Secretary is the head of this department."

Q: "In what form was the disclosure made—to a newspaper or to—"

CR: "I have nothing beyond what I gave you earlier that—which is that it was not a defense secret but rather related to diplomatic relations."

Q: "How was he located? Did he—did some investigative body discover him or did he—"

Q: "Did he come forward?"

CR: "It was uncovered through an investigation."

Q: "Is this the first time this has been done? The Secretary has been talking about this quite a lot lately."

CR: "This is not the first employee to have left the Department because of unauthorized disclosures."

Q: "Can you give us any—"

CR: "But I cannot give you any further details."

Q: "Dates or precedents?"

CR: "Nothing else."

Q: "'A non-career employee,' does that mean a political employee?"

CR: "I think that's a fair assumption."

Q: "Chuck, when you say he was not the first to have left the Department for unauthorized disclosures, is he the first employee to have been fired for doing that as opposed to resigning?"

CR: "As I say, I don't have all the details as to what the circumstances of others may have been."

Q: "[Inaudible] . . . publicizing this, and you are unwilling to tell us if there have been a dozen in the last four or five years, or one hundred, or one thousand? Why are you coming out now?

CR: "I'm not leading you toward any specific number. The reason this one is being publicized is for the reason, of which I think you are all aware, as Secretary Shultz made very clear, at the Overseas Writer's Club the day before yesterday. He says, 'We've got to find the people who are doing it,' and in this case, we have."

Q: "It is intended to deter others, the public announcement?"

CR: "As you'll see in my statement, I ended by saying, let me reiterate it—I didn't commit that to memory—the Department will continue to deal strictly with any of its employees who have made unauthorized disclosures of classified information."

Q: "I'm talking about the public announcement; is that intended as a deterrent?"

CR: "I have nothing else for you on that."

Q: "Listen, could I just ask a quick question? I'm not clear. When you say that he is not the first that has left the Department because of unauthorized disclosures, is he the first that has left the Department because of unauthorized disclosures while Mr. Shultz has been secretary of state?"

CR: "I don't have that."

Q: "Could you give us more information on how many in the past have left?"

CR: "I'll take a look in a very general sense."

Q: "May I ask a question, please?"

CR: "Yes."

Q: "You have said that there is no intent to penalize him further, but it seems to me that by making this public—and undoubtedly his name will be disclosed by someone—that he will have a stigma which will follow him all of his life. Will this not be a harsh penalty?"

CR: "That is part of the price that the individual would have paid for this case under any circumstance—"

Q: "Then, why has he been singled out instead of others too?"

CR: "—and whether or not I had made this announcement, I'm sure it would have been a matter of public record very shortly. And as a consequence, in the spirit of openness, you asked us to tell you what we can."

Q: "I think since you raised this issue, and you've not given us any details, I think you really—"

CR: "I object to that, Bernie. I've given you a considerable amount of detail—maybe not all the detail you wanted."

Q: "No. You've said it's a diplomatic matter, not a defense matter."

CR: "I've told you—"

Q: "Yes."

CR: "—something about his status in the Department."

Q: "Well—"

CR: "I've told you something about the investigation in response to several questions."

Q: "But I think we have to have some sense of how serious this is because the Secretary has been blasting away in the last week or so about disclosures of covert activities and things like that, which a reasonable man could say could endanger national security. All you've said is it's a diplomatic matter. And as we know, diplomatic stuff is discussed with reporters constantly; and almost all of it has some kind of phony or unnecessary classified label. How serious a matter—could you give us some sense, was some major agreement imperiled by this?"

CR: "No, I can't."

Q: "Chuck, this comes up at a very convenient time in the Secretary's campaign against leaks. How long has this case been pending? It seems very convenient."

CR: "I would not want you to believe that it was convenient in the sense that you're implying at all."

Q: "Chuck, can you give any indication—is there a special investigatory team or operation set up to do this? And do you know that there are going to be other people who will also be terminated?"

CR: "There is nothing special. It was investigated through the normal channels available to this department under the circumstances."

Q: "Chuck, has the news organization which was involved in disclosing this information been made aware of this penalty?"

CR: "I don't know."

Q: "Chuck, was this information ever published? All you said was that it was disclosed to the news media. Do you know if the information was ever published? Was the information ever made public as opposed to disclosed to the media?"

CR: "As I say, all of this goes to helping everyone identify this in an ever more expeditious fashion, and as a consequence, I'd just as soon not reply to any of those stories from here."

Q: "Let me follow that up by asking on what basis you are withholding. Is it classified information? Whether the information was published? Is his name classified information? Would disclosure of any of those details subject the disclosee, the discloser, to possible termination?"

CR: "These are policy decisions, Ralph."

Q: "Is it the case that polygraph tests are being given now in the Department to try to ferret out news leaks even though this [inaudible]—"

CR: "I believe you're all aware of the department guidelines on use of the polygraph and those remain fully in effect."

Q: "So polygraph tests are being given regularly?"

CR: "That has not been Department guidelines. If you're creating new Department guidelines, then you should read the old ones. And those were available in a Department notice, which was circulated throughout this building, which I had here a minute ago."

Q: "Probably not for the news media, huh?"

CR: "The Department of State uses polygraph examinations on a voluntary basis in the course of counterintelligence, criminal, and special investigation."

Q: "Does that cover news leaks?"

CR: "Pardon?"

Q: "Does that mean news leaks?"

CR: "Special investigations would cover that category."

Q: "Most of the leaks that have gained some publicity recently have had to do with Libya or the West Berlin discotheque bombing. Would you be willing to rule out that it did not have anything to do with this?"

CR: "As I say, I would lead you toward a diplomatic matter."

Q: "Chuck, can you say whether this was the result of a complaint from some country with which we had ongoing diplomatic negotiations or other contacts?"

CR: "No, I can't give you any other details. OK? Any other subject?"

Q: "Does the Department have any comment with regard to the culpability of the news media in particular, not only with regard to leaks in particular, the NBC case of interviewing a terrorist who threatened the life of the president of the United States, and then refused to identify the location of that interview, and the whereabouts of this terrorist, Abu Abbas?"

CR: "Are you asking for an instant replay?"

Q: "I'm looking for a comment from the State Department with regard to the culpability of the news media not only publishing what they know to be leaks and classified information but also engaging in activities like NBC was guilty of just last week."

CR: "On that case, I had comment at that time, and I don't have anything that would go beyond that. In this case, I've said nothing about the news media, its culpability, or otherwise, and I don't have any comment to offer."

Q: "Chuck, you said that the person didn't take a polygraph test. Did they refuse to do so?"

CR: "As I said, I have nothing else to that."

Q: "Could I just ask one question? Did we inform any government of this action?"

CR: "No comment. I'm not sure what the relevance of it is, but—"

Q: “Well, I mean, has it come as a complaint from a country—”

CR: “I had that question before—”

Q: “—and did we notify a country that, in fact—”

CR: “—at which point I said I had no comment.” (Laughter)

Q: “Can I follow up on that last question on the polygraph? If we put your answer that no polygraph was taken together with your answer on the policy of polygraphs and your steering us in the direction that special investigations cover this sort of case, it’s pretty hard not to draw the conclusion that he was asked to take the polygraph test. Can you offer us any guidance on that score beyond what you’ve already said?”

CR: “No. You can draw your own conclusions.”

Q: “Chuck, George wants to know if this is your last briefing.” (Laughter)

Q: “At this level—I’m sure we can look it up, but would this cover, like, a Deputy Assistant Secretary? You said ‘middle-level political appointee.’ What would, say, a Deputy Assistant Secretary—”

CR: “I gave you his rank.”

Q: “Would that be, say, a Deputy Assistant Secretary? A GS-15?”

Q: “Yes.”

CR: “I’m to tell all of you what a GS-15 is?”

Q: “Well, just what, a Deputy Assistant Secretary, Assistant Deputy, or what?”

CR: “Deputy Assistant Secretaries outrank GS-15s.”

Q: “Do you have any other announcements?”

Q: “Could you give us an example of a GS-15?”

CR: “That’s all the announcements I have.” (Inaudible) (Laughter)

Q: "How many GS-15s are there? OK. You're finished?"
CR: "I'm finished."

For the next couple of minutes the press and the press spokesperson discussed issues in Paraguay, Syria, and the Jewish Knesset and problems in the Bekaa Valley in Lebanon. But shortly it was back to the question of the leaker.

Q: "Chuck, could I just ask you a quick question back on this employee? Do I understand that he is employed by the Department of State here in Washington, or can he be a Department of State employee in any other country?"
CR: "He was employed by the Department of State here in Washington."
Q: "Can I ask you also on that question, because on diplomatic relations there is so much dialogue between the press and officials of this Department, at least until today, in which clearly material which has not been made previously public knowledge is discussed, such as exchanges on various subjects. Is there some guideline you have on what a State Department official is authorized to discuss with a newsman?"
Q: "Or not?"
CR: "I can't help you on that beyond saying that this was an unauthorized disclosure of classified information."
Q: "But that happens probably all the time, because classified—I mean, can you give some sense to how classified?"
CR: "If it happened all the time in the sense you are speaking about, we would probably have many more dismissals than we've had."

Q: "Chuck, can I just follow one thing? Could you say—can you recall any similar announcement of such a dismissal from the Department—public announcement? Not a case but an announcement?"

CR: "I can't recall any."

Q: "How long have you been here?"

CR: "Since July of last year. Any other questions?"

The journalists took a break from this issue and asked questions concerning Soviet problems, Saudi arms sales, and bilateral relations between the United States and Mexico. But they could not let it go.

Q: "Secretary Shultz in his speech at the Overseas Writers Association the other day, when the question of leaks came up, said that anyone who was leaking should be fired, but he said that he would defer to the Justice Department with regard to any action on it."

CR: "With regard to prosecution."

Q: "OK. So is there any indication that the Justice Department is pursuing this in agencies other than the State Department? For example, is there something that's going on which is also covering the Pentagon, the White House, and so forth? As an administration-wide—"

CR: "I'm not sure why I should have any information on that or why you are referring to this as something new in terms of administration-wide policy. We here in this Department as well as other Departments have said that unauthorized disclosures have to be stopped."

Q: "I'm just wondering—"

CR: "Prosecution in any specific case is a call for the Justice Department to make. In this case I said that there would be no prosecution."

Q: "I'm just talking in terms of individuals from the Justice Department being invited in to conduct investigations in these various agencies with regard to this particular problem."

CR: "These investigations are conducted as always, and that's with the—at least for the large part—with the internal resources of the Department. But one can only presume that in investigations the total resources are available if necessary."

Q: "Chuck, has the Secretary of State or any other official in this Department had to either apologize or explain this case to any particular government?"

CR: "No, I don't have anything on that, Ralph." One unrelated question and back to the leak.

Q: "Chuck, did the fact that he's a political appointee limit his or her right of appeal or any kind of—does it make it easier to terminate them? Is there a difference between—"

CR: "I don't have an answer to that, Matt."

Q: "—between career and political?"

CR: "Every political appointee, obviously, serves at the pleasure of the Secretary."

Q: "Was there any deal struck about the secretary not naming this person in exchange for this person keeping quiet later on and not having further conversations with the press?"

CR: "I said earlier this was a policy decision, and I said it was not my intent to publicly embarrass the person in specific terms."

At this point in the daily press briefing, around 1:04 p.m., the press stopped questioning Charles Redman about the dismissal of the unidentified department employee who had leaked information. The press did not know if the leaked information was actually published or if it was provided as a basis for a larger story. The press, in a rare instance, became the subjects of a breaking news story, and they were obviously uncomfortable. The thrust of the questions suggested that the unofficial relations they enjoyed with senior State Department officials at the deputy assistant secretary level might be in jeopardy. Why? Because many of the journalists' stories concerning foreign policy issues in which senior government officials were quoted depended on those deputy and assistant secretary officials. The journalists' probing questions were clear indications of the anxiety they suffered that afternoon as they tried to determine who among their treasured, unnamed sources had been dismissed. Not to fear; the burned GS-13 was, in fact, of no ultimate consequence to the ongoing hidden relationship between State Department officials and the media. Despite the firing, leaking by senior and midlevel department officials would continue unabated.

On June 3, 1986, Mr. Penn and his new lawyer, Seymour Glanzer, presented themselves for a prearranged interview in room 2422. The room's bleak décor had not changed one iota. We sat down and reviewed the agreement that our prime suspect's lawyer had crafted with L, in which Mr. Penn agreed to cooperate with the investigation. It seemed that he would answer any and all questions that I had in relation to his involvement in the unauthorized disclosure of BA

2228. What considerations, if any, had he received in return from the legal advisor's office? I was not told, but I would learn in short order. I glanced at his lawyer, then to Mark, and finally told Mr. Penn, "Tell me the whole story."

Mr. Penn said that when he read the cable from the American embassy in Buenos Aires on the morning of April 4, he was angered by Speaker O'Neill's conduct in Argentina. He said, "I think it is highly improper for members of Congress to go overseas and publicly criticize the administration."

"But the cable's contents are properly classified and restricted and you are obligated to protect that information," I said.

"Well, I believe that by having pertinent contents of BA 2888 in the public domain, the public would better understand the administration's critic's tactics."

Our suspect—now an admitted liar and potential felon—initially telephoned the offices of Evans and Novak and, unable to talk to them directly, was told to mail the information directly to their office. He typed an anonymous letter, which disclosed the contents of the telegram, and mailed the letter later that day. When he was not contacted in return, he called William Kritzberg on the morning of April 7 and left a message to call him back. They were not able to confer until 11:00 that night when Mr. Penn disclosed parts of the cable to Kritzberg. The next time he spoke to Kritzberg was during a lunch on April 15 when they had a general discussion about unauthorized disclosures. The conversation was telling for many reasons.

Kritzberg warned Mr. Penn that there would be an investigation of the leak because Robert Kagan had told Kritzberg that there would be an investigation. I do not know why Kagan tipped the journalist off about my investigation, and I was not authorized to ask him.

Kritzberg also told Mr. Penn not to worry about his latent fingerprints being on the BA 2888 telegram as these would "wear off." That statement was hard to hear without laughing out loud. Mr. Penn also disclosed telling White House presidential speechwriter Anthony Dolan about the cable and its contents (so much for Nicholas Platt's comment that his colleague at the NSC was sure the cable was not passed to the "West Wing").

I asked Mr. Penn why he leaked confidential information to journalists who had no business reading privileged correspondence.

Without hesitation, he said, "A senior congressman should not be criticizing and undermining the president of the United States before a foreign leader."

I bit my tongue to keep from asking—if the Speaker of the House had been a Republican and the president a Democrat pushing a policy he objected to, would he have leaked that cable? Instead I asked, "How do you square your unauthorized disclosure with your security acknowledgement form that you signed, in which you agreed not to provide classified information to unauthorized individuals, which I have here in front of me?"

I pushed his signed security form across the table for Mr. Penn to scrutinize. He did not look at it and slid the form over to his lawyer. Glanzer read it with interest for the rest of the interview.

Mr. Penn was unable or unwilling to answer the question. It is my belief that he felt badly only because he got caught and would have continued to leak as future opportunities presented themselves.

His answer to my final question still sticks in my mind. I was confident that Mr. Penn was responsible for at least two other leaks, so I wanted to take advantage of his presence in the room to clear up some of my other unauthorized disclosure investigations. I said to Mr. Penn, "Let's talk about two other newspaper articles in which department cables were disclosed to the press."

Mr. Penn looked at me without blinking. "Upon the advice of my attorney, I will not answer the question." He then dropped a bombshell. He smiled, leaned back in his chair, and said, "I have been specifically advised by the staff of the department's legal advisor not to discuss any additional disclosures with you or your office."

This was the first time that I discovered that L had been working a "plea agreement" with the subject of our investigation without a single consultation with my office or the Department of Justice. It was a sleazy, unprofessional, and cowardly act. But Mr. Penn had provided me with what I already knew and confessed to what I had previously confirmed about L.

The secretary of state was screaming about punishing leakers, but the State Department's legal office, supposedly representing the organization's core governance values, wanted no more publicity and certainly no more investigations. I badly wanted Mr. Penn to give me more information about who else was leaking in S/P and elsewhere. I was terribly disappointed I could not pursue those other characters. The interview was over, so I stood up but did not offer my hand to either Messrs. Penn or Glanzer. I would have liked to offer another part of my hand to L.

I submitted my final report of the investigation to Director Dittmer and went about my other inquiries involving other department employees suspected of misconduct or criminal activities. Spokesperson Redman should have been commended for withholding the identity of Mr. Penn during his May 16 grueling by the press corps, who were relentless in their attempts to discover the name of the poor soul. It was the right thing for Redman to do.

However, the next day, May 17, the *Baltimore Sun-Times* reported in an article written by Jerome R. Watson and entitled "Employee fired by State Dept. for News Leak":

"As part of its new campaign against unauthorized news leaks, the State department yesterday fired a speechwriter for disclosing the contents of a classified cable from the U.S. Ambassador to Argentina. Department spokesman Charles E. Redman said the fired employee, a political appointee, had apologized to Secretary of State George P. Shultz and would not be prosecuted. But he said 'criminal prosecution will be undertaken in future cases if appropriate.' He said the leaked material in this case did not involve military secrets.

"Redman declined to name the employee, the news agency that received the leak or the nature of the material. But administration and congressional sources speaking on condition of anonymity identified the speechwriter as Spencer C. Warren of the State Department's policy planning office.

"Redman said only that an internal investigation had fingered the culprit. The announcement of the firing apparently was intended to dramatize Shultz's determination to stem leaks."

If I was asked then, or were to be asked now, to comment on the validity of the identity provided in that *Baltimore Sun-Times* article, I would have to respond that "I can neither confirm nor deny the accuracy of the newspaper's story."

CHAPTER ELEVEN

I readily admit that the BA 2888 unauthorized disclosure investigation resulted in a satisfying conclusion despite the lack of a prosecution by DOJ, and Mark and I were pleased to have witnessed a rare victory over those government officials who choose to ignore their sworn pledge to safeguard classified information. And Director Dittmer's reason for selecting me to lead the BA 2888 inquiry was clear because one year before the Novak article, I had managed to identify the Foreign Service employee who had leaked sensitive information to a *Los Angeles Times* reporter assigned to Africa.

In 1984, thousands of Ethiopian Jews, called Falashas, from the region of Gondar, trekked out of Ethiopia, which at the time was under the brutal rule of pro-Moscow leader Mengistu Haile Mariam. To escape starvation and political repression, refugees formed camps in Sudan, filled with half-starved women and children claiming to be one part of the Jewish Diaspora. Tel Aviv took notice. Operation Moses was Israel's solution for repatriating many thousands of African Jews to the promised land of Judea. It was a clandestine effort, spearheaded by the Israeli government but financed and facilitated by Washington, to transport the Falashas, or black Jews, from Africa to Israel. While eight thousand were ultimately saved, over four thousand perished during the march from Ethiopia into Sudan.

The nuts and bolts of the operation consisted of moving the Falashas from Ethiopia across the border into Sudan and quietly transporting them aboard unmarked C-130 aircraft to Israel.

This effort could not have been achieved without the direct knowledge and cooperation of a number of Sudanese government officials. As in any such tricky scenario, success depended on money and silence, and the Israeli government was prepared to provide one in order to gain the other. Because the Israelis did not have any diplomatic representation in Sudan, it fell to "unofficial" Israeli citizens to work with whoever might be available in Khartoum to handle the logistical arrangements.

By March 1984, a USAID employee, on assignment to the American embassy in Khartoum as a refugee programs officer, was fully involved in Operation Moses. While "Mr. Reaves's" local Arabic language skills were nil, he had been in Sudan so long that some of his embassy colleagues believed he had gone native. What the embassy eventually realized was that Mr. Reaves was working intimately with Sudanese and Israelis in keeping the Falashas airlift alive, without the knowledge or approval of the US ambassador.

The embassy had its first inkling that Mr. Reaves was the point man in this operation when he approached the embassy's RSO, Peter Gallant, and asked that the combination to his office's US government-supplied Mosler security repository be changed, a routine request that occurs every six months or when an officer with knowledge of the safe combination leaves the embassy on permanent rotation. When RSO Gallant arrived at Mr. Reaves's office and opened the security repository's fourth drawer to access the safe's Sargent and

Greenleaf lock mechanism to change the combination, he noticed what appeared to be in excess of one-half million dollars in US cash, neatly stacked in rows. When questioned about the purpose for having such a significant amount of cash inside his office safe, Mr. Reaves replied, "This is an operational issue that I am dealing with." That was a diplomatic way of saying the discussion was over. While uncomfortable with the quantity of cash, RSO Gallant had no further responsibility in the matter. He changed the combination, and there were no further conversations about the bundles of twenty- and fifty-dollar bills in Mr. Reaves's safe. RSO Gallant went about his duties and Mr. Reaves went about his—both official and unofficial.

Mr. Reaves was involved in the part of Operation Moses that would move one to three thousand Falashas from holding camps in Sudan to a secluded airport where operatives would prepare the way for the final trip to Israel. In order to keep the Sudanese camps supplied with food, water, and security, money was needed. Someone to coordinate the airlift operation was also needed, and that person was Mr. Reaves.

At the start of Operation Moses, Sudanese president Jaafar Nimeiri and his vice president and chief of state security, Omar Tayeb, were described as being staunchly pro-American. But the extent of their knowledge or involvement or support of Operation Moses remains an open question. As it turned out, it did not matter. In April 1986, while President Nimeiri was visiting Egypt, his sixteen-year reign of corruption and civil rights abuses came to an end in a military coup.

One must ask the question whether *Los Angeles Times* reporter Charles T. Powers's two articles, "U.S. Evacuates Ethiopian Jews. Last Group of Falashas Secretly Airlifted from Sudan to Israel," published on March 25, 1985, and "Ethiopian Rescue: An All U.S. Operation Airlift Plan Came from Officer in Sudan, not Israel," published on March 27, 1985, helped precipitate the coup against President Nimeiri by neoconservative Islamists. Perhaps it was just coincidence.

Powers's final article in the *Los Angeles Times*, published on July 7, 1985, and titled "Saga of Secret Airlift Ethiopian Jews: Exodus of a Tribe," did not help matters.

As the coup unfolded, the US embassy, under the direction of career ambassador Hume Horan, wisely decided that it was time to downsize the official staff and send back to the United States nonessential personnel and family members. One of those individuals was USAID employee Mr. Reaves. In late 1984, the Israeli government, as the result of deteriorating regional conditions, was clamoring to increase the number of Falashas departures to Israel. It determined that the only way to do so was to locate a remote yet secure airfield in Sudan to house large groups of Falashas and where the unmarked C-130 aircraft could arrive and depart in relative safety and obscurity. The Israeli government lacked the necessary diplomatic avenues even to approach the Sudanese, and that act could have risked disrupting the modest shuttle operation that was already underway. The Israeli government approached the US government, seeking an intervention on its behalf. The White House readily agreed to do so. Consequently a senior US government official arrived in Khartoum to tell Ambassador Horan that the White House had given its blessing to a robust Operation Moses. But as a result of the ordered departure of embassy personnel, Mr. Reaves was effectively removed from any decision making or operational role concerning the airlift.

RSO Gallant, who remained behind during the evacuation, was contacted by Gayle Fowles, Reaves's assistant. She told him that she had been asked by Reaves to go over to his house to tidy things up and clean out a "gun locker" beneath his bed. Due to the dangerous street conditions, Fowles asked RSO Gallant to accompany her. Once inside the residence, the two embassy officials discovered that the gun locker contained high quality shotguns, hunting rifles, handguns—including a .44 magnum Smith and Wesson six-shot revolver equipped with a scope—and a Galil (Israeli) assault rifle, along with gold coins and tax-free Israeli war bonds, one of which was valued in excess of $100,000. As the embassy officer was making an inventory of the weapons from the locker, Reaves's houseboy, who had remained in the house after Reaves left Sudan, came into the bedroom with a fully loaded AK-47 and asked the officer if he wanted another one of Reaves's weapons.

While Reaves's home was being inspected, I was once again up in Director Dittmer's office. This time I listened to a tirade about how upset the Black Dragons were with the latest series of leaks, which involved classified and highly sensitive department information quoted in the *Los Angeles Times* articles. In no uncertain terms, I was told to initiate an investigation and do whatever possible to identify the responsible person. The unauthorized disclosures in the *Los Angeles Times* were directly responsible for the termination of the US-backed airlift of Jews from Ethiopia. Leaks have serious human implications.

This one was easy. One quick telephone call to RSO Gallant, and the mystery leaker was identified. Khartoum was not a city in which foreigners pass unnoticed. Journalists and diplomats receive particular scrutiny from both security personnel and those involved in the tourist industry. The RSO confirmed that Reaves and Charles Powers, the *Los Angeles Times* reporter working in Khartoum, were known to have socialized while both worked in Sudan.

During this conversation, I discovered that Reaves had a "gun collection," and since it was maintained on US government territory (the house's rent was paid for by the US government) in apparent violation of embassy housing regulations, I directed that everything discovered inside the gun locker, except for the AK-47, be packed up and shipped to my office.

It was high time to call Reaves in for a friendly chat. On July 11, 1985, he sat across the conference room table from SA Nanette Kreiger and me and spun quite a story.

"I do not deny that I had a limited social and professional relationship with Powers," Reaves said. "I never provided him with any classified information until the night Powers told me that he was going to publish a story concerning the secret airlift of Falashas out of Ethiopia via Sudan."

"Go on," Nanette encouraged.

"Unfortunately Powers had been able to piece together a fairly detailed and accurate story of Operation Moses," Mr. Reaves said. He explained that he told Powers that if the story went public, it could end the program prematurely, and he asked Powers to postpone printing the story until the airlift program was over. "I needed Powers to delay his story, so I promised to flesh out the details of Operation Moses, to include a visit to the remote airfield, if he delayed publication." Eventually Powers accepted most of Reaves's proposal and Reaves later fulfilled his promises. Powers got everything he could have hoped for and more out of the deal. Then he returned to the United States.

I asked Reaves who had given him permission to release classified information to a journalist. I also asked who had authorized him to take Powers to a restricted military airfield. He wavered a bit and finally said that US ambassador Hume Horan was aware of his dilemma with

Powers and had authorized him to "do whatever was necessary" to protect Operation Moses from public exposure. When I told Reaves that I thought his previous comments suggested that he and Powers had finalized their "non-disclosure until the right-time agreement" during one conversation, he disabused me of that notion and said it took place over several days. He acknowledged that he was the primary source of leaked information and signed a sworn statement to that effect.

I then turned my attention to the weapons and monies. The gold coins were eventually returned to Mr. Reaves as well as the shotguns, rifles, and handguns that he had legally registered in the United States. The fully automatic Galil assault rifle was not. Neither were the two thirty-round magazines. He explained that he kept a large cache of weapons because he was an avid hunter and Sudan offered great game opportunities. He said he paid for hunting guides and services with the gold coins as they were an acceptable form of payment by the locals. The issue of the Israeli war bonds was purposefully not raised because the subject was outside the scope of my investigation. But I have to admit it was difficult to keep a straight face listening to Reaves's explanation of the connection between the guns and the gold coins.

Nanette and I shared a good laugh together after he left the interview room. She would eventually become my immediate supervisor a decade later when she was assigned as the director of DS/CI and would supervise me in the investigation into the missing laptop from INR that contained nuclear-sensitive information. Her aggressive style was highly appreciated.

On July 25, 1985, at 10:00 a.m., a distinguished yet highly annoyed Hume Horan, the US ambassador to Sudan, reported to HST room 2422 to explain his understanding of Operation Moses and its nexus with Reaves. He was not happy to be called in front of investigating agents to explain a highly political and sensitive matter that should have never become public, much less in the context of a leak case. In precise words and a slow monotone, Ambassador Horan said, "I did not authorize Reaves to review the details of Operation Moses with Powers or anyone else for that matter."

"Would you provide a sworn statement to that effect?" I asked.

He slowly unscrewed the top to his fountain pen and said, "Give me a piece of paper so that I can write and sign a statement."

Whom do I believe—Ambassador Horan or Reaves? Ambassador Horan continued his distinguished career and served as our ambassador to Saudi Arabia and as a deputy assistant secretary of state in the Bureau of Consular Affairs before retiring from the State Department in 1998. After working as a Middle Eastern affairs analyst for BBC, NPR, and MSNBC, among other news agencies, he served from May to November 2003 as a senior advisor on religious and tribal issues to Ambassador L. Paul "Jerry" Bremer at the Coalition Provisional Authority in Baghdad, Iraq. His son, a former officer in the Marine Corps who worked closely with DS in Europe, became an FBI agent with whom I subsequently worked closely on numerous foreign counterintelligence investigations from 1997–2002. Ambassador Horan passed away and was buried on July 30, 2004, in Arlington National Cemetery.

I believe that Mr. Reaves was disappointed to discover in late 1984 that he was being removed from any future involvement in Operation Moses. He had been working in Sudan on numerous USAID projects since 1980. I am convinced that he wanted to continue to be part of an historical event. I further believe that Reaves, without seeking or obtaining permission from the US ambassador, provided sensitive information to a reporter from the *Los Angeles Times*. Because Reaves was a USAID employee, the results of my investigation were turned over to that agency's security personnel for whatever action they deemed appropriate. I was never told if he received any administrative punishment or adverse action or if he was turned over to the Department of Justice for review. It was my understanding that Mr. Reaves was allowed to continue working for the US government. His identity was not leaked to the press.

Unfortunately the story of the *Los Angeles Times* articles on Operation Moses did not end there. On January 28, 1986, in an article entitled "Trial Tests Sudan-U.S. Relations," the *Washington Post* reported that former Sudanese officials were now on trial for their participation in Operation Moses. Much of the prosecution's case came directly from the *Los Angeles Times* articles, and selected portions were quoted in the courtroom to bolster the new regime's case, especially against Omar Tayeb. According to those who had known him before the coup, Mr. Tayeb had lost over sixty pounds while waiting out the four-month-long trial. The trial, which was televised locally, was also used by the prosecutors to take some potshots at Ambassador Hume Horan, who had recently returned to post. One fallacious sentence in the *Washington Post* article was this line: "Sudanese were shocked last year at the disclosure abroad of a joint Israeli–American civilian charter airlift of the Ethiopian Jews, called Falashas, and then of a follow-up U.S. Air Force evacuation of those left behind earlier." Of course, this was sheer nonsense. What the article failed to mention was the fact that the Israeli and American media made the disclosure. Without the media's revelations, the trial of the former Sudanese officials would not have been possible. Leaks have serious consequences.

The real reasons I believe that Director Dittmer called me into his office in 1986 to review the Novak leak was not only because I had solved the *Los Angeles Times* leak but also because I had identified the US government employee in 1983 who was leaking department economic reporting by the bagful. Truth be told, I was probably the most successful investigator at the time dealing with purported high crimes and misdemeanors that most senior officials did not really want solved. Every time I managed to pinpoint another perpetrator, I was persona non grata in the office. As they say—"no good deed goes unpunished."

★★★

Well before the *Los Angeles Times* leak, Director Dittmer had frog marched me into his office to hand me a batch of newspapers, advising that the Black Dragons were again whining and whimpering about unauthorized disclosures of embassy cables in a newspaper. In a series of articles commencing in late 1982, S. Karene Witcher, a staff reporter for the *Wall Street Journal* (*WSJ*), divulged a significant amount of sensitive foreign financial information provided to our embassies by foreign leaders. A number of US ambassadors were advising the Black Dragons that the articles purloined from their classified cables were adversely affecting US bilateral relations, and they were demanding action. The Black Dragons had contacted Director Dittmer and insisted that an investigation be conducted, and in late 1982, I was directed to initiate a preliminary inquiry into the matter.

After reading several *WSJ* articles in the department's reference library, I returned to our classified telegram inventory records center and located the cited embassy cables. I discovered that eight of

Witcher's articles in 1982 contained information derived from classified State Department cables.

The first article of note appeared in the September 13, 1982, edition of the *WSJ* under the title "Havana's Efforts to Reschedule Its Debt Meeting Difficulties, U.S. Officials Say." The Havana US Interests Section's principal officer, John Ferch, was quoted from a classified cable that the Cuban Foreign Ministry told heads of foreign diplomatic missions in Havana that Cuba "attempted to seek special treatment" in rescheduling its foreign debt because Cuba represents "a special case." The so-called "U.S. Officials" are never identified further in the *WSJ* article.

Quoting from department cables, another article noted that US ambassador to France Evan Galbraith reported that the issues surrounding Cuba are "very sticky to sort out for several reasons" and that French financial officials had their own take on the problems. (Galbraith served an interesting tour in France as US ambassador where he was quoted in 1985 as saying "Foreign policy is too important to be left up to Foreign Service Officers," all the while receiving four separate public reprimands by the French government for his undiplomatic behavior.)

Another article quoted from a US Embassy London cable saying that Raúl León Torras, president of Banco Nacional de Cuba, had hoped "to conclude debt rescheduling agreements with creditor governments and banking institutions within ninety days." (Luckily for us, Kendall Myers was still working only at FSI at this time.)

Of investigative interest was the *WSJ* article entitled "U.S. Banks Reportedly Felt Threatened into Joining 4 Billion Credit to France," in which Witcher quoted extensively from an October 1982 Paris embassy classified cable, which she did again in her December 7, 1982, article

"U.S. Preparing a Rescue Package for Yugoslavia." Three weeks later, Witcher quoted from a classified November US Embassy Ankara cable in her December 27 article entitled "Turkey Asks for More Relaxed IMF Pact; U.K. Faults Cuba's Plan to Reschedule." Not only was Witcher obtaining classified cables originating from our embassies in Latin America but also from our embassies in Europe. The compromised cables were being leaked at a frequency and in numbers I had never encountered before. The White House was getting hammered over the head big time.

My initial review of the articles and cables was interesting in that the quoted embassy cables concerned different countries and cut across divisions and bureau jurisdictions within the department. The only common denominator in the department was the Bureau of Economics, Business, and Agricultural Affairs. The bureau had a vested interest in the information, but it seemed an unlikely source. With US embassies around the world reporting on the issue, the agencies most concerned with debt were the International Monetary Fund, the World Bank, and the US Department of the Treasury—and only the latter organization had access to classified State Department cables; the information was generated from these cables by non-State Department US personnel assigned to our embassies primarily for consumption by non-State personnel. My preliminary conclusion was that the culprit was someone working for the Treasury Department or the Federal Reserve.

Why did my investigative instincts lean this way? As in the case of BA 2888, I was initially convinced that the leak originated outside the State Department because, once again, it made absolutely no sense for a department employee to make life difficult for his or her colleagues serving overseas by leaking sensitive bilateral negotiations. Leaks destroy trust; only someone not involved in the sensitive negotiations would have so recklessly endangered the embassies' success. I was not looking for a department employee; however, I lacked investigative authority to conduct an inquiry at the Federal Reserve or the Treasury Department. Previous experience told me that any request for investigative assistance to any other federal agency normally was passed to the inspector general's office, which lacked the experience or resources, or frankly the interest, to assist. I informally alerted my FBI colleagues of my findings.

I continued to monitor the *WSJ* for future articles under the Witcher byline and discovered a March 11, 1983, *WSJ* article by her entitled "Jamaica Reportedly at Odds With the IMF; Economic Growth Could be Depressed" that quoted extensively from another classified embassy cable. I also discovered a January 1, 1982, *WSJ* Witcher article entitled "Mexico's Belt Tightening Could Cause Social Unrest, U.S. Diplomats Are Told," which lifted classified quotes from another department cable.

My inquiry resided in the freezer until Director Dittmer called me up to his office (again with serious knots in my stomach) in early 1983. He thrust the latest Witcher missive into my hands. The April 15, 1983, *WSJ* headline read, "Venezuela Seen About to Seek IMF Loan As Oil Price Decline Buffets Its Economy." Over 40 percent of the article contained quotes from two classified Caracas embassy cables. Unusually candid in describing economic conditions in Venezuela, the cables' contents were supported by comments made in confidence by Venezuela's finance minister, Arturo Sosa, to senior US embassy officials. After the article had been published, Sosa had summoned US ambassador George W. Landau to his office and in an agitated manner lectured the ambassador about how such *WSJ* stories endangered bilateral diplomatic relations. Leaks have serious consequences.

Sosa made clear that he was speaking to the US ambassador at the personal direction of President Herrera. He stated further that the Venezuelan government was now unwilling to share confidences with the United States on these issues until it was assured that the leaks would stop. He concluded by saying that prior to the leaked story his government was willing to share confidential information with the United States, but now his standing with certain international bankers to refinance his country's debt had been undermined. Ambassador Landau sent a cable asking that the department undertake whatever measures it could to ensure the protection of its classified messages.

"Robert," Director Dittmer asked, "what is the status of your *WSJ* investigation?"

"Zero, sir," I meekly replied. "No suspects, no trail, nothing. The distribution of the leaked cables both inside and outside the department makes it impossible for me to conduct an investigation. This case is not going to move forward unless the FBI gets involved."

At the mention of the FBI, Director Dittmer rolled his eyes and grimaced. He was no fan of the FBI.

"Sir," I went on, "I don't think the culprit is a State Department employee, and therefore I lack jurisdiction or professional weight to pursue my leads or to get any other agency to help me investigate these leaks, and—"

"The problem, Robert," Director Dittmer interrupted, "is that the seventh floor is complaining about the State Department's lack of credibility in safeguarding sensitive foreign government information."

I was curtly dismissed. Back to my cubicle.

Fortunately another case was dropped on my desk that would eventually help me discover the most likely source for Witcher's articles. In May 1983, the *Atlantic* magazine published an article titled "Embassy cables—How the U.S. Embassy Reported an Economic Crisis in Kuwait to the State Department," in which the author, Edward Jay Epstein, quoted liberally from five classified US Embassy Kuwait cables that described in unflattering terms the country's leaders and certain social and economic conditions in Kuwait City. Epstein wrote, "A secret cable sent on October 10 states, 'The stock market . . . so enveloped Kuwaiti society that one could not sit down with a Kuwaiti for more than 30 seconds without the subject being raised. Cabinet meetings were disrupted as ministers excused themselves to call their brokers. . . . Young aggressive Kuwaitis . . . became billionaires in a matter of months; Kuwaiti women found an activity they could profit at and enjoy. . . . Kuwaiti society—with the perceived blessing of the government—indulged in an orgy of greed that knew no bounds.'"

I checked for the cable in question and, yes, the quotes were accurate. Epstein continued his unauthorized disclosures: "An Embassy cable said that 'those who stayed out of the market were ridiculed for their conservatism and backwardness, and young Kuwaitis found new heroes in the high-rolling nouveau riche traders from lesser known families.'" This too was an accurate quote. He continued, "The U.S. Embassy, basing its reports on sources within the government, reported, 'Keeping the populace at ease, and preserving local liquidity were two priorities satisfied beyond the government's expectations by the stock market rise. Government leaders and the Sabahs, of course, also found enjoyment in making huge gains from their own activities in the market.'" But he did not stop there; the article went on to quote from another cable: "'The banks in Bahrain,' the Embassy said, 'including several of American ownership, such as Chase Manhattan and American Express, found that they had lent money on worthless bits of paper. An impending real-estate bubble, furthermore, threatened the banks' solvency. . . .'" And finally, "another U.S. Embassy Kuwait cable reported that 'Jassim al-Marzouk is one of the more active market players, and is regarded as one of the more corrupt and influence-peddling prone high officials.'"

It was clear to me that Epstein had photocopies of four separate classified cables originating in 1982 from our embassy in Kuwait City and one sent from the department and that he selectively quoted from several sections of those documents. A quick check revealed that he had written an article for the *Atlantic* just two months previously in which he revealed sensitive OPEC policy deliberations, but, upon additional checks, these were his only articles talking about Middle East financial issues. I was convinced, just as I was regarding the leaks in the Witcher articles, that no department officer would leak the cables quoted in the *Atlantic* because of the inevitable backlash his or her Kuwaiti embassy colleagues would suffer from Kuwaiti government officials and their sources, just like the BA 2888 case. Department professionals would not subject their own kind to such diplomatic unpleasantness—a Schedule C employee, perhaps, but not a fellow FSO.

Out of nowhere, Epstein and Witcher were suddenly reading 1982/1983 department cables. Could the US government source for Witcher and Epstein be the same person? I was intrigued by the possibility, and after many hours of research, the potential answer pointed north. After traveling to Boston and toiling away anonymously in the archival records at Harvard University, I believed that I found a strong paper connection between Witcher, Epstein, and a current employee of the Treasury Department—my number one suspect agency. In fact, the Treasury Department, which is normally on distribution for any department cable that analyzes international economic or financial issues that affect the United States, had for some years assigned a small number of its officers to serve at US embassies to report independently on economic issues of specific interest to the Treasury Department. In diplomatic jargon, they were titled as financial attachés. I had another undiplomatic word to describe my suspect.

Subsequent to my Harvard University discovery, my Witcher/Epstein inquiry led me to Sy Oglesby of the Treasury Department's Inspector General Staff. On May 17, 1983, we sat down and reviewed my preliminary findings. Following our session, we agreed to contact the FBI—I did not inform Director Dittmer of my bold decision—to ask my FBI colleagues if they wished to assign a liaison agent to our investigation in case the list of suspects included individuals working for other US agencies besides the state or treasury departments. We were pleased when the FBI readily agreed to participate. At the first joint DS/FBI/Treasury meeting held in my office, many investigative options were offered and debated. At one point, I suggested that a possible method of identifying the leaker would be to install a "tap and trace" device on Epstein's and/or Witcher's office and/or home telephone lines. Prior to our meeting, Bernard Johnson, a special agent assigned to our New York field office, had provided me with the New York City telephone listings in question. While the tap and trace devices would not capture any conversations, they would record all the telephone numbers to and from Witcher's and Epstein's office and home telephone numbers.

After I offered my tap and trace suggestion, I was politely informed by the FBI agent that I was out of my mind. Technical operations were reserved for espionage cases—such as Myers and Keyser—and NSA metadata operations, not unauthorized disclosure investigations. There were no other technical options available to our team. Oglesby and the FBI representative told me that they hoped that future interviews would help identify a suspect and that I was to remain the "lead agent" in the ongoing investigation because only State Department information had been leaked to this point. Lucky me!

I continued to work with Oglesby until we jointly reached the conclusion that there were only two possible suspects—both Treasury officials. One of the suspects was a Treasury official assigned to the National Security Council at the White House, the other a Treasury attaché assigned to a US embassy in the Middle East. At this juncture, all possible investigative leads had been exhausted, and there was nothing left for me to do as the two suspects were beyond my investigative reach. Director Dittmer was not pleased, but this time I had cover. Just before I had informed Director Dittmer of the status of my inquiry, the FBI agent assigned to our mini-task force stated that he was satisfied with the conclusions of my investigation and the bureau would assume control of the case.

Some months later, an FBI agent assigned to the case advised me he had reached the same conclusions concerning the two Treasury officials and that he had been authorized by FBI headquarters to ask both employees if they would submit to a polygraph examination. In early spring, during the course of the first polygraph examination, the Treasury official reassigned to the NSC denied having provided classified department documents to any US or foreign journalist. According to the FBI's report, the Treasury official indicated "no deception" to the relevant questions during the interview. This Treasury official quietly continued with his career without any adverse consequences.

The FBI also informed me that a decision had been reached not to send a polygraph team to the Middle East for the examination of the second Treasury official but rather to wait for his expected return to Washington, DC, in late 1983. Shortly after his arrival in DC, the Treasury official/financial attaché was contacted by the FBI and, without knowing the substance of the investigation, agreed to be interviewed. During the interview he was asked if he had disclosed classified department secrets to either foreign or US journalists. While denying he had been the source of the Epstein or Witcher stories, he declined to submit to a polygraph examination. Some weeks later, he unexpectedly resigned from the US Treasury Department.

Was this Treasury official the source of the leaks? He certainly denied leaking classified department cables to Epstein or Witcher. My belief in his culpability was based on facts lying somewhere between "reasonable suspicion" and a "balance of probabilities" but nothing approaching a "beyond a reasonable doubt" standard. However, I was never called upon again to investigate any articles authored by Witcher or Epstein that quoted from classified department cables after the Treasury official's resignation. Maybe the Treasury official detailed to the National Security Council who had passed the polygraph examination had decided that one close call was enough. Regardless, the news disclosures stopped. In one fashion or another, I had helped to close another leaking faucet.

★★★

A unique case started in 1985 when an IC representative telephoned me, while I was the acting chief of the Special Investigations Branch, to advise that the IC had recently "processed" information that had to be reviewed immediately by my office. During the early 1980s, our office, due to its small size and lack of recognition, investigative jurisdiction, and, I must admit, credibility, had minimal contact with the IC. I was intrigued that an IC entity would call us directly. I immediately arranged for a meeting the following day.

Two IC security officials arrived as scheduled and provided me with documentation indicating that one of their officers reported he had overheard a State Department employee telling a Japanese diplomat, during the course of a Washington social function, the bottom line figures for the upcoming Reagan-Japanese prime minister trade negotiations. While the IC source was uncertain as to the identity of the department employee, the documented conversation revealed the beliefs, opinions, and attitudes of the department officer in regards to the upcoming negotiations. The phrases attributed to the unidentified department official were indicative of an individual with an axe to grind. Comments were highlighted in the IC document, such as "the lions have been put back in their cages," referring to those US officials wanting tough negotiations with their Japanese counterparts. The department officer was certainly not in favor of President Reagan's public policy on trade talks with Tokyo. Given the size of the department's cadre of Japanese specialists, especially the small number of those calling on their Japanese embassy counterparts, my suspect pool was tiny. Following my discussion with the IC representatives, I briefed Director Dittmer about my meeting with the IC officials.

"Robert," he said, "start an investigation, although you know you will never solve this one."

Ah, Director Dittmer, always the encouraging soul. Returning to my office, I opened a file folder, wrote out SB12-0185-100-0059 on the tab collar, and started a new unauthorized disclosure investigation.

With a little bit of digging, it became clear that the only people in the department who would be intimately involved in the upcoming negotiations were officers assigned to EAP—Don Keyser's future assignment as PDAS. With an invaluable insider source within EAP, I quickly was able to reduce the possible suspects to three individuals, and only one whose outspoken views concerning the upcoming negotiations were well known. The US had been making economic concessions to the Japanese government ever since Prime Minister Kishi Nobusuke visited the United States in 1957. Maybe it was time to level the playing field. Or maybe not.

However, before interviewing the suspects, I needed to interview William Sherman, who was the deputy chief of mission in Japan with me from 1978–1980, and now the deputy assistant secretary for the region, to determine whether members of his staff had been authorized to discuss negotiation topics with their Japanese embassy counterparts. But before that interview took place, I had to alert Director Dittmer that my inquiry was getting very close to implicating or touching Black Dragons. Surprisingly, without any hesitation, he authorized me to go ahead.

My discussion with DAS Sherman, conducted on the afternoon of January 9, 1985, was slightly strained as it became crystal clear to him that I was pursuing an unauthorized disclosure of sensitive information investigation and that one of his subordinates was my prime suspect. I was sure that he wanted to protect his employee from an overzealous investigator such as myself (shades of Kelly/Keyser). However, in the end, DAS Sherman was the consummate professional; he could not confirm or deny if the leaked information was "classified information" (shades of Kelly/Keyser). I needed to draw my own conclusions. Later that afternoon, I contacted "Edgar," suspect number one, and arranged for a 9:30 interview the following day.

Edgar appeared on time at room 2422, and SA Michael Posillico and I amicably started the interview. All said and done, Edgar acknowledged that he had reviewed with his Japanese embassy counterpart the suggested importation quotas of Japanese cars into the United States. Even before the negotiations started, the Japanese had been handed a huge advantage in terms of the US position. It was a nice starting point in a game of cards knowing how the deck was stacked. Edgar explained that, in fact, his disclosure (was it classified or just damn sensitive?) would ensure that the negotiations were successful (shades of Kelly/Keyser). Had the secretary of state approved this diplomatic disclosure? Most importantly, Japanese face saving had been assured. Was American saber-rattling about Japanese car imports all show for the public and Detroit? Did President Reagan have a public narrative for the US public and a private narrative for the Japanese government? Maybe concessions by the Japanese in other areas of negotiations would be forthcoming as a result. I thanked him for his candor and honesty, wrote up the interview, and forwarded the final report of investigation to Director Dittmer, who never discussed this investigation with me ever again—odd indeed.

Edgar's career appeared unaffected by his actions, and he moved up to the most senior ranks of the Department of State. So maybe this was actually an authorized leak, and neither I or the IC sleuths had a need to know. Maybe DAS Sherman was giving me a hint that afternoon of January 9. I think to this day that Director Dittmer and I stumbled into something that was way over our collective pay scales.

All I know is that in 2013, Japanese car companies sent over 1.5 million vehicles to the United States while fewer than thirteen thousand US cars were sold in Japan.

★★★

The leak cases just never stopped. It got so bad that on one occasion even I was suspected of having leaked a story to a national newspaper. Director Dittmer called me into his office on October 17, 1990, when I was the SIB chief, and handed me a copy of that morning's *Washington Post* federal page with an article entitled "Ex-Bush Aide Quits As Zimbabwe Envoy" boldly circled in red ink. Agitated, face flushed, arms gesticulating wildly, he shouted, "Robert, did you leak this story?"

I slowly and carefully pored over the newspaper article. According to the story, prepared by Ann Devroy, "Steven Rhodes, a senior adviser to President Bush when he was vice president, has resigned after less than five months as the U.S. Ambassador to Zimbabwe because of what the State Department describes as 'personal reasons.' Rhodes, 39, was recalled to Washington in August after the State Department received an accusation from Zimbabwe that he had been involved in an incident involving drugs earlier in the summer, a senior administration official said yesterday. The official said he was not under criminal investigation in either country. The official said Rhodes resigned after 'discussions' with State Department authorities here over a two-month period. A spokesman for the department, Adam Shub, said Rhodes submitted his resignation to Bush October 4.

"'As in any case in which a resignation is submitted for personal reasons, it is the department's practice not to comment on the reasons involved,' Shub said.

"Shub said Rhodes has what amounts to a ninety-day grace period before he leaves government. Reached at a hotel here, Rhodes declined comment.

". . . Officials would not provide further details of the alleged drug incident. 'There was an incident involving drugs,' an official noted. 'Discussions were held. He is now gone. That is all we have to say about it.'"

What could I say to Director Dittmer? To be sure, I was the lead agent responsible for investigating "the accusation" as the *Washington Post* so carefully phrased it. All such accusations must be vetted, especially if made against a serving US ambassador. The results of my investigation, conducted with technical assistance from the FBI, had been submitted to Director Dittmer in late September 1990. I guess "the discussions" between Ambassador Rhodes and the department were initiated as a result of my investigative report.

Director Dittmer knew that my final report had been restricted to his office and those with whom he shared it. The contents of the investigation were highly restricted to preserve Ambassador Rhodes's privacy, yet someone in the department felt no such compulsion. While the article was not entirely accurate, only a Black Dragon who had access to my investigative report would have revealed selected portions of the final report to the *Washington Post* staff. Ambassador Rhodes was a political appointee, just like the fired BA 2888 leaker, and not a true Black Dragon and, as such, could be sacrificed for an indiscretion. I assured Director Dittmer that I had not discussed any information concerning Ambassador Rhodes with anyone outside my office, except him. I was not the source of that leak. Why would I be? To this day, I am baffled as to why anyone in the department would leak the story to the *Washington Post.* For what it is worth, I would happily serve at an embassy under Ambassador Rhodes's leadership. Fortunately I was not asked to conduct an unauthorized disclosure investigation into this particular leak.

During my career, I assisted with at least another twenty-five or so significant department loss and leak investigations. Some remain very sensitive as the identities of the leakers and the correspondents who received the classified information are known to the FBI and DS. Some still remain under investigation. Some department leakers will not be prosecuted, even though their identity is known, because DOJ and the State Department are unwilling to confirm in a public courtroom the authenticity of the information disclosed or, even worse, to defend why the information was classified.

★★★

There is a whole category of leaking, much of which could be considered classified, that occurs between reporters, officials, and even DS agents on overseas missions. My good friend Sid Balman Jr., with whom I shared coaching duties for nearly a decade with our children's soccer teams, was United Press International's diplomatic and national security correspondent during the 1990s, which meant that as part of his duties, he travelled on all overseas missions with presidents Bush and Clinton and Secretaries of State James Baker, Lawrence Eagleburger, Warren Christopher, and Madeleine Albright.

As part of the regular "spin cycle" on those trips, top aides to the president or secretary of state would come to the press section of the plane and impart nuggets of information about the story they wanted to create from a trip—say, to Syria for peace negotiation, China for a discussion of trade relations, or Brussels to work out NATO's Balkan war planning. They mostly spoke on background as "senior US officials" or maybe "Western diplomatic sources" if the news was so classified or so sensitive that they did not want any fingerprints on it. If it was really sensitive, they would corner one particularly influential reporter near the bathroom—usually the likes of Tom Friedman of the *New York Times*, Barry Schweid of the Associated Press, or Steve Hurst of CNN—and leak something they were sure would end up at the top of that day's news lineup.

But some stories leak out in unusual corners of those airplanes. Sid was travelling with Warren Christopher back from consultations in Moscow during the mid-1990s with Russian Foreign Minister Andrei Kozyrev. There was a full agenda of disputes, including the Balkans and the Middle East peace negotiations that the two diplomats addressed with varying degrees of success. Sid went to the restroom on the Air Force VC-137, the military's version of the Boeing 707, immediately after then-Assistant Secretary of State Martin Indyk, who was largely responsible for Middle East policy. Imagine Sid's surprise when he clicked the door locked behind him and saw an eight-page document clearly marked "top secret," a virtual blow-by-blow of the meetings with the Russians that Indyk had left behind. As Sid describes, it was a "reporter's pot of gold at the end of the rainbow." But he had been around the block a few times as a reporter, and he didn't want to end up in hot water for what some might view as stealing a classified document. Sid wrote most of the narrative in his reporter's notebook, then tore up the document and threw it in the trash, thus ensuring his deniability and preserving his scoop. Further Sid waited a few days once back in Washington, to insert a little more space from the flight, before he reported a series of stories that caused quite a diplomatic stir in Moscow and Washington.

Indyk's department security clearance would be suspended on September 12, 2000, by DS for mishandling classified information while he was assigned as the US Ambassador to Israel. I was the DS/CI deputy director working along with DS/SIB chief Robert Hartung for the 1999 investigation into allegations of Indyk's "... sloppy handling of classified information ..." while serving as assistant secretary of state for Near Eastern Affairs and as our ambassador. But when Robert and I interviewed Ambassador Indyk on October 25, 1999, about his adherence to department security guidelines concerning his handling of classified information, this airplane episode was completely unknown to me. Reportedly Indyk's top secret security clearance was re-instated at the direction of President Clinton.

CHAPTER TWELVE

When I was a young special agent, one of the first department conundrums I had to resolve was a case where "top secret" documents were being shared among convicted felons in a federal institution near Washington, DC. In this instance, the department thanked God that interest in foreign policy was not particularly high among the inmate population. Unlike comic books, drugs, and shanks, which could be easily traded for favors or contraband, the classified department documents held little or no value for the run-of-the-mill prisoner. Put another way, bureaucratic prose of a highly sensitive nature was not the currency of the prison. Not surprisingly, the office eventually identified as being responsible for losing the classified information was none other than the Bureau of Intelligence and Research (INR).

This loss of highly classified department documents received its first public exposure when a *Washington Times* article dated November 10, 1983, entitled "Shultz Orders Hunt for Person who Let Secret Papers Go to Jail" reported that Secretary of State George Shultz, who was informed of the situation during a refueling stop in Alaska while traveling to Japan, had ordered an investigation into the circumstances surrounding the loss of our government's most sensitive information. It was another black eye for the department—one that caused much snickering and finger pointing among the Washington pundits and politicos.

Seven days before the *Washington Times* article appeared, I was seated behind my massive oak desk, poring over unsolved investigations, when my telephone rang.

"Special Agent Booth," I answered, "Special Investigations Branch, Department of State, how may I help you?"

"I am Corrections Officer Charles Wrice at Lorton Reformatory. I have been calling everybody in federal law enforcement, and no one seems to be willing to help."

Lorton Reformatory—that would be the District of Columbia's severely overcrowded and outdated prison built in Occoquan, Virginia, which holds DC's most vicious and violent prisoners. Nothing but nothing good happens there. No wonder no one wanted to talk with him. Why was he calling the State Department?

"Well then," I said, "why don't you tell me your story, and let's determine who should be talking to you."

"Listen, about one month ago, I found these government documents in an old metal file cabinet being refinished by Lorton inmates."

"Oh, really?"

"Yeah, and when I told my Lorton supervisor about it, he told me to forget it. And when I called the FBI's Alexandria Field Office and talked to "Jerry" he just brushed me off. And when I called "Sally" who works at the Department of Justice, she claimed they had no jurisdiction. That's why I am calling you."

Oh no, I thought, *I have a looney on the other end of the line.* "OK, and why are you calling the State Department?"

"I think these are State Department papers. Some papers have 'State Department Telegram' written on the top, and I have one in my hand right now."

It was possible I have a real problem here, I thought. "Can you start to read from the top left of one of those papers for me?"

Corrections Officer (CO) Wrice proceeded to recite a time and date group and additional acronyms that were consistent with a State Department telegram that was less than ninety days old.

I interrupted him, asking, "Is there a large marking in the middle on the top and bottom of the page?"

"Yeah," he replied, "Secret."

"And any words after the subject line on the left side?"

"Grenada, but the one that I think you might be interested in is one that talks about a suspected KGB agent traveling in Europe."

Someone is going to die here, I thought. "Excellent, you have reached the right office."

I quickly asked him when he could drop by my office for an interview, and he agreed to visit the next day.

At 3:45 p.m. on November 4, I escorted CO Wrice to room 2422, deep in the bowels of the department, to be questioned by SA Michael Considine and me. Mike—6′4″, basketball standout, and graduate of SUNY Brockport—had a constant smile and gentle comportment. We had served together on the secretary of state's protective detail in the early eighties and enjoyed each other's company.

Once seated around the square walnut table, CO Wrice spun the tale. According to the CO, sometime in early October 1983, he discovered classified documents inside a file cabinet located in Lorton's Old Furniture Building (OFB). For years, the US government had sent old or slightly damaged furniture to be refurbished by the inmates housed at Lorton as part of the corrections agency's rehabilitation and cost reduction programs—the "Idle Hands are the Devil's Tools" dictum, I supposed. In this instance, it turned out the department was bedeviled by a significant loss of ultrasensitive information thanks to gross negligence on the part of INR employees. According to CO Wrice, on the day in question, he was assigned to stand post in the saliport in the maximum-security area of Lorton Reformatory. Around 9:00 p.m., he was told that the maximum-security prisoners did not have linens or other sundry items in their cells and that Lieutenant J. Gibbs had authorized CO Wrice to scrounge for the necessary items. Images of James Garner in the movie the *Great Escape* filled my mind.

During his search, while walking between One Block and Three Block, he noticed that the back and front gates of the walkway were open and the OFB front door facing the flagpole was also open. CO Wrice explained that it was possible an inmate could have been trying to hide inside the OFB, so he radioed Officer Coleman in tower 7 directly above the OFB to advise that he was going inside to conduct an inmate search. Even though he found no inmate inside, CO Wrice remained suspicious of the unlocked door and believed that contraband may have been secreted somewhere inside the OFB.

In the midst of a search through the numerous pieces of furniture in various stages of refurbishment, CO Wrice opened a file cabinet and discovered classified documents inside. He removed some of the papers, which he recalled were stamped with "TOP SECRET" and "SECRET" markings. He suspected that his discovery was significant enough to contact his direct supervisors, Lieutenant Gibbs and Captain Durham, to alert them to his finding. His initial alert did not appear to generate any interest, and after thirty minutes, CO Wrice called back seeking guidance. He received an oral reprimand from Captain Durham for being away from his assigned post.

CO Wrice left the documents in the file cabinet, locked the OFB front door, and returned to his post. He immediately prepared a memorandum describing the incident and at the end of his shift left copies with three lieutenants and Captain Durham. Worried that he might not be believed, he kept one department telegram marked "Grenada" in his Lorton cabinet locker.

Listening to his story, I mused that his locker was probably more secure than a cabinet in INR. The following day, CO Wrice discovered that William Plaut, the Lorton administrator, had obtained a copy of his memorandum. Yet over the ensuing weeks no one came forward to question him about the documents.

But worse was the fact that he started to hear yard talk that some of the prisoners had discovered the classified papers. CO Wrice explained that although Lorton regulations mandate that all inmates be escorted in the OFB, as a matter of practice, the uniformed guards did not watch inmate electricians and plumbers. Approximately one hundred civilian contract laborers and painters had also been in the building since September to refurbish cells in Lorton. He conceded that the guards were supposed to have rosters of all inmates authorized to access the OFB, but they were not accurate or up to date.

On October 26, 1983, following the announcement that US military forces had invaded the island of Grenada, CO Wrice became convinced of the documents' authenticity. The next day, while assigned to his normal post, he returned to the furniture building and removed all the papers from the file cabinet, made photocopies, and returned the originals to the cabinets.

"Like I said," he explained, "I called lots of FBI officials at various buildings and the lady at the Justice Department's civil rights division but with no results."

"So what led you to our office?"

"Well, I was told that someone from the State Department had come to Lorton to pick up some of the papers but that no one was interviewed, nothing else happened. No one did anything. State Department documents floating around inside a prison, being traded among convicts, and nothing happens."

Mike and I stared at each other as we realized that whoever picked up the documents had done so with the mission of keeping the incident out of the public's eye. I was coming face to face with the department's strategy for covering up its losses of classified materials. One week following my interview with CO Wrice, I would interrogate that "someone," who acknowledged that he traveled to Lorton to retrieve classified department documents. His name was included in my final report of the investigation.

"So afterwards nothing was done and I was upset," CO Wrice said. "I decided to fix this thing by finding out who in the State Department needed to know about this. I mean, convicted murderers Elroy Lewis, Connie Wilkens, and Sampson in Block 6 are sharing the papers."

"You have done the right thing. This office will immediately open an inquiry, and we need to stay in touch." After a moment, I added, "This case could get pretty dicey. Would you prefer that we keep your identity confidential in this matter?"

"I would," he said.

He readily agreed, and we scheduled a meeting for the following week. After we escorted him out of the building, I briefed my immediate supervisor, Bernd Schaumburg, the SIB chief. I went home for a good night's rest—or so I thought.

Imagine my shock after getting home around 7:30 that night and turning on my bedroom television to hear a reporter announce: "Tonight, exclusive on WTTG-5, we talk with a Lorton Reformatory official who says he found classified State Department documents inside the prison."

At 11:00, Channel 5's lead story started with an image of CO Wrice standing outside the State Department's diplomatic entrance talking with a television reporter. It seemed that Mike and I had been set up. CO Wrice commenced the story by saying, "A few minutes ago, I finished talking with special agents Booth and Considine, and they. . . ."

That was how the rest of late-night Washington found out about the Lorton documents. So much for CO Wrice's request for confidentiality in this matter. About halfway through the WTTG-5 broadcast, SA Walter Deering of our General Investigations Branch called to wish me a good day in the office next morning. His teasing call was one of many that night. The calls from the DS seniors were much less humorous.

The question I pondered into the wee hours of the morning was this: did CO Wrice plan for the television interview beforehand, or did it result from a serendipitous encounter with one of the many reporters who congregated at the diplomatic entrance in the late afternoon to film their pieces before their deadlines? Who knew? Who cared? I was in the hot seat, regardless.

Secretary of State George Shultz had ordered a "full-scale investigation" into the matter, and I needed to find cover fast. Too bad security blankets were hard to find for young, vulnerable special agents—even inside a security organization.

The following Monday, I was at the FBI's Washington Field Office at 0630 to discuss investigative jurisdiction issues with FBI special agent "Tim." It was decided that since the documents were recovered at Lorton Reformatory, any investigation fell under the statutory definitions of 18 USC 793—FBI territory. The FBI would assume primary investigative responsibility. I had successfully dodged a big bullet that could have been fatal to my short tenure in security.

Shortly thereafter, the department's spokesman, Alan Romberg, advised the press corps the documents found in Lorton Reformatory had been discovered inside surplus State Department furniture that had been sent to Lorton for refinishing. He also acknowledged the cabinets and documents originated from the department's Bureau of Intelligence and Research. He noted that in the first week of August 1983 a team of contract laborers had been escorted to INR office space to remove "empty" office cabinets and used furniture, and they "inadvertently removed one full but unsecured safe."

What Romberg left unsaid during the press briefing spoke volumes. Many pertinent and embarrassing questions came to the minds of those sitting in the room. Who were the INR specialists responsible for ensuring that all furniture leaving the INR space did not contain classified materials? Did anyone in the bureau alert anyone in authority that there was a missing safe chock-full of highly classified materials? Who handled the inventory of "top secret" documents in INR? What were the internal controls for releasing office equipment and furniture outside a controlled access area? What roles and responsibilities did senior INR management have in assuring an effective security program within the bureau? If sensitive documents could just vanish without the loss being noticed, one certainly could question the security practices in INR.

Romberg indicated that it was the department's "assumption" that most of the recovered documents had not been "compromised." If the department seniors assumed "top secret" papers left unprotected for a month in a federal prison had not been compromised, then what constituted a compromise of national security information? The press briefing had nothing to do with explaining what happened; it was all about controlling damage to the department's credibility and image.

On November 10, 1983, Lorton officials, with the assistance of federal investigators, searched the cellblocks of inmates and were able to retrieve several government classified documents. The Lorton documents were eventually identified as the most sensitive papers in the US government's arsenal. Unfortunately INR could not positively identify all the documents lost or compromised. Slowly, and to the great relief of the department seniors, the episode disappeared from the national headlines.

When the FBI finally determined that there was insufficient evidence to proceed with a criminal case, the mess was turned over to the department for resolution. Instead of asking DS to conduct an inquiry, the State seniors handed off the investigation to the department's powerless inspector general's office, which did not have independent statutory authority like the other executive branch IGs at the time. Although spokesman Romberg had stated that any employee identified by the investigation as being culpable would be subject to "appropriate disciplinary action," no one was reprimanded. Senior INR officials just swept everything under the rug.

The only significant result of the inquiry was the codification in the Foreign Affairs Manual, the department's internal regulations, of how properly to inspect and certify a security repository before it was to be removed from the department's inventory. The change resulted in a requirement for safes and file cabinets to be thoroughly inspected for classified materials before they were retired and removed from service. The new regulation also called for any furniture removal to be documented in writing. Plain commonsense would have sufficed.

★★★

Another incident involving loss of classified information took place at the US consulate in Udorn, Thailand, in the early seventies. It's not one I can personally vouch for, as the event took place before my time. However, it serves as a cautionary tale. Again, negligence and a failure to follow security rules caused a loss and compromise of classified documents. It also ended up with the department making an unintentional donation to the local economy.

At the time, the US consulate was a tiny outpost in northern Thailand with only two Americans and half a dozen Thai employees. The Vietnam War had raised its profile given US military operations in the area that supported war efforts in Cambodia and Laos. The consulate did not have the luxury of shredding equipment in those days, but it did not generate or receive much classified material. The consulate practice for destroying such materials was to burn them in a fire pit on the grounds of the compound.

The American secretary would gather the sensitive papers to be destroyed, and a Thai employee would light them. Burning the papers was an approved method of destruction provided they were thoroughly destroyed and could not be reconstructed in whole or part. However, the flaw in the process was the American secretary, who immediately returned to the consulate without witnessing the destruction.

The Thai employee would then put out the fire and salvage the unburned documents. Everything had value, and the Thai could not understand why the Americans were stupidly destroying something worth a few *bhat* in the local marketplace as scrap paper. Apparently recycling was a well-established green practice even then. The arrangement went on for some time until one day an entrepreneurial Thai contacted the consulate.

The Thai gentleman politely asked the consular officer if the US government wanted to buy back its classified documents. It seemed that the Thai consular employee had been selling the paper to the local fish monger in downtown Udorn. State Department confidential and secret memoranda and cables were now wrappings for Mekong carp and other delicacies sold at the local market. The Thai gentleman bought all of the market's scrap paper and was now offering to sell it back to Uncle Sam. Reportedly the department paid several thousand dollars ransoming its own secrets! Luckily for us, the literacy rate for English in rural Thailand was rather low.

★★★

Department officials have an uneven record when it comes to safeguarding department secrets. For many years since 1982, whenever my FBI colleagues and I shared cups of coffee over numerous conference room tables to discuss serious counterintelligence breaches, I had to submit to "friendly fire" from my counterparts who complained that department employees were simply not serious about following security regulations that prohibited taking sensitive documents outside the HST in file folders, envelopes, briefcases, and purses. I endured the comments with grace and silence. That is, until 2001, when I had the pleasure of chiding them about the fact that John O'Neill, the FBI's special agent-in-charge (SAC) of the New York City Field Office's national security division, was under criminal investigation for the loss of classified documents. In the summer of 2000, local thieves stole a briefcase crammed with sensitive documents concerning IC counterintelligence and counterterrorism investigations that O'Neill had left behind in his Tampa, Florida, hotel room following an FBI meeting. Fortunately for all concerned, it was recovered by local law enforcement officials and returned to the FBI within twenty-four hours of its reported disappearance. Unfortunately for SAC O'Neill, the DOJ determined that his lapse of judgment was serious enough to move forward with a criminal investigation. Upon conclusion of the investigation, the DOJ decided not to prosecute O'Neill, and he retired shortly thereafter. (O'Neill became the head of security at the World Trade Center in New York City and perished in the September 11, 2001, attacks.)

When the FBI agents could no longer tolerate my hectoring, they dropped their department "briefcase caper" bombshell on me.

On September 28, 1995, a US delegation comprising Undersecretary of State Peter Tarnoff, his special assistant Daniel Russel, and Office of Chinese and Mongolian Affairs director Jeffery A. Bader (who later submitted a letter of support for Don Keyser to the US District Court) exited a vehicle in front of the Permanent Mission of the PRC to the United Nations (PRCMUN) in Manhattan. They had arrived for a scheduled 1:00 p.m. meeting with Chinese vice foreign minister Li Zhaoxing. Once inside, the US diplomats were escorted from the lobby to a conference room. At the conclusion of the forty-minute discussion, Tarnoff asked for a private discussion with Li and all other US and PRC officials left the ground floor conference room. Ten minutes later, the US delegation left the PRCMUN and then, according to my FBI colleagues, truth became stranger than fiction.

Traveling back to the US delegation's Waldorf Astoria hotel headquarters, the group determined that Tarnoff's briefcase, crammed with classified US-PRC position papers, was missing. The trio decided that Tarnoff had lost custody of the briefcase sometime that morning. They recalled that Tarnoff had a meeting with the Indonesian foreign minister in the "D" conference room located in the basement of the United Nations (UN) building before they left for the PRCMUN. Russel, being the junior officer, was tasked with trying to locate the briefcase. A department vehicle took Russel to the UN, where he proceeded to the basement area to conduct a quick search. Finding nothing, he decided to go across the street to the US Mission to the UN (USUN). At no point did any one of the trio inform UN security or DS about the missing briefcase.

At this point, Russel took a US Mission vehicle to the PRCMUN and went inside to ask the Chinese receptionist if he could talk to PRCMUN official Liu Xiaoming. When he was advised that she was unable to reach Mr. Liu by telephone, Russel asked if she would escort him back to the conference room as he may have inadvertently left a "notebook" behind. According to my FBI colleagues, the receptionist looked at Russel and asked if he meant a "briefcase" and dutifully produced Tarnoff's briefcase, which was inside a shopping bag that was on the floor next to the receptionist's desk.

Russel took the shopping bag from the receptionist and left the PRCMUN building. Once inside the USUN vehicle, Russel opened Tarnoff's briefcase and found a department Skypager, Tarnoff's glasses, and approximately fifty "secret" and "confidential" documents inside.

The first thought that ran through my head as I heard this part of the story was that, of course, gentlemen do not read each other's mail. The MSS officers inside the PRCMUN would never violate diplomatic mores. So all is good in the world. Well, maybe not.

Once back at the Waldorf Astoria, Russel handed the briefcase to Tarnoff's executive assistant and promptly forgot the whole episode—at least until the FBI came calling three weeks later. When interviewed by the FBI, the trio had trouble keeping their stories straight, but in the end, DOJ declined prosecution. The FBI's report was turned over to the department, where Richard Moose, the undersecretary of state for management (the department's fifth ranking official and responsible for all budgetary, administrative, and personnel matters), was tasked to determine how to conclude the inquiry.

I almost laughed out loud when the FBI mentioned Richard Moose's name. That would be the same Richard Moose who in the spring of 1980, while serving as assistant secretary of state for African affairs, was confronted by an irate passenger aboard Braniff flight 704. Apparently Moose was reading classified documents during the flight when a passenger, who happened to be an IC official, challenged him and warned that he should not be handling classified documents in full view of the public. Moose told the passenger that he was indeed reviewing classified material but he needed to work on an urgent draft and was too busy to discuss the matter further. Moose's attitude infuriated the US government employee. Once the plane landed, the IC official went to the Braniff counter, identified himself, determined Moose's identity (by seat assignment), and informed the department of the encounter. Moose received an oral admonishment for his Braniff caper from Ben Read, the undersecretary of management, on August 18, 1980. (Moose would resign from the department in 1996 following the disclosure of his relationship with a member of his staff [not his wife] with whom he traveled on official business.)

DS recommended that written admonishments be issued to the PRCMUN trio for their failure to notify the department that classified documents may have been compromised. Moose determined that a written admonishment was too drastic of a punishment for such an offense and, instead, Assistant Secretary of State for Diplomatic Security and career Black Dragon Anthony Quainton was directed to administer an "oral reprimand" to Tarnoff. The FBI's story was too much for me to believe, and I dismissed this FBI "urban legend" until I was informed years later that when Tarnoff reported to the DS executive office to receive his mandated tongue lashing, Quainton was in his full Black Dragon glory. Quainton dismissed his special assistant, SA Thomas McKeever, from witnessing the closed door "punishment session."

★★★

On March 9, 1998, in an article entitled "Agents Investigate State Department Security Breach," the *Washington Post* reported that DS and FBI agents were investigating an incident where an unidentified man appeared outside the secretary of state's executive office and walked off with "top secret" documents in full view of two secretaries. An unidentified official exclaimed, "No one has drawn the conclusion that this was benign, but clearly this did not represent the MO of any spy. It was not clandestine. We do not know whether any national security information has been compromised." At that time I was deputy chief of DS/CI and would have to disagree with the anonymous department officer who briefed the press about the incident.

Around 7:00 a.m. on February 5, 1998, an individual described as standing over six feet tall, wearing eyeglasses, and sporting a pony tail with a State Department identification card dangling from his neck by a metal necklace, entered the 7-2 corridor just outside Secretary of State Madeline K. Albright's seventh floor executive office. Without introducing or identifying himself or even saying "Good morning" to Shirley M. Hachey and "Susan" that morning's office managers, he walked over to a wooden credenza on top of which was an accordion file with nineteen folders, one of which contained that morning's National Intelligence Daily (NID). Nicknamed the "Super Pouch," the CIA's "top secret" NID contains NSA reports and reports about clandestine operations conducted by the CIA and DOD, including National Reconnaissance Office satellite photography. The State Department's copy of the NID, which normally consists of ten to twenty pages, is transported by a CIA courier in a locked canvas-style briefcase. The documents are turned over to INR, which quickly sorts through and identifies the information most affecting America's foreign relations for immediate delivery to the secretary of state. Arriving at her office in the morning, it is the first official documents the secretary of state peruses.

The unknown individual, dubbed "Mr. Brown Tweed Coat" (BTC) by later investigators for the jacket he was described as wearing that day, started to comb through the folders, much to the discomfort of the two office managers, who did not recognize the individual. About two minutes after his initial appearance, Hachey asked BTC if she could be of help. He responded, "We have got to keep this paper moving," a common department phrase, and he continued his search of the folders for about another minute.

At that point, Hachey stood up and asked BTC more forcibly if he needed help. Sensing that his time was running out, without saying a word, BTC removed all the NID documents that were in a folder, tucked them in a brown vinyl briefcase, walked out of the secretary's suite, and proceeded down a narrow corridor lined with the framed portraits of former secretaries of state. He hasn't been seen or heard from since.

Minutes after BTC departed the secretary of state's suite, the two office managers sensed something was amiss. As one would tell the FBI and DS agents later, it was clear to her that BTC was thumbing through the classified papers in search of one specific document. They reported the incident to their supervisors, who reacted calmly to the incident with the false belief that BTC was from INR and had come to take specific documents back to their office. William J. Burns, the executive secretary for the secretary of state, called "Mary" in INR and asked for her assistance in verifying if an INR employee fitting BTC's description had been sent by INR to retrieve documents from the "Super Pouch."

The description of BTC did not fit the profile of anyone Mary knew in INR, so she conducted a few telephone calls to INR employees asking if anyone had personally gone, directed someone to go, or knew of anyone who had gone to the secretary's suite to review "Super Pouch" documents. No one admitted responsibility. A little nervous at this point, Mary transmitted this e-mail message to over 320 department employees at 1:05 p.m.:

"S/S [the Secretary's Office] called a little while ago to say that a tall man wearing glasses had come up and taken some things out of their INR pouch this morning. They would like me to verify that the person in question is from INR. Calls to the usual suspects who routinely take intelligence up and back from the 7th floor have not turned up the answer. Would the person who went up to S/S please let me know so I can put their minds at ease. Thanks much."

By the close of business that evening, neither INR nor the secretary of state's office had notified DS about the missing NID, and Mary had received only a couple of disclaiming e-mails.

By late morning of Friday, February 6, a full twenty-four hours after the loss of the "'top secret" NID documents, after no one in INR confessed to being BTC, and after having received fewer than twenty-five e-mail responses to Mary's request for assistance, INR and the secretary's office began to raise the alarm. Even though DS had a full time SA assigned to INR to assist with security issues, SA "Chip" McElhattan was kept in the dark until late Friday afternoon. Finally around 4:00 p.m., the deputy secretary's office called DS and SA Thomas McKeever, the director of investigations and counterintelligence, was notified. DS/CI was alerted to the loss of the NID around 4:30 p.m. and immediately started to devise an investigative plan.

There was no question in my mind, given the description of events that had transpired the day before, that BTC had been directed by a very bold foreign intelligence agency to search for a specific document. Was it information concerning our forthcoming war with Iraq or the role of NATO peacekeepers in ex-Yugoslavia? Moreover, BTC sported a State Department identification badge around his neck. Did we have another department employee who was a clandestine penetration agent? DS/CI was ready to begin interviews, but as I started to make my preliminary telephone calls to INR officials in the HST, most people had gone home for the weekend or were not answering their phones or e-mails. It was nearly 6:30 p.m. If my small squad of six DS/CI agents had walked over to the HST and had attempted to enter nineteen separate INR office spaces unannounced, waving badges, talking about missing documents while trying to obtain interviews, we would have looked worse than the Keystone Cops. My decision was that the investigation would have to wait until Monday.

Promptly at 7:00 a.m. on Monday, February 9, DS agents met in SA McKeever's tiny but orderly office space to review the situation. To my delight and amazement, "Chip" McElhattan had started his own inquiry late Friday and over the weekend and, with the assistance of SA John Finnegan, had already interviewed the two office managers and developed additional information. But the long and short of it was that we quickly decided that since the missing documents were "stolen" US government documents and not "missing" department papers, the FBI needed to be involved. Theft of classified documents is not just every day, ordinary, regular theft. Section 1924 of Chapter 93 of 18 United States Code (Title VIII), Section 808, makes it a felony, punishable by a fine up to $1,000 and imprisonment for not more than one year, or both, if an individual without authority knowingly removes classified US information with the intent to retain the material at an unauthorized location. That was how the FBI became the lead investigative agency in the BTC matter with DS assisting.

Suspicions quickly fell on one disgruntled FSO but were dismissed. The CIA was circulating the rumor that BTC was a department employee who was threatening to leak sensitive materials if "his/her concerns are not accommodated." The FBI interviewed hundreds of sources, administered polygraph examinations, and even searched the private residence of a government employee. All to no avail.

Whoever did take the NID documents did so purposefully. BTC is without question a foreign intelligence penetration agent. Despite deputy spokesman James Foley's assertion that "[w]e certainly take the incident seriously and we are determined to get to the bottom of it," we did not. I wonder if BTC still works inside the department.

PART 4

Inside the Castle

The King hath note of all that they intend by interceptions which they dream not of.

—William Shakespeare

CHAPTER THIRTEEN

In 1999, the SVR deployed a team of clandestine intelligence officers (IOs) working under diplomatic cover at its Russian embassy in Washington, DC, to penetrate the HST and install a high-quality transmitter in a seventh floor conference room. The seventh floor houses the offices of the secretary of state and most other senior department officials. A technical penetration by a foreign intelligence agency of a guarded US government building in the middle of our nation's capital was no small feat.

Responsibility for the security lapses allowing the successful SVR operation falls squarely on the shoulders of senior members of the State Department whose administrative decisions opened the doors of the department to clandestine IOs who took advantage of their largesse—and America's secrets. In this instance, the Black Dragons' ill-considered actions directly contributed to the relaxation of access control measures at the HST that facilitated the SVR IO's penetration of the building.

I was involved from the beginning in a joint DS/FBI counterespionage operation to uncover, exploit, and eventually seize the transmitter and neutralize the Russian technical intelligence officer overseeing the mission. It was called Operation Sacred Ibis, and it was one of the most significant cases of my career.

★★★

In 1992, Sheldon J. Krys, then assistant secretary of state for the Bureau of Diplomatic Security, directed DS's Office of Domestic Operations to issue unclassified Circular C92-19, dated June 24, 1992, which was sent to all department personnel. The Black Dragons had handpicked Krys, a career Foreign Service officer with minimal security, intelligence, or law enforcement experience, for the job. The circular read, "Effective immediately Russian and Romanian diplomats no longer require an escort while in DOS facilities. They will [be] processed the same as any other visitor. This leaves no countries on the required escort list."

The circular was issued on the heels of an April 2, 1992, unclassified memorandum sent from Douglas L. Langan, the executive director of the Bureau of European Affairs, to James W. Sandlin in DS's Domestic Operations branch, requesting that building escorts be eliminated for Bulgarian diplomats: "With the rapid political evolution of Bulgaria, we no longer see a legitimate security need to require building escorts for Bulgarian diplomats. Accordingly, we ask that you lift this requirement effective today and advise the appropriate guards and reception personnel. We are considering whether to lift this requirement for the remaining two countries on the required escort list: the Soviet Union and Romania. We anticipate a firm response soon."

Senior State Department officers had come to the erroneous conclusion that a mere three years after the dismantling of the Berlin Wall and a forty-year Cold War, Russian, Bulgarian, and Romanian diplomats, including their intelligence officers, were suddenly trustworthy, benign individuals. The DS rank-and-file officers strongly disagreed with the decision but were powerless to countermand it because the leadership of the department's security organization was firmly in the hands of the Black Dragons.

So why did Langan anticipate a firm and positive response to his request "soon?" The answer was simple: his professional colleague Sheldon Krys and the building's senior management had already discussed the foreign diplomat escort policy and decided it must be changed. It was a done deal beforehand. Prior to Langan's memo and Kris's directorship of DS, senior department officials had unsuccessfully argued with their DS counterparts that the end of the Cold War meant that the outdated and rigid security practices should be relaxed to accommodate changing times and a new geopolitical reality. As far as they were concerned, Russian diplomats no longer represented a threat to the State Department.

Until Krys's June 1992 ruling, diplomats from Russia and other former Soviet bloc countries were required to present themselves to the department receptionist at the HST diplomatic entrance. There they would identify themselves and provide the name of the department official being visited. The receptionist would then call the receiving office, confirm the visit, and ask for the name of the department escort, who would then come down to the reception desk at the diplomatic entrance. The escort would shepherd the diplomat past the uniformed guards and security checkpoints.

Most DS managers expressed the belief that the real impetus for the change came from Kris's Black Dragon colleagues as well as, and importantly, the building's support staff, who simply did not want to be bothered with the onerous, time-consuming task of escorting Russian diplomats and others to and from the diplomatic entrance on C Street.

Shortly thereafter, Krys left DS and supreme Black Dragon Anthony Cecil Eden "Ace" (the nickname for him used by many in DS) Quainton assumed the mantle as the assistant secretary of state for diplomatic security in 1992. Ace joined the State Department in 1959 after completing his BA from Princeton (1955) and BLitt from Oxford (1958). Rising rapidly through the ranks of the Foreign Service, he served as US ambassador to the Central African Empire (1976–1978), Nicaragua (1982–1984), Kuwait (1984–1987), and Peru (1989–1992). Assuming the leadership of DS, he immediately began to implement a closely-held program to cut DS resources, technical counterintelligence missions, budget, and personnel (specific numbers redacted by State); at the same time, he attempted to transfer DS's criminal investigative and protective authority to the FBI, USSS, and other federal agencies. The Black Dragons were becoming nervous about DS's evolving law enforcement and security responsibilities and feared that DS's new missions—counterterrorism, dignitary protection, and criminal investigations, including assignment to nationwide multi–law enforcement agency Joint Terrorism Task Forces—detracted from the traditional role and image of the State Department. They claimed that the changes were for budgetary reasons and that the White House's mandate to "reinvent the government" with the "peace dividend" produced by the end of the Cold War meant, among other changes, that DS's core missions needed to be re-evaluated, but the DS agents were not convinced.

In 1993, Ace began downsizing the Office of Counterintelligence by reducing agent and analyst positions by half and the budget by 75 percent (specific numbers redacted by the State Department). The numbers alone spoke to his intentions to gut the organization. Assistant Secretary of State David Carpenter testified before Congress in 2000:

"Following the fall of the Soviet Union, DS was authorized to hire only a handful of agents, engineers, and civil service security personnel. Twenty percent of DS positions worldwide were reduced. Rules and regulations concerning security were loosened to the point that holding employees accountable for security issues became more difficult. . . .

"Let me give you a few examples of how DS programs were streamlined during that period. Among the activities affected was our office of counterintelligence. The number of positions was reduced from 41 to 26 and funding for the program was cut from $225,000 to $65,000. Staffing for programs in the Department that handle procedural and informational security issues was reduced by more than 50 percent. . . . The Department's reaction to imposed fiscal constraints and a popular opinion that the Cold War had ended and now the world was a better place had devastating consequences for DS programs."

When news of Ace's enthusiastic stewardship of the scorched earth program for DS became known to the special agents, he became perhaps the most reviled individual ever associated with DS. Lacking any law enforcement background, he was distrusted and disliked by the rank and file agents. He left DS in December 1995 and assumed the position as the director general of the Foreign Service. His potential nomination as US ambassador to India in 1997, where he had served as a young officer from 1966–1969, was effectively torpedoed by stealthy DS special agents. He retired from the Foreign Service shortly thereafter. Ace would later admit that his actions as assistant secretary for DS "effectively ruined [him] with a large number of people" in DS.

The Ace directives represented an abrupt about-face from previous attempts to build up the DS counterintelligence force, which directly resulted from the fallout of the 1987 arrest and eventual conviction of former US Embassies Moscow and Vienna Marine security guard Sergeant Clayton J. Lonetree for spying for the SVR. Secretary of State George Shultz put it succinctly when he said on April 8, 1987: "We didn't break into their embassy; they broke into our embassy. They invaded our sovereign territory, and we're damned upset about it."

The buildup of the DS counterintelligence function continued in 1988 in response to the FBI/DS investigation of career FSO and suspected SVR penetration agent Felix Bloch, the former deputy chief of mission to our embassy in Vienna. Barely five years later, the Black Dragons had determined that the Russian bear was in full hibernation.

Perhaps Messrs. Langan, Krys, and Ace had forgotten that scarcely seven years earlier President Ronald Reagan ordered the expulsion of eighty SVR, GRU, and Ministry of Foreign Affairs Russian diplomats working in the United States in an attempt to disrupt their hostile intelligence operations inside the United States. The SVR's successful recruitment of American agents resulted in the arrest of over twenty Americans in 1985 alone, the so-called "Year of the Spy." Maybe according to the Black Dragons, Russians IOs working under bogus diplomatic cover no longer represented a counterintelligence threat. Under Ace's leadership, Circular C92-19 was revalidated. Having worked and socialized with clandestine IOs—both friendly and unfriendly types—assigned to foreign embassies during his numerous overseas tours, how could Ace so easily forget that intelligence services routinely used their Foreign Ministries to infiltrate their agents as bona fide diplomats in Washington, DC, and elsewhere? To Ace, this well-known practice obviously did not present a serious security risk after 1992. But then again he was merely carrying out the will of the Black Dragons who ran the department. He was not about to cross swords with them over such a trivial matter, which would have been a career limiting act of disloyalty. And he had the US ambassadorship position in New Delhi in sight.

The DS officers responsible for administering the now-defunct security escort program were appalled by the decision but powerless to overturn the Krys and Ace edicts. The deed was done, and Russian diplomats (and SVR IOs) soon wandered freely inside the HST. One department official recalled that in December 1995 a Russian diplomat showed up unannounced in his office with Christmas gifts of chocolate and flowers for the office staff. At another point, Russian diplomats' unfettered access to offices and staff was such a nuisance that a career department officer, "Gladys," who worked in the European Bureau, contacted DS to complain about the lack of security controls. Some department staffers could see the forest for the trees despite the myopia of certain Black Dragons.

The results of the relaxed escort policy were clearly evident to most of us—the security of the HST had been compromised by ill-advised policies and facile bureaucrats. Although early indicators suggested that the SVR had reduced its reliance on former Eastern European proxies to run a variety of intelligence operations against the United States and that previous aggressive SVR behavior under general secretaries of the Central Committee of the Communist Party to the Soviet Union Yuri Andropov and Konstantin Chernenko seemed to wane following the breakup of the former Soviet Union, there was no evidence suggesting that the governments of either Mikhail Gorbachev or Boris Yeltsin were any less intent on obtaining sensitive information concerning their political, diplomatic, military, or commercial competitors. To believe otherwise was just wishful naiveté. Until a complete ideological purge of the former East German, Polish, and Bulgarian security services could be accomplished by the fledgling democratic governments, the former intelligence bosses and midgrade officers in those countries still owed their positions and political allegiance to the SVR. Consequently it retained considerable clout in that part of the intelligence world.

Langan's flawed justification in asking for the suspension of the escort rules was due to the "rapid political evolution" in former Soviet bloc countries. That artful statement suggested the State Department would be less aggressively targeted by the SVR and its surrogates.

Obviously Langan and Ace were unable to predict the rapid ascent of one ex-SVR thug named Vladimir Putin, giving credence to the notion that career diplomats should leave the department's security program in the hands of security professionals. Contrary to what these gentlemen liked to believe, when it came to clandestine collection, most foreign intelligence operatives, both friends and foes, assigned to diplomatic missions in Washington aggressively attempted to exploit American diplomats and other targets of opportunity.

So how, why, and under what circumstances did I first find out that the longstanding HST Russian diplomat escort rule had been abolished? In the summer of 1998, SSA Don Sullivan, assigned to the FBI's Washington Field Office managing one of the counterintelligence desks, called me to arrange a meeting. Tall, lanky, and soft-spoken, Don had worked Russian counterintelligence for the better part of his career. In the near future, we would work together on the Robert Hanssen case before Hanssen was arrested and convicted for espionage in 2001. (However, his most important duty would occur years later when he retired from the FBI and moved to Nashville, Tennessee in the late 2000s. In 2009, Don, I, and our spouses had a delightful reunion over brunch where he accepted his new surveillance responsibilities, which were to discreetly monitor my daughter, Chloe, who attended Vanderbilt University from 2009–2013. Apparently it worked, as she graduated without reportable incident.)

By 1998, Don and I had already worked together on a variety of Soviet intelligence issues, and I had come to appreciate his aggressive counterintelligence stance. I always welcomed his calls. Don told me that he wanted to share some intriguing information that his FBI surveillance team had recently developed regarding Russian diplomats spotted in the vicinity of the HST. A few days later, I was sitting in his WFO office as Don explained the significance of the details contained in the papers strewn atop his overflowing desk.

Patiently and concisely, Don identified seven specific Russian diplomats and their vehicular itineraries when they left the Russian embassy, located on Wisconsin Avenue in the northwest section of Washington, DC, and drove to various destinations in DC, Virginia, and Maryland.

Don explained that the FBI surveillance team had recently noted that certain Russian diplomats were now entering the HST with a frequency and duration dramatically inconsistent with what the FBI had observed for the previous twelve months. More ominously, Don said, "Unfortunately for you, a high percentage of those Russian diplomats walking around the department are strongly suspected to be SVR IOs operating in the United States under diplomatic title."

"This is a tricky one, Don," I said. "Bona fide Russian diplomats visit the State Department for a variety of legitimate reasons and some will be IOs." I could tell from Don's expression that he was not happy with my answer. "Well, in reality," I added, "IOs serving under diplomatic guise abroad, for any country, would perform similar activities to protect their clandestine personas."

"I get that, Robert," Don said, "but how do we, the FBI, or you in DS account for the sudden influx of Russian IOs inside the HST in such a short period of time?"

"I honestly don't have a good answer right now, but any Russian IO threat is minimized by the department's strict escort policy." Oh, how I would later come to regret that ignorant reply!

Only after returning to my office and researching the access control issues for the HST did I discover Circular 92-19. While Russian diplomats were not authorized unescorted access to the White House, NSA, CIA, the Pentagon, or DOJ, they could freely wander the halls of the US Department of State for as long as they wished without fear of challenge. There wasn't any similar reciprocity by the Russian Foreign Ministry in Russia for US diplomats assigned to Moscow. *Quid pro quo* simply didn't exist in that country's foreign affairs lexicon. All I could think of was that the State Department had somehow adhered to an overly generous interpretation of America's "Open Door" policy.

In 1998, David Carpenter, a career United States Secret Service special agent who had been the agent-in-charge of President Clinton's protective detail, was appointed as the new assistant secretary of state (A/S) for the Bureau of Diplomatic Security. I was pleased with Carpenter's appointment as we had worked together in Strasbourg, France in 1995 in anticipation of President Clinton's arrival in the city. I found him to be not only personable and professional but also someone who understood and appreciated personal protection and physical security in a way few department managers do.

In November 1998, in direct response to the bombings of the American embassies in Tanzania and Kenya and in consultation with his professional DS staff, Carpenter issued a new visitor escort policy via a State Department notice on November 17, 1998. The notice significantly tightened the escort rules, including restrictions on foreign diplomats.

According to SA Patrick Donovan, A/S Carpenter's executive assistant, a hurried telephone call from Daniel Russel (the same PRCMUN Russel), a member of Undersecretary Pickering's staff, less than forty-eight hours after the issuance of the department notice, resulted in the revocation of Carpenter's notice. According to Donovan, who left the department in November 2009 to become director of security for Chevron, the undersecretary's staff had received a number of irate telephone calls from offices complaining about how staff would be burdened with time-consuming escort duties that would also have a chilling effect on friendly diplomats visiting the State Department. In testimony before Congress in 2000, Carpenter stated that Pickering called him "within hours" of the distribution of the policy. According to Carpenter, Pickering indicated that "[p]eople felt it would be too confining and it wasn't doable and [Pickering] asked [Carpenter] to withdraw it."

Consequently a new escort policy memorandum, modified and reviewed by Pickering's office, was issued on November 23, 1998. This policy categorically stated that there would be no escort requirement for diplomats, regardless of country of origin. Counterintelligence and counterterrorism concerns and just plain commonsense failed to win the day on the issue.

I had served at the American embassy in Paris from 1992 to 1995 and had not worked inside the HST since 1986. I was completely ignorant as to the escort rules governing visitors to the building. However, in Paris, all foreign diplomats who visited the US embassy for any reason, including French Ministry of Foreign Affairs (MFA) officials, were escorted to and from the reception desk by an American officer. The French MFA, in kind, enforced the same policy. On one occasion in April 1994, I was a member of a US delegation that attended a meeting at the French MFA at the Quai D'Orsay, and the entire delegation was issued French MFA identification cards and escorted at all times within the building. Even the French MFA viewed counterintelligence rules seriously—including concerning their allies. The US Embassy Paris escort policy was in force at all our embassies and consulates but paradoxically not at the HST.

Don and I quickly reconstructed how Russian diplomats were now treated under the new policies when they presented themselves to the reception desk at the HST. Whenever a diplomat arrived at the HST front desk, he or she presented some form of identification to one of several receptionists who were seated behind a large wooden structure in the middle of a massive lobby festooned with the national flags of all the countries with which we have diplomatic relations.

The rest of the lobby was controlled on both sides by turnstiles, which were activated by department identification cards equipped with secure electronic chips and monitored by armed security guards manning the visitor access gate. The receptionist would check the daily logbook to determine if the visitor had been pre-cleared for entry inside the HST. If so, the foreign diplomat would be issued a white, stick-on paper lapel day pass and directed to the security x-ray machine located next to the visitor access gate. A uniformed guard at the screening station would then x-ray the contents of the diplomat's briefcase for explosives or other weapons. But other personal items such as cell phones and other electronic devices were permitted according to the security protocol.

The diplomat next walked through a magnetometer or "Walk-Through Metal Detector," as the department aptly called the device, before proceeding beyond the physical security barrier. This was done for purposes of form rather than substance because no diplomat activating an alarm was ever physically searched. That would have been a downright ungracious act in the eyes of the establishment. Having cleared the supposed screening process, the foreign diplomat was then trusted to proceed to the appropriate office inside the HST without an escort.

Certain department offices were designated as controlled access or Sensitive Compartmentalized Information Facility (SCIF) areas due to the nature of the operations occurring behind closed doors. Gaining access to these offices might be more difficult but not impossible. Much of the building was wide open and ripe for the picking. There was a lot of low-hanging fruit for those ballsy enough to take advantage of the department's lax security procedures. And the orchard was huge because the HST is the third largest office building in the Washington region, after the Pentagon and the Ronald Reagan Building.

Sadly my only other direct and very tragic encounter with the department's access rules occurred in 1985 when bureaucratic inefficiencies resulted in the death of a State Department employee. In February of that year, Carole Doster, a forty-four-year-old secretary, requested that the building security office issue her dependent son, Edward Steven Doster, a temporary department pass. The pass acted as a department identification card allowing the holder to enter the building without having his or her possessions searched by the security guards. Why she requested the pass remains a mystery because, unfortunately, as we would discover later, young Edward had physically abused his mother and displayed episodes of violence inside her house where he still lived. On May 30, less than ninety days after requesting the temporary pass for her son, she feared for her life and submitted a memorandum requesting that it be withdrawn. At the time, the department didn't have an automated identification system, and revocations of passes depended on keen-eyed guards memorizing visitor faces and checking the photos on the "do-not-admit" board. Keeping track of all of those who had been denied access to the building over time was a virtually impossible task in the pre–electronic identification card era.

On the afternoon of June 21, 1985, I received a frantic call from the DS executive office directing me to report to the seventh floor of the building, where sounds of gunfire had been reported. I was the only agent in the Special Investigations Branch at the time, and I quickly grabbed my Smith and Wesson Model 19 .357 revolver and holster, stuck both inside my belt, put on my coat to conceal the weapon, and dashed out of my second floor office and up the internal staircase.

Almost out of breath and not knowing what to expect, I opened the seventh floor stair door, took out my revolver, and cautiously glanced out at one of the nine corridors crisscrossing this floor. The hallway was uncharacteristically deserted and quiet. My heart pounding, I carefully walked down the hallway, hugging the right side corridor until I came to the first intersecting hallway. Peering around the corner, I spotted a fellow DS agent and called out to him.

"John." I waved my hand above my head. "Robert . . . over here."

He recognized me instantly—we had served together in Beijing during the mid-seventies—and responded, "Somebody just shot an employee and shot himself in the office behind me." He pointed to the door behind him.

I asked if he needed help, but he told me that a police officer was already inside. I assumed the frantic call to my office was a bit late, so I holstered my revolver and approached my colleague.

"Want to go inside?" he asked. "I guess your office will be involved in the upcoming investigation."

I nodded and opened the door to see a police officer standing over the body of a young man. We shared a few words, and he said that it appeared that an unidentified man had entered the building using a temporary pass and smuggled in an AR-7, .22 long survival breakdown rifle initially developed for the US Air Force. The grim-faced officer looked at me, pointed to a woman's body lying on the floor, and said, "Seems pretty clear that this young man shot this woman and then committed suicide. Pretty odd. Since he could not have been walking around the building with a rifle in hand, this guy probably snuck the broken-down rifle into the building in some kind of bag and assembled it in one of the custodian closets or restrooms on this floor."

Since there was no further need for me in the office, I offered to inspect the adjacent restrooms for any evidence linked to the shooting. However, just before leaving the office, I glanced at the Wang desk computer and noticed that the screen displayed a chronology of incidents involving physical abuse. Upon closer inspection, I noticed that the abuser was simply identified as "E."

Walking back into the hallway, I advised John of my mission and immediately entered the men's room closest to the office. In an almost comedic scene, I took out my badge, opened the door, and announced, "Federal officer, anybody inside?"

It was empty of people. But lying on the floor next to a trashcan were a gym bag and towel. I quickly stepped outside and said, "John, I think we need to secure this bathroom now and get technicians up here pronto."

He said, "I will secure access to the bathroom from here and alert the investigators that we might have some possible evidence to tag outside the office."

We would later learn the identities of the deceased man and woman—Edward Doster and his mother, Carole. The bag I found in the restroom turned out to be the one Edward had used to conceal the AR-7.

That terrible incident ended my brief involvement with these unfortunate deaths. It would be my last association with the State Department access control system until some twelve years later and ironically on the same floor of the HST. As a tragic footnote, it was later determined by the State Department's Office of Inspector General that Carole Doster's May 30 revocation memorandum had not reached the guards' desk by June 21.

When the locks and gates to the castle are not working, the consequences can be enormous.

CHAPTER FOURTEEN

As we belatedly discovered, there were all too many occasions when Russian diplomats would unexpectedly appear at the HST's diplomatic entrance without prior notification and request entry to the building. As long as the receptionist was able to contact someone inside the building to vouch for the visitor, the unannounced diplomat was admitted in the same manner as a pre-cleared one. In essence, one telephone call permitted a diplomat unescorted access inside the HST.

There were obvious problems inherent in the system. For example, how was the HST receptionist able to confirm that a phone call to pre-clear a foreign diplomat actually came from inside the building? In other words, a Russian diplomat speaking perfect American English could call the receptionist, identify him or herself as a building employee, state that he or she was expecting a Russian diplomat at such-and-such time, and authorize access. Following the telephone call, the receptionist would routinely enter the Russian diplomat's name in the logbook and await the visitor's arrival. The then-existing telephone system used by the building's receptionists didn't distinguish between internal and external calls. A legitimate department officer could call the receptionist from a restaurant, a residence, or elsewhere to set up a future meeting at the building. It was all a high-risk game of trust that the SVR would eventually exploit.

It was simply too much to expect the SVR or any other competent intelligence service to respect our honor system. The sad fact was that a diplomat from any country could wander aimlessly or purposefully throughout the State Department following a meeting with his department counterparts unless he or she was escorted down to the diplomatic entrance. A review of the security logs for the previous two years failed to disclose a single instance in which a wayward diplomat had been confronted or challenged by department staffers or a security officer. Later on, after the discovery of the transmitter, a "senior official, speaking on conditions of anonymity" and providing background information to the Associated Press, advised that the department's inspector general found that visitors were "not routinely escorted to the offices in which they claimed to have appointments."

What the inspector's report did not explain was why nothing was done to stop this trend, even as the anonymous senior US official explained, "Under the old system…visitors were cleared at the front desk by telephone and could do what they wanted. This was the problem."

Senior department management was aware of this counterintelligence problem and did nothing. It would soon become DS's embarrassing nightmare before the IC.

In early spring 1999, the counterintelligence concerns were painfully obvious to the joint DS/FBI team that was formed to address the issue. But maybe it wasn't just the Russians we had to worry about. The new team would immediately initiate a program to monitor physically the arrival and departure of all Russian diplomats and a few select other foreign diplomats who might pose an intelligence threat to the department's security. That task was easier said than done. How could we accomplish our mission without alerting our Russian and other friends to the surveillance?

Fortunately the HST's C Street diplomatic entrance was often surrounded by a large press corps, including teams of crews equipped with tripod mounted cameras and boom mikes. Why not disguise the FBI and DS personnel by equipping them with handheld cameras and video equipment and mingling them among the scores of journalists, tourists, and sightseers? Add to that mix the frequent arrival and departure of foreign diplomats with motorcades and bodyguards, and we had all the covert cover we needed. We just had to decide what cars to park on C Street and what to wear or carry around our necks. As a matter of fact, even we had difficulty sorting out the various players hanging around the diplomatic entrance without a scorecard, so any possible Russian counter-surveillance team would be thoroughly confused.

DS/CI was able to coordinate with our DS Domestic Operations counterparts so that the receptionists assigned to the diplomatic entrance were alerted to our interest in monitoring the arrival and departure of diplomats, particularly Russian ones. We wanted no sudden change in welcoming protocols to alert our friends to our sudden interest in their presence.

Within two weeks of my first meeting with Don, the DS/FBI surveillance team had cobbled together an operational strategy in which we would photograph Russian diplomatic vehicles parked in front of the C Street entrance and then photograph the diplomats themselves as they entered and exited the building. Three days into the joint DS/

FBI project, I received a radio message from a young DS special agent who was a member of the team.

"Robert," he excitedly exclaimed, "we were just notified that a Russian diplomat has shown up unexpectedly at the reception desk, and the diplomat has been telephonically granted unescorted entry to a department office. Somehow he evaded us and entered the HST unnoticed."

The receptionist alerted us to his presence as planned. However, our surveillance team in bogus press corps mode hadn't detected his arrival. The team also noted there weren't any vehicles sporting Russian diplomatic plates in the reserved diplomatic parking spaces in front of the building. Part of the operational plan was to determine the exact make and model of vehicles driven by specific Russian embassy officials. At times, this particular task turned out to be a high-stakes game of three-card Monte. The money card was sometimes elusive, and we weren't always certain if we were watching a Russian shill or mark.

I hung up the phone and walked over to the desk of SA Steve Jenkins, my senior branch chief, and said, "Let's take a nice walk outside and get some fresh air." He looked at me quizzically because he had known me for over twenty years and that was something I simply did not do. While I used the nearby GWU Smith Center gym three days a week for many years, a power walk during the day was not my routine. I quickly explained that we needed to "gear up" and search Twenty-First and Twenty-Third streets between Constitution Avenue and C Street in hopes of locating a "YR"-plated vehicle, which signified a car registered to the Russian embassy, because—as I told him—"we have a live one about." The look of relief on his face was immediate.

Part of the plan was to observe the interiors of any Russian diplomatic cars for intelligence clues or indicators. Steve and I donned our suit coats to conceal our Sig Sauer pistols and Motorola two-way radios equipped with the ubiquitous plastic wires and earpieces. "We will be around the C Street entrance in about five minutes," I alerted our surveillance team by radio as we left the building on its Virginia Avenue side. "Keep us updated, please."

As Steve and I rounded Twenty-Third and C streets, we began to scour the license plates of parked cars, looking for any diplomatic license plate beginning with YR. Nothing suspicious in Washington, DC, about two SAs on a dignitary protection detail taking a walk in the vicinity of the HST. DS or US Secret Service special agents, it did not make any difference; our cover would hold.

It was a mild morning, and I was delighted by the fact that I could take advantage of the surveillance team's call for a rare trip out of the office. We walked along with the National Academy of Sciences building to our right, looking for vehicles of interest. Suddenly a voice boomed in my earpiece: "Robert, don't look around or act suspiciously because the Russian target is right behind you!"

DS/CI special agent Thomas Haycraft, a member of that morning's team, had spotted the Russian diplomat exiting the HST and, while discreetly following him, saw us ambling along a block ahead. There was no questioning the importance of his instructions, so I did my best tourist imitation by looking to the right and pointing to the Albert Einstein statue on the academy grounds. My finger-pointing must have been a lucky stroke of genius because a few seconds later Steve and I were overtaken by a middle-aged man wearing a sports coat and white shirt sans tie who paid us no attention. He quickly entered a car, bearing YR diplomatic plates, parked about thirty yards ahead of us. Before we could walk past the car, the Russian diplomat pulled out of the parking space and sped away, denying us any opportunity to peek inside the vehicle.

We all enjoyed a good laugh over the incident when the team regrouped in the DS/CI conference room that afternoon to go over the day's events. In some respects, we felt like the characters out of the Spy vs. Spy cartoons in *Mad* magazine. Perhaps that description was apropos since the comic strip was created by Antonio Prohias, a Cuban national who fled to the United States in 1960 only days before Fidel Castro took control of the Cuban free press.

Regardless of the accuracy of the characterization, everything went well since we did not get burned right out of the box.

The perplexing question was why the Russian diplomat came unannounced to the department and stayed only ten to fifteen minutes. Regrettably the Russian was allowed entry to the building before a member of the team could follow him inside. We were not disposed to interview the department employee authorizing his admittance to the building. Had we done so, word of our interest in the diplomat's activities would have spread throughout the building within hours and ended any chance of determining exactly what the SVR was up to. It was a calculated risk but a risk we decided to take.

Given manpower and time constraints, the joint FBI/DS surveillance team could be deployed only three times—for two-week periods—in the ensuing months. But it was clear to senior DS and FBI counterintelligence officials that the sudden influx of Russian IOs and diplomats entering the building was unusual. Complicating our efforts to ascertain the real purpose of these visits was the fact that it was virtually impossible to follow the Russians once inside the building without giving ourselves away.

We had already decided not to brief the department's Russia desk officers about our operation, fearing our suspicions would be inadvertently leaked or our inquiry would be terminated by Black Dragons who would find our activity manifestly undiplomatic.

One intriguing incident occurred when the team filmed a known SVR intelligence officer under diplomatic cover entering the diplomatic entrance followed some forty minutes later by a bona fide Russian diplomat. We subsequently learned they had attended different official functions, yet they were photographed leaving together and entering the same Russian diplomatic car parked in the department's parking lot reserved for foreign diplomats. Entering a diplomatic car together under the shadow of the HST appeared to be a terrible gaffe in their intelligence tradecraft. On second thought, it suggested to us the total disdain that the SVR held for the department's security program. Photographs of Russian diplomats carrying briefcases or large bulging envelopes were endlessly analyzed for any hint of espionage, without resolution. We continued plodding along, going nowhere fast. But other activities turned out to be even more disconcerting.

Early one morning the team observed a Russian diplomat entering the diplomatic entrance lobby and walking over to a table on which an internal State Department telephone was located. To his immediate left and right beyond the security barriers were located two of the State Department's memorial plaques. Unveiled in 1933 by Secretary of State Henry Stimson in the Old Executive Office Building located next to the White House, the original plaque held sixty-five names and honored those members of the State Department's family who were killed in the line of duty or under heroic or inspirational circumstances. Starting with William Palfrey—lost at sea in 1780—and ending with Ambassador Chris Stevens and his three colleagues, who were killed in the attack directed against our Special Mission Compound in Benghazi, Libya, on September 12, 2012, the plaques now list 244 names. While Washington pundits like to poke fun at our "Daiquiri Diplomats," many of the men and women serving our diplomatic mission overseas have paid the highest price in service of their country. I don't think our Russian diplomat noticed or cared.

Shortly thereafter, a second Russian diplomat entered the lobby and presented himself to the receptionist, asking that he call a certain number to obtain telephonic access. Not needing to check the number as it was a five-digit department line, the receptionist dialed the number. On the first ring, the first diplomat picked up the telephone on the lobby table and authorized his accomplice entry. As this was so unexpected, the team was unable to have an agent follow the Russian diplomat inside the building. The Russian stationed in the lobby, well-known to the FBI as an SVR IO, spoke fluent American English and wouldn't have aroused any suspicions. He calmly walked out of the building after concluding his job. If nothing else, the SVR knew how to exploit vulnerabilities—both the human and technical varieties. In any event, we'd been hoisted by our own petard once again. It was frustrating to watch and not be able to do anything about it.

Another time, members of the joint team were in the lobby reviewing a number of activities when one of the FBI agents spotted an Aeroflot (Russian Airlines) official and long-suspected SVR IO walking unescorted behind the first floor security barrier. An immediate review of the receptionist's log failed to disclose any entry approval or preadmittance authorization for the individual. Despite our best efforts, we were unable to determine how the Aeroflot official obtained access to the building and where he was headed, if anywhere in particular. The cloak-and-dagger stuff had gotten downright embarrassing!

But then, as suddenly as it started, the number and frequency of visits by Russian diplomats and suspected IOs to the HST, both announced and spontaneous, diminished significantly. While we confirmed that the Russian presence clearly represented a potential counterintelligence issue, neither the FBI nor DS was able to determine with any certainty what the SVR might be doing inside the building. Regardless, I believed that the Black Dragons needed to be alerted to our findings even as inconclusive as they were. The joint team's conclusions regarding the HST's security weakness and a possible SVR operation inside were presented to Peter Bergin, the director of the Diplomatic Security Service, who immediately recognized the significance of our findings. I had replaced Peter as a security officer at USLO in Beijing in 1975 and we had maintained an excellent professional relationship.

At the conclusion of my presentation, Peter directed me to obtain permission from the FBI to use its photos and analytical documents in a briefing that I should be prepared to provide to senior State Department management. On May 20, 1998, with the FBI's photographs, documents, and blessings in hand, I accompanied DS deputy assistant secretary Wayne Rychak to the seventh floor to join a meeting chaired by undersecretary of state for political affairs and former US ambassador to Moscow Thomas Pickering. The meeting was arranged in record time, undersecretaries having full schedules and my message having nothing to do with interesting foreign policy matters, only boring physical security concerns.

Quickly laying out spreadsheets containing target names, times of arrivals and departures, and incriminating black and white photographs, I concluded the briefing by saying, "Both we and the FBI are convinced that the SVR is up to no good, but so far we have failed to uncover the specific reasons why these Russians visitied HST so frequently."

Undersecretary Pickering and his staff stared at me in silence. Following a very long forty-five seconds, Pickering turned to Rychak and said, "Have your technical security staff reset the finger-coded magnetic locks installed on internal office doors so that the release time is reduced from five to three seconds."

Rychak replied immediately, "Yes, sir, starting today, Mr. Pickering." It seemed that in Pickering's mind, this security "enhancement" would discourage any Russian diplomats from "piggybacking" behind a State Department employee, thus gaining access to restricted areas or SCIFs inside the HST. Poof—the Russian presence inside the State Department was now mitigated. Undersecretary Pickering, the third most senior official in the State Department, evidenced little interest in our operation, asking a few questions and glancing at the photographs and documents that I had presented. Speeding the lockup time on doors was the solution to uncontrolled SVR officers inside the building. Rychak similarly seemed unconcerned by the joint FBI/DS counterintelligence team's findings. My enthusiasm for the job was quickly heading south.

As we prepared to leave, one of Pickering's staffers asked a question about another counterintelligence concern that I included in my briefing. Completely by happenstance, the DS/FBI team had identified an Israeli diplomat who had a habit of leaving his sponsoring office in the department and heading unescorted to the HST ground floor cafeteria. With a cup of coffee in hand, the Israeli diplomat would wave over and engage in supposedly spontaneous conversations with various department employees. The department employees didn't seem the least bit concerned to have an unescorted Israeli diplomat hanging out at his home away from home.

I advised Ambassador Pickering, "DS/CI cannot find a single contact report from department officers about any US–Israeli HST cafeteria talks."

"And why do you think that is?" one of Pickering's advisors shot back.

"Well, I think it is clear that these discussions have not been reported by the employees because they simply do not believe the Israeli diplomat poses a security threat despite the fact that he is probably on intelligence gathering missions." All department employees receive an initial employment and periodic security briefings about these exact sorts of unexpected encounters, both here and at our embassies overseas, and their responsibilities to submit written reports to DS. I was asked to name the Israeli diplomat, and after I did, two of the staffers started to laugh.

One said, "Yeah, that's Benny, all right." Another staffer explained, "Everybody knows Benny quite well."

I stared in silence as they continued to talk. The same staffer said, "I am not surprised at all to hear that Benny is conducting his debriefings in the heart of the State Department. He is a ballsy guy, all right."

Maybe it was a laughing matter to them, but I simply could not believe the apparent lack of concern by senior department officers for the Israeli intelligence gathering activity occurring inside the HST. Had I missed the punch line? Was it just me? Then again, maybe in their minds, there just wasn't anything worth stealing from naive department officers in the cafeteria.

Years later, in 2005, Benny—better known by his real name, Naor Gilon—was the political counselor assigned to the Israeli embassy and implicated in a twenty-six-page FBI indictment for receiving US classified documents from Pentagon Iranian analyst Lawrence Franklin, who was indicted for espionage in having passed classified information to lobbyists Steven J. Rosen and Keith Weissman, members of the American Israel Public Affairs Committee (AIPAC). AIPAC is the most potent pro-Israeli lobby in the United States, rivaling only the National Rifle Association and the AARP in asserting its political will on Congress. Classified information obtained at the Pentagon by Franklin was shared with Rosen and Weissman, who allegedly passed selected portions along to certain journalists and the Israeli government. Even after the indictment, Gilon continued to attend official meetings at the State Department and Pentagon.

As an accredited diplomat, Gilon could not be arrested by the FBI or tried by the DOJ for any suspected violations of federal or state law unless his diplomatic immunity was specifically waived by his government—something no country would do for its coveted intelligence collectors. All diplomats carry one "get out of jail free" card wherever they go and whatever they do, or so the Vienna Convention guarantees.

In October 2005, following a guilty plea in which Franklin acknowledged meeting at least eight times with Naor Gilon as well as with AIPAC lobbyists, federal judge T. S. Ellis sentenced him to twelve and a half years in prison for passing classified information to unauthorized persons. Due to his cooperation with the government, his sentence was later reduced to probation. In 2009, the Department of Justice dropped the charges against Rosen and Weissman for conspiring to violate the provisions of the 1917 Espionage Act, believing it could not prevail in a criminal proceeding against them and desiring to avoid "the inevitable disclosure of classified information that would occur."

I did not get the feeling that my warnings were appreciated or understood by Undersecretary Pickering or his staff, but then again they weren't security specialists, nor were they in the business of implementing regulations that made it difficult for department officers to conduct diplomacy in an open forum. Before leaving, we convinced Pickering that we could offer a sanitized version of our report to department bureau directors in order to alert them to the fact that the building and its personnel were vulnerable to hostile intelligence targeting. Something was better than nothing. Undersecretary Pickering stood up, thanked us for our time, and ushered us out of his office. We had been summarily dismissed with our tails tucked between our legs. For what it was worth, I still had some pride and didn't let the door hit me on the way out.

As we walked out of Pickering's seventh floor office, I turned to Rychak and asked, "They don't get it, do they?" He didn't reply.

Following the meeting with Undersecretary Pickering, John Tello and I provided a number of briefings to department office directors and managers attempting to reinforce the idea that we needed their support in implementing a stronger escort policy. To my surprise and satisfaction, most bureau and office directors immediately instituted additional office-specific safeguards regarding escorts and updated contact reporting briefings to ensure that younger, unsuspecting, and inexperienced FSOs were briefed on how to interact with foreign diplomats, especially those with a shopping list of questions and smiling behind a cup of HST cafeteria coffee.

With the Russian diplomat building access caper behind us, my attention shifted back to a number of counterintelligence cases that had been put on hold in the interim. However, my diversion from the building's entry control issues would be short-lived when, in early 1999, I received a telephone call from a senior FBI SSA alerting me to expect a phone call from one of their agents assigned to the Washington Field Office. Shortly thereafter, I received a call from FBI special agent "Andy," who asked if I'd already been contacted by his headquarters. I calmly said that I had and that I was all ears.

Andy said that he was prepared to share with me particularly sensitive information but that it could not take place over the telephone but only in a SCIF. I invited Andy to drop by my office (a SCIF) at his earliest convenience. Several days later, he laid out a series of photographs on my desktop that simply astounded me. Andy pointed to a black and white photograph of a middle-aged man sitting on a wooden bench in a nondescript park.

"That individual is Stanislav Gusev," he said, "a suspected SVR technical officer serving in Washington under diplomatic cover."

I picked up the photograph and inspected it closer. Gusev looked about 5′5″ tall, slightly balding, with solid white hair and a relaxed pear figure.

"This picture was taken of Gusev as he sat on a park bench located outside the State Department," Andy continued.

Suddenly I recognized the bench and surrounding area. The DS/CI office was located just across Virginia Avenue from the HST. From my office, I could actually see the park bench that was in the FBI photograph. *What was going on here?* I wondered.

"How old is the photo?" I asked.

"It was taken in early 1999." Tapping his finger on another photo, Andy said, "Look at this picture. Do you see that Gusev has his hand in a black bag placed on top of the park bench?"

I nodded.

"Well, it's the FBI's belief that the bag contains electronic gear that is being manipulated by Gusev in order to activate a listening device located inside the HST."

Now it was my turn to stare and say nothing. Maybe Undersecretary Pickering was just as dumbfounded by the FBI black and white photos I had shown him much earlier. The photographs were taken by specially trained FBI personnel, and they strongly suggested that the SVR was up to its old tricks. I finally asked how the FBI had initially spotted Gusev.

"A bit of luck, actually," Andy replied. "A member of one of our FBI surveillance teams who was familiar with the photographs of suspected Washington, DC, based IO's observed him sitting on a bench located near the HST and alerted his supervisors of his suspicions." Shortly thereafter, the FBI flooded the area with surveillance teams to confirm if, in fact, the man spotted actually was the SVR intelligence officer Gusev, long of FBI interest. It was indeed!

According to Andy, the surveillance teams not only confirmed Gusev's identity, but they also noted that Gusev had a habit of parking his four-door, white Chevrolet Malibu bearing Russian diplomatic plates in the area bordering Twenty-Second and Twenty-Third streets and Virginia Avenue, on the opposite side of the HST's C Street diplomatic entrance. The FBI team recorded Gusev removing several large, black canvas bags from the car's trunk, then sitting at one of several park benches facing the building's northeast façade. The FBI captured on film how Gusev's hand would disappear inside one or two of the handbags while he manipulated an earpiece firmly attached to the side of his head. Looking at the photos, it appeared as though Gusev was playing a game of one-handed poker; except in this case his gaze never left the building's façade, and never once did he look directly into the bags.

Andy explained that this unusual behavior was observed a number of times over a period of several months. One of the funniest episodes caught on video was of one of Gusev's attempts to pose as a simple tourist passing the time reading a newspaper on a park bench. There was only one problem. During the twelve-minute clip, with one of Gusev's hands inside the gym bag, he pretended to read a newspaper—but he held it upside down!

Andy explained that his team recently noticed that Gusev had finished with his bench gymnastics and was now visiting the vicinity of the HST in a whole new mode. As highlighted by FBI photographs and videos, Gusev's new routine was to drive slowly up Virginia Avenue in his Chevrolet, now sarcastically tagged as the "Malibuski," in an attempt to find an open parking space with a direct line of sight to the building's northeast façade. FBI photo examiners noted that a tissue box, which never seemed to move even during turns, was affixed conspicuously to the backseat panel just under the rear window. Instead of taking out black canvas bags, Gusev now took out shiny metal quarters to feed the parking meter and then went on a two-hour walk around the GWU campus.

The FBI logs noted that Gusev's visits varied in time but mostly took place in the morning hours during the business week, though for some reason never on a Friday. The only consistent pattern was that he always parked his car with a line of sight of the HST's northeast façade. Andy pointed out one photograph that captured Gusev reaching with one hand under the car's dashboard. He explained that Gusev performed the maneuver every time he left the car for his two-hour constitutional. The FBI technical analysts assumed that Gusev was activating some sort of device, one that was not a standard accessory from the Chevrolet parts catalog.

Andy finished his presentation and leaned back in his chair. He didn't have to say anything else or review any more photographs or videos with me. The photographic evidence was damning. There was no doubt about it. The SVR had successfully installed a technical device inside the HST.

I asked Andy, "How many people in the State Department know about the FBI suspicions?"

He smiled. "Only Secretary of State Madeleine Albright, Deputy Secretary Richard Armitage, A/S David Carpenter, John Tello, and now you."

Andy's purpose in briefing me was to determine if a joint DS/FBI counterespionage team could mount an operation to uncover, exploit, and eventually seize the "bug" and neutralize a Russian intelligence officer to boot. My first concern was how the State Department could, as large and porous as it was, keep such a highly sensitive inquiry from being leaked to the press or, worse, back to the Russians. I was extremely concerned that another media leak à la Felix Bloch would permanently rupture the excellent working relationship we enjoyed with the FBI. It was still widely assumed in the IC that someone in the State Department had thwarted the FBI's espionage case against Felix Bloch by indiscreet comments to the press or an intentional tipoff. My other concern was that if our office became actively involved in this investigation, then most of the operational activity would occur inside the building, and the fourteen special agents assigned to my staff would be working long and hard hours. We already had a full investigative caseload, and this case would snow us under even more. I took less than five seconds to give my answer—DS/CI was going to be a player! I fervently hoped that my immediate supervisor, John Tello, who was out that morning, would agree to my pledge of assistance. At worst, he'd likely shake his head in exasperation and go for a long stroll around the GWU campus to let off steam. Maybe he would accidently bump into Gusev!

Andy returned the photos and logs to his briefcase and promised to get together our first, formal interagency meeting within the next seventy-two hours. Operation Sacred Ibis was about to get underway.

CHAPTER FIFTEEN

I relayed my conversation with Andy to John Tello upon his return to the office. He smiled, mumbled "Welcome aboard," and immediately agreed that we needed to assist in the investigation using all possible DS/CI resources at our disposal. I was off the proverbial hook for already committing DS to the case. When we discussed office priorities and resources, I quickly pointed out that my primary job as the office's deputy would not allow me to run the day-to-day operational aspects of Sacred Ibis. We both agreed to assign the case to SA Paul Gaffney, the office's branch chief responsible for monitoring hostile intelligence activities in Latin America and Europe.

As a twenty-year career DS veteran, Paul had been assigned as a section chief in DS/CI after a highly successful tour as the RSO at the US Interests Section in Havana. He had also served in Moscow from 1986 to 1988 in a newly created counterintelligence position within the embassy's security office.

During Paul's tenure in Russia, Marine Security Guard Clayton Lonetree's espionage efforts on behalf of the SVR were uncovered. Since a significant portion of Sergeant Lonetree's activities occurred in Moscow, Paul was responsible for coordinating the department's participation in the multiagency espionage investigation—something he would have to do with Sacred Ibis. Paul and I had served together on Secretary of State Alexander Haig's protective security detail in the early 1980s, and I had total confidence in his judgment and was comfortable with his personality and temperament. He was an ideal fit for the job from my perspective. It was also quite fortunate for us that he wasn't married at the time because for the next few months, he would have to sacrifice his evenings and weekends to the mission at hand. Once briefed, Paul readily agreed to lead the investigation.

The first order of business was to determine exactly where in the HST the SVR had planted its transmitter. Initially Paul worked alone in obtaining the building's blueprints and floor plans in order to identify every nook and cranny on the northeast side of the building. "Discretion" and "secrecy" were every counterintelligence officer's watchwords as we had learned from bitter experience. In previous investigations, when DS/CI agents asked department officers questions or requested documents, the inevitable rumors and gossip quickly emerged, destroying any chance of confidentiality. People naturally talk, yet Paul managed to avoid drawing undue attention to his work. He painstakingly identified those offices in which classified information would likely be discussed since we not-so-cleverly surmised that the SVR transmitter had to be located in an office in which sensitive conversations took place. A cursory review of the HST's floor plans revealed a significant amount of square footage occupied by restrooms, hallways, stairwells, utility closets, elevators, storage rooms, open seating areas, and public office spaces. Fortunately Paul's survey concluded that the actual number of potential conference rooms and individual offices, referred to as "target spaces," was not that large.

Once the target spaces were identified, the FBI determined that it was time to resort to technical detection measures. This part of the operation was successful due to the excellent help of Joan Lombardi, DS's executive officer, who made available office space for the technical countermeasures aspect of Sacred Ibis without raising any eyebrows. The exact nature of this help remains classified. However, less than forty-eight hours after activation, suspect radio emanations from a location near a window on the seventh floor of the HST's northeast façade were detected. The next morning, John Tello, John "Fitz" Fitzsimmons, our valued security engineering officer, and I sat down with our FBI colleagues to determine the next course of action based on the spurious radio signal. The decision to act was immediate.

Around 11:30 p.m. that same day, Paul Gaffney ushered a team of FBI and DS special agents and technical specialists into the Bureau of Oceans and International Environmental and Scientific Affairs (OES) seventh floor conference room to conduct a search of the premises. Within an hour, the team located an electronic transmitting device encased in a section of the wooden chair rail—a waist-high molding designed to establish proper scale and proportion in a room as well as protect a wall from chair marks—surrounding the room. This bogus piece of chair rail was secured to the wall just below the conference room's seven-foot-tall windows facing Virginia Avenue. The entry team was impressed by the SVR's due diligence. They had reasonably duplicated a piece of decorative wood molding that closely matched the existing chair rail. Better yet, the fake molding was hidden from sight behind the conference room's ceiling-to-floor window curtains. Regardless of whether the curtains were opened or closed, they always concealed that specific corner of the room where the bogus molding was affixed to the wall.

Even if an employee or member of the cleaning staff had pulled aside the curtain, a slightly mismatched piece of molding wouldn't have raised suspicions. A potted plant over six feet tall stood directly in front of the curtain, discouraging anyone from reaching around it. The clandestine SVR survey team had done its job well. It was a textbook example of surreptitious emplacement.

Countermeasures detection equipment and highly sophisticated photographic devices were trained on the molding by the entry team, and they immediately confirmed the existence of the clandestine transmitter, fitted with multiple batteries, embedded inside the wood. Since there was nothing else to do, the entry team quickly and quietly withdrew.

Senior administration officials were alerted to the discovery of the listening device, and within seventy-two hours, the most senior representatives of the FBI, CIA, NSA, and DOJ were hastily convened into a large SCIF located within the JEH building to determine how to respond to the discovery of the SVR transmitter. John Tello and I were the only two State Department officers present that morning, and the ensuing debate, while cordial, was intense. We remained quiet throughout the discussion, strongly suspecting that regardless of any decision reached by the gathered intelligence community, DS/CI would now be asked to make a significant contribution in the investigation.

As the assembled body debated the discovery of the transmitter, the potential harm arising from its operation, and a potential US government plan of action, my mind wandered and I asked myself—why the OES conference room? We knew that Russian diplomats had attended meetings inside the conference room during the course of bi- and tri-lateral negotiations, but OES is not considered a hard target for the SVR.

We would quickly learn that any number of people and internal department units could use the conference room for non-OES related topics. Paul Gaffney had reviewed the OES conference room sign-up book and determined that many sensitive discussions took place inside the room. The information captured by the SVR was eclectic and diverse. Some was classified, some was personnel sensitive, and some was mind-numbingly mundane. In my opinion, the information compromised in the OES conference room did not give the Kremlin a tactical or strategic edge in anything, luckily for us.

During the lively debate, certain attendees preferred to exploit the device by offering up disinformation in future staged conferences, hoping to disrupt and confuse Russian analysts.

Some FBI officials opted for a quick arrest of Gusev and an immediate examination of the transmitter while others suggested that the device be disabled and see who would show up at the conference room to repair or retrieve the device. Finally the technical folks argued that the top priority was immediately to remove and inspect the device and learn its design capabilities in order to develop appropriate technical countermeasures. They insisted the transmitter be removed that very afternoon.

Several hours later, it was agreed to leave the transmitter in situ. However, the OES conference room and listening device would be monitored electronically on a twenty-four hour, seven-day-a-week basis until the DOJ determined that all legal and technical issues associated with the discovery of the device had been thoroughly reviewed for a potential prosecution. The participants further agreed that FBI technicians would install the necessary electronic surveillance monitoring equipment in the conference room so that DS special agents could remotely monitor the room and make an "arrest" should any individual attempt to service or handle the device during the surveillance.

As we departed the JEH building, John Tello and I discussed how best to inform our agents of their new and time-consuming task. Both of us were uneasy about the open-ended nature of the commitment our office had just made. Our anxiety greatly increased when we realized just how forceful our message must be to the office staff concerning their need to practice extraordinary discretion and discipline in the months to come. The adverse consequences of an inadvertent disclosure of the operation were just too great to let our guard down.

The only thing more boring than sitting in a windowless room in the bowels of the HST for hours on end watching live video feeds coming from inside the OES conference room during the workday was doing the same mindless camera watching during the evening and midnight hours over very long weekends. The tedium was mind numbing and excruciating. But the miniature television cameras and audio devices expertly installed inside the conference room, without the knowledge of department personnel, worked beautifully. From the moment the cameras were activated, DS/CI agents carefully monitored and recorded every single second of activity and conversation that took place in the OES conference room. For months on end, every DS/CI agent took turns participating in the tedious task.

Personal sacrifices became routine during this time frame. I recall that while enjoying my Thanksgiving dinner with my mother, wife, daughter, brother, and sister-in-law, I had not touched my glass of wine—a highly unusual sacrifice for me—when just before the pies arrived, I stood up and announced that I had to go to work. My brother, Tom, a savvy Justice Department lawyer for over twenty-five years who usually had an insightful appreciation for my work, just gave me an odd look as I geared up for the job.

On another occasion, it was reported that one of the duty agents, Christopher Lyons, serving on yet another boring overnight shift, was overheard by his teammate to be moaning over and over again: "This bullshit is never going to end!" The frustration levels of those who protect and serve are incredibly high most of the time.

With DS monitoring the conference room, the FBI continued to watch Gusev. That exercise resulted in some funny moments. There were times when the FBI surveillance teams alerted me that Gusev was trying to find a parking space on Virginia Avenue. My office faced the northeast façade of the HST with an unobstructed view of Virginia Avenue, and sometimes I casually rested my forehead on the office window and watched Gusev park his car and feed the meter before leaving for his walkabout. I had to admit it was somewhat amusing to watch an SVR agent at work while drinking coffee and conducting business with colleagues.

On another occasion, John Tello almost literally bumped into Gusev inside the CVS pharmacy located just thirty yards around the corner from our office. Once, while walking up Twenty-Second Street, John and I caught the now familiar sight of Gusev approaching us from the direction of GWU's Smith Center on his way back to the parked Malibuski. We held our laughter until the next block while we reflected on the sheer lunacy of it all.

Many different federal agencies were involved in the Sacred Ibis investigation, and DS/CI played an important role in the overall operation. The ultimate decision on how best to exploit and ultimately conclude the operation rested with the DOJ and the IC. Luckily all good things must come to an end, and in the case of Sacred Ibis, it was none too soon for us. When DOJ decided it was time to roll up Gusev and remove the transmitter, John called all of the agents into DS/CI's conference room and advised them that the game was about to end. The relief on everyone's face was obvious. They had accomplished their tasks with dedication and without mistakes and could now look forward to spending evenings and weekends at home. There were only a few final details left to resolve before the case was officially wrapped up.

The legal and administrative issues surrounding the impending detention of a clandestine intelligence suspect are daunting and unique in every espionage investigation. One unusual aspect of this case was that taking possession of the transmitter and the recording devices located inside the Malibuski was more important than grabbing Gusev. As an accredited Russian diplomat, Gusev could be detained for only a few hours at most and would have to be released to the custody of his embassy. Ditto for the Malibuski; it is the private property of the Russian embassy. The electronic devices were the true prize in this game of spy vs. spy.

Just to be on the safe side, the DOJ determined that in order to prosecute Gusev successfully, if the Russian embassy for some bizarre reason waived his diplomatic immunity to meet the legal definition of espionage, it would be necessary that a conversation transmitted from the OES conference room to a recording device in Gusev's Malibuski had to be classified at the "secret" level. DOJ forwarded its tasking to our office.

Ultimately John Tello identified Fran Saunders, DS/CI's branch chief for counterintelligence analysis, to prepare an authentic classified briefing that she and her staff would deliver inside the OES conference room. As Sacred Ibis had been a closely held investigation even in our small office, I vividly recall the shocked look on her face when I disclosed to her the existence of the transmitter and her upcoming role in the final hours of the operation.

She then smiled and said, "I have watched you and John for the last several weeks, and I had suspected that something big was going on because of the everyday wholesale change in the work routines of the agents." Being a true professional, she had never attempted to violate the need-to-know doctrine and ask questions of John and me. "I can have a plausible script ready within twenty-four hours," she said.

One last hurdle to be jumped was to figure out how DS/CI could ensure that Saunders's team could enter the OES conference room and carry out the twenty-minute "secret" level conversation required to meet DOJ's legal threshold for "the transmission of classified information." Timing was absolutely crucial to success. The OES conference room might be occupied by a meeting when it was time to commence the "secret" DOJ ordained conversation, so we had to prepare for that possibility. A fire drill, an electrical problem, an environmental concern, or other lame excuse for evacuating participants from the room were some of our options. OES, which was administratively responsible for managing the conference room, intentionally had not been briefed on the Sacred Ibis operation for fear that an inadvertent comment or action by OES personnel would unravel the operation. So we could not rely on its help in the ruse. We arrived at a solution in typical government fashion—we would cross that bridge later and hope we didn't burn it behind us.

In preparation for Gusev's detention and the examination of the SVR transmitter, a team of DS and FBI technical specialists was identified to wait inside the same cramped observation room manned by the DS/CI OES surveillance team. The FBI wanted the technical team to enter the OES conference room to commence an immediate forensic and technical inspection of the device following Gusev's detention.

With the final details worked out and the agents and technicians readied, we agreed that Gusev would be detained sometime in the last week of November. Since he frequently visited Virginia Avenue on Monday mornings, we all agreed that his rollup date would be pegged for November 29, 1999—if things went well.

At 6:30 a.m. on November 29, I visited members of the joint DS/FBI technical team, who sat on the floor of the cramped observation/monitoring room surrounded by bags of electronic equipment and tried not to interfere with the DS agents still conducting video monitoring of the OES conference room. There was a sense of urgency in the air as everyone speculated what the next few hours would bring. Shifting back to my office, I spoke with analysts Tom Lalley and Fran Saunders about their upcoming dramatic roles as "senior officials" discussing twenty minutes of classified information inside the OES conference room. In an attempt to calm the nerves of the members of the bogus team, I jokingly asked if they had ever committed espionage on behalf of a foreign power. I warned them that their voices would forever be recorded on SVR equipment. They appeared confident and said they looked forward to being actors in this psychodrama.

Finally I spoke with SAs Kent Trogden and Jon Norsworthy, DS/CI's representatives on the FBI's detention team, and completed confirmation of our readiness by speaking on a secure line with SA Ollie Ellison, who was assigned to the Sacred Ibis Command Post located at the FBI's WFO. Everything was set, and everyone was ready to pounce. But like Godot, Gusev never came.

Monday came and went. So did Tuesday. There were no Gusev sightings. In fact, no suspicious cars bearing Russian diplomatic plates were spotted in the vicinity of Virginia Avenue. Suddenly all activity associated with Gusev and the State Department ceased.

Something seemed desperately wrong. My first guess was that a leak had occurred. Had someone made an indiscreet comment to the wrong person on the phone, perhaps at a high-powered luncheon or during a classified meeting?

We had been notified that Secretary Albright had already briefed James Rubin, the assistant secretary of state for public affairs and chief spokesman for the State Department who was married to CNN correspondent Christiane Amanpour. Rubin's relationships with the press left a number of us in the investigative community with a sense of unease. Fearful of an unauthorized disclosure to the press, I had personally voiced my misgivings about briefing the department's public affairs office any earlier than five minutes before Gusev's detention. But decisions of this nature were made, for better or for worse, by the secretary of state.

By Friday, December 3, the mood among the FBI/DS team was dour, to put things mildly. I visited the surveillance room the previous day only to be greeted by a group of sullen individuals sitting in a room littered with empty coffee cups and fast food wrappers. No one spoke, but the resignation of defeat was in the air. I asked a quick, "Is everything OK?" and made a quicker retreat into the hallway before I heard the replies. I advised A/S David Carpenter about the grim possibility that our prey had slipped away. I reviewed the situation with John Tello who, as usual, maintained his professional composure while counseling patience.

That weekend seemed like the longest of my career, as I feared the inevitable finger pointing was about to begin, especially given the massive effort and manpower resources that had been devoted to Sacred Ibis. My wife, Lori, sensed my discomfort and guessed correctly that something at work wasn't going well. Monday morning came and went, and the tension in the office and the observation room was fierce. On Wednesday, December 8, after arriving in my office to confirm that all personnel were in place around Virginia Avenue and near the OES conference room, I remained in a foul mood. The FBI and DS simply couldn't continue this manpower-intensive wait-and-see operation much longer, and I was already wondering who would be singled out as the number one scapegoat responsible for its failure. The answer was easy: me.

How had the Russians found out about the investigation? Five days before the proposed rollup, Gusev had calmly fed the parking meter on Virginia Avenue and took his usual two-hour stroll. It appeared that we had missed him by one weekend

In the midst of my frustration and disappointment, I remembered that I needed to talk to SA Ollie Ellison, who was still assigned to the FBI's Sacred Ibis Command Post, about an unrelated matter. Around 9:15 a.m., I finally got Ellison on the telephone and exchanged pleasantries before talking shop. We were careful to use an encrypted secure telephone line, which is critical in these circumstances.

No sooner had we begun to talk than Ollie blurted out, "Robert, I am getting a frantic hand signal from my FBI counterpart. Gusev has just been sighted leaving the Russian embassy in the Malibuski and appears headed in the general direction of the State Department!"

I slammed down the phone, leaped out of the office, and looked around for help, only to discover that I was the only agent around—a pretty old and frustrated one at that. Anxiety hit me fast. Where the hell was everybody? The sense of urgency hanging over the detention and removal operation had diminished over the past ten days to the point that early morning enthusiasm had been replaced with slow-paced purchases of coffee around the normal 8:45 a.m. startup time. Hurrying down the corridor and peeking into empty cubicles, my worst fears were confirmed. I was alone and panicking!

At that moment, Paul Gaffney opened the main door to the DS/CI office space, coffee cup in hand and resignation on his face. I literally screamed, "Gusev's mobile," the code words to conclude the final phase of the operation.

At first, he refused to believe me, having been exposed to my warped sense of humor for the better part of twenty years. As he brushed past me, his only response was "Right." It took three or four tries before he realized that Gusev's arrival was imminent. Calmly putting down his coffee on the secretary's desk, he said with a wink and smile, "Don't worry. I know what to do." He buttoned up his trench coat and hurried out of the office, heading in the direction of the HST surveillance room filled to capacity with eager agents and technical specialists.

The DS/CI agents were alerted by cell phone and handheld radios to move immediately to their predetermined locations. Those DS SAs assigned to work with their FBI counterparts needed to hook up with them ASAP or sooner. John Tello had returned to the office to escort the bogus briefing team to a preselected location adjacent to the OES conference room. Thank God everything fell into place as planned and practiced. Within five minutes of my call to SA Ellison, I spotted Gusev's car from my office window as it slowly traveled north on Virginia Avenue heading in the direction of the John F. Kennedy Center for the Performing Arts, apparently in search of a parking spot. I alerted our agents by encrypted radio that the Malibuski had circled the block and was now attempting to park in a space diagonally across from the CVS pharmacy. I then instructed John to move his "briefing team" into the OES conference room. As luck would have it, there were no meetings scheduled for the morning, and the DS/CI team promptly took their seats around the conference table and began the putative classified discussion.

As Gusev pulled his car into an empty parking space on the north side of Virginia Avenue, he managed to bump a van parked in front of him as he jockeyed for the perfect position. Earlier that morning, the FBI had parked a nondescript white van equipped with TV cameras in order to capture Gusev's final acts on film. By the greatest of coincidences, the empty parking space picked by Gusev happened to be the one directly behind the FBI surveillance van—the very one he had just bumped! When I later reviewed the surveillance film, I couldn't help but laugh out loud seeing Gusev's face behind the Malibuski's front windshield as his car jostled the FBI van. The recorded, hushed comments of the FBI surveillance team inside the van were not so polite. Gusev kept moving his car two feet forward and then one foot back, turning his wheels toward the street, and then swinging back in. All the maneuvering was making me nervous. I was afraid that either he had spotted the FBI surveillance van or else he couldn't properly align his receiver with the transmitter located in the OES conference room. In either case, I worried that he might call it a day. In those few moments while he was attempting to perfect his parallel parking, Gusev pushed my panic buttons.

As my anxiety grew and choice expletives poured from my mouth, my secretary, Theresa Black, having just been briefed on the essentials of the case, teased me unmercifully.

"Mr. Booth, this one isn't so important, is it?"

"Well, kinda. Yeah, it is."

"No one will get fired if it is screwed up, right?" She had a huge Cheshire smile on her face.

"Just me."

I kept staring out the large pane of glass to the street below and announced to no one in particular, "This is probably the only time in the history of espionage that the conclusion of a spy case has occurred at the door steps of the affected agency's counterintelligence office."

"Is that good, Mr. Booth?" Theresa continued. "Can I get something for you, coffee or a relaxant? You are not going to survive this morning if you continue like this."

Gusev was still inching his car backward and forward while my blood pressure was seconds away from going over the top.

Finally Gusev exited the car, closed the door, and pulled a palmful of quarters from his pants pocket. Wearing a light gray winter jacket and dark gray pants, he carefully fed the parking meter until the two-hour maximum time limit was reached. He gave one quick glance over to the HST and headed north on foot to Twenty-First Street. I just rolled my eyes, shook my head, and took a deep breath, much to the amusement of Theresa, who thought I was going to stroke-out any second.

Approximately twenty minutes after Gusev left for his walk, the final act in this long and complex investigation began to unroll. As I watched, a nondescript vehicle containing three occupants and traveling south on Virginia Avenue suddenly pulled a U-turn and jerked to a stop next to Gusev's vehicle. Two men quickly got out of the car and opened the Malibuski's front passenger doors. Within seconds, both cars drove away in tandem. The FBI had just seized Gusev's vehicle. I alerted Tello by radio, "John, time to dismiss your bogus briefing team and usher the technical team into the OES conference room."

At 11:34 a.m., as he was returning to his long gone Malibuski, Gusev was detained by a team of DS and FBI agents near the GWU Smith Center. Numerous students, office workers, and shoppers calmly walked around the small group of five people, blithely unaware of what was happening even though one of the FBI agents had a pair of handcuffs dangling at her side. A Russian-speaking FBI agent advised Gusev that he was being detained on suspicion of being involved in espionage activities against the United States. I don't know if he was read his rights or not. Gusev politely declined to engage in any conversation beyond a few "yes" and "no" responses and an occasional nod or shake of his head.

Two unwitting but highly cooperative Secret Service Uniformed Division officers happened to be driving by in their marked police cruiser and were pressed into service by DS SA Jon Norsworthy. They were asked to assist in the rollup by diverting all vehicle traffic away from the street corner so as not to have cars stop or slow down to gawk at the developing spectacle on the sidewalk.

The back-and-forth street theater continued for about two minutes before the FBI gave the signal to take Gusev into custody. Neither handcuffs nor physical force were used as Gusev meekly stepped into a strategically parked government vehicle that immediately sped off in the direction of the FBI's Washington Field Office.

SA Ellison called some minutes later to confirm that Gusev had just been brought into WFO. That gave me license to leave the now deserted DS/CI office and walk over to the OES conference room. Using my identification card to enter the building via an employee entrance on D Street, I finally allowed myself to relax and reflect on what had just happened. There was no leak, an SVR clandestine intelligence officer had been detained, and technical equipment located inside the Malibuski was now in the hands of the IC who was about to inspect a Russian transmitter and its receiver. In the tiny world of counterintelligence, which few people truly understand, it just didn't get any better than this.

In response to my gentle rapping on the OES conference room door, John opened it and let me in. The conference room was now technically a crime scene and investigative protocols needed to be observed. My first duty was to sign my name on an access sheet attached to a clipboard resting on top of the massive conference room table. This was a necessary drill should, in any future court hearing, a defense attorney attempt to prevent the introduction of the transmitter as an item of evidence claiming "chain of evidence" issues, "contamination," or some other legal impediment. There were only eight FBI and DS personnel present. Everyone walked carefully around the assorted technical equipment that was focused on the chair rail molding, which was now fully exposed because the right-hand side window curtain had been pulled away and draped over a chair. Conducted in accordance with precise forensic protocols, the piece of molding containing the transmitter was gently pried from the wall.

A cursory inspection revealed that the eighteen-inch piece of fake molding was coped on one end and had a mitered return at the other that had been attached to the wall with two nails and a bead of adhesive. Contrary to numerous public reports claiming that the bogus molding was an exact copy of the existing molding, it was not. The profile of the bogus molding mildly resembled that of the authentic molding but its staining was lighter than some of the surrounding pieces. Frankly those physical differences would not have raised anybody's suspicions because the rest of the room's chair rail molding had mismatched stains and profiles as well. Maybe the expressions "lowest bidder" and "good enough for government work" helped the Russians conceal their device among carpentry work that was not of the highest caliber. In 1998, certain portions of the OES conference room's drywall partitions, cove base, ceilings, doors, and chair rails had been reworked by a company tentatively identified as Consolidated Engineering Services, and perhaps the Russian diplomats walking around unescorted inside the HST used the renovation to their advantage. We simply didn't know.

Further on-site inspection by the FBI revealed a tiny pinhole in the molding that was quickly identified as a microphone hole. At that point, no further destructive analysis could be undertaken, and it was time to remove the device and take it to an IC laboratory specifically created to examine such things. Published reports emerged suggesting that the transmitter was one of great design and sophistication. This simply was not the case. FBI assistant director Neil Gallagher would tell members of the press gathered for a State Department briefing held on December 9, 1999, that ongoing technical examinations were needed to gauge the sophistication of the device; the "space-age technical bug" myth persists to this day. In reality, the transmitter consisted of individual components of high quality, but it was nothing more than a simple microphone powered by a series of flat cell batteries attached to a transmitter that was activated by a radio frequency actuator/transponder emanating from the Malibuski. There was no burst transmitter, no satellite relay, no 200-year-life batteries, and no other Buck Rogers technology—just basic tried and true tradecraft used by the SVR for decades.

Just before leaving the conference room, I shot a glance over to John Fitzsimmons, our lead engineering officer in the operation. We both smiled and shook our heads, knowing all too well that within twenty-four hours, the press and Congress would have a field day talking about lax State Department security practices. Leaving the technical cleanup to the FBI, John and I walked across Virginia Avenue to our office to confront the ordered chaos.

Pairs of DS and FBI SAs had started to interview jointly all individuals who may have had access to the OES conference room, starting with the janitorial staff and finishing with OES's highly cooperative assistant secretary of state. The teams fanned out through the HST to determine if anyone had any insight or information as to how the device could have been clandestinely introduced into a restricted conference room. While cooperative, like the three wise monkeys in the parable, no one volunteered to speak, hear, or see any evil. Not surprisingly, physical security was not of interest or of prime concern. Not a single lead was developed from the interviews conducted with hundreds of department employees.

John and I were worn out at this point and decided that the only good we could offer at this stage of the investigation was to get out of the way of the investigating agents and head off to the GWU Smith Center gym for a good workout. Many of the DS/CI SAs watched with disbelieving looks on their faces as we hoisted our gym bags over our shoulders and walked out of the office. But frankly there was nothing more John or I could contribute at this juncture. The ongoing investigation was now nothing more than a straightforward exercise in attempting to elicit information. About ninety minutes later, we returned to discover that the FBI and DS SAs had conducted themselves with great skill, just as expected. My blood pressure had returned to normal.

Unfortunately I had already reached the conclusion that the interviews were not going to be productive. If the SVR had planted the device inside the OES conference room without any inside assistance over a year ago, it was my belief that precious little could be obtained from interviewing people about events that may have occurred that long ago. Worse yet, if a department co-conspirator had aided the SVR, he or she had not aroused any suspicions with his or her fellow colleagues. The interviews of department employees were not going to advance the investigation. John and I were of different minds on this particular issue and as to whether the planting of the SVR transmitter had occurred with inside assistance or not. I am sorry to admit that thirteen years have gone by, and neither of us has changed his mind about who is right.

While the transmitter was being removed from the OES conference room, Gusev was claiming in broken English to his FBI WFO interview team that he was an accredited Russian diplomat protected under the provisions of the Vienna Convention. He would not engage in conversation beyond this.

Gusev's assertion of immunity wasn't at all surprising. The claim of diplomatic immunity was a standard retort proffered by any foreign diplomat accredited to the United States under such circumstances. American diplomats assigned overseas make the same assertion when confronted by a foreign counterintelligence service or law enforcement agency. The Vienna Convention cuts both ways.

All attempts by the FBI to elicit Gusev's cooperation with even the simplest of questions were unsuccessful. But after it was clear to him that the official "interrogation" was over, Gusev's demeanor became jovial and gregarious. His command of English improved as well. In fact, he was so disarming that he convinced one of his interviewers to part with a FBI commemorative lapel pin as a souvenir of his visit to the enemy camp. There was nothing else to do but release Gusev to his embassy and send him packing back to Russia.

The State Department contacted the Russian embassy at approximately 1:32 p.m. to advise a surprised Russian official that the FBI was currently detaining a certain Mr. Gusev, who claimed to be a Russian diplomat, for violation of the espionage laws, and could the embassy kindly confirm his identity and official status. Clearly the Russian embassy official had no clue what was going on and even asked for clarification as to the spelling of Gusev's name. Once provided, the dumbfounded Russian official promised to call back shortly.

Both the DS and FBI agents laughed at the apparent discomfort occurring inside the Russian embassy. We imagined the words exchanged between the Russian ambassador and the SVR rezident about how the Motherland would now have to apologize to Secretary of State Madeleine Albright over the latest SVR transgression against the department. It took the Russian embassy over an hour to coordinate its response. The long delay likely occurred because few, if any, of the legitimate Russian diplomats were aware of what the SVR rezident was up to, especially regarding the installation and monitoring of a clandestine transmitter in the HST. But now they were responsible for responding to a diplomatic snafu and cleaning up the mess left by one of their brethren from the dark side of diplomatic life.

The social and professional wall separating bona fide Russian diplomats and their SVR counterparts within an embassy is quite rigid and formidable. But from an operational security standpoint, the divide was absolutely necessary to avoid compromises of ongoing

SVR activities. "Good fences make good neighbors," however that translates into Russian.

When a Russian embassy official finally called back, it was to acknowledge that Stanislav Gusev was, in fact, an employee of the Russian embassy protected by the provisions of the Vienna Convention. The official stated that embassy representatives would arrive at WFO to escort Gusev back to its embassy. About forty-five minutes later, two Russian officials walked into the WFO lobby and presented themselves to the receptionist sequestered behind a booth surrounded by bulletproof glass, all under the watchful eye of armed FBI police officers. The Russians glumly announced they were ready to take their colleague home. Gusev was brought down to the lobby and turned over to his embassy colleagues, who whisked him away. Two smiling senior FBI officials sat outside on the three-foot-high granite wall surrounding the FBI field office and waved discreetly as he passed. *Do svidaniya*, Comrade Gusev!

Later the same afternoon, Thomas Pickering, the undersecretary of state for political affairs, the same official whom I briefed earlier about unescorted Russian IOs and legitimate diplomats wandering inside the HST, summoned Russian ambassador Ushakov to his office to protest Gusev's "incompatible with diplomatic status" activities inside the United States. In addition, Pickering informed the Russian ambassador that Gusev was now declared *persona non grata* by the US government and had ten days in which to leave the country. Ironically the discussion took place less than a hundred yards from the conference room where the Russian had managed to plant the listening device.

Gusev would depart the United States aboard a regularly scheduled Aeroflot flight from Dulles International Airport without fanfare or press coverage before the expiration of the ten-day State Department deadline.

On December 9, 1999, Neil J. Gallagher, the assistant director in charge of the FBI's National Security Division, and DS A/S David Carpenter provided an on-the-record briefing to the press concerning Sacred Ibis. Later Messrs. Gallagher and Carpenter would brief Congress in public session about the basic facts of the investigation. In February 2000, I would accompany Wayne Rychak, the same DS executive present during my brief visit to Undersecretary Thomas Pickering's office, to a closed meeting held by the Senate Intelligence Committee to discuss the security failures and vulnerabilities identified during operation Sacred Ibis.

In typical tit-for-tat diplomatic fashion, on December 10, Russian first deputy foreign minister Aleksandr Andreyev summoned US ambassador James Collins to the Russian Foreign Ministry in Moscow to express his country's "categorical protest" of Gusev's illegal treatment by US law enforcement agencies. Andreyev complained further "the actions of the American authorities are a gross violation of the Vienna Convention and diplomatic relations and obligations, which the United States has assumed under the convention."

Andreyev's démarche to Ambassador Collins did not address the substance of DOJ's allegations of espionage but instead complained of the mistreatment suffered by one of its embassy officials. Several days after the Collins-Andreyev tête-à-tête in Moscow, I was able to share an unofficial transcript of the conversation with my IC counterintelligence colleagues, and we couldn't help but chuckle at the scripted, diplomatic verbiage used by the Russians when they were caught red-handed trying to steal our secrets. We were also aware of the fact that our government had essentially used the same language when its clandestine intelligence officers serving abroad under diplomatic cover were caught with their equally red hands in the Russian bear's cookie jar. It was just part of the gamesmanship between adversaries bent on stealing each other's secrets.

Both the national and international media were quick to report the incident, asking how it was possible for the SVR to penetrate the security confines of the State Department and place a "listening device" in a room located in the same corridor as the secretary of state's personal office. It was a logical question and one that confounds the Diplomatic Security Service to this day. Some news outlets speculated that Gusev's detention and return to Russia was in retaliation for the December 1, 1999, detention and forced expulsion of Cheri Leberknight, a second secretary assigned to the US embassy in Moscow. According to the Russian domestic security service, Leberknight was an alleged undercover CIA intelligence officer who had been "caught red-handed while conducting an espionage operation" inside Russia.

In my opinion, the great success of this case was that for the first time in counterintelligence history, the US government had captured an electronic device called an "actuator" that caused the transmitter to transmit. Clandestine transmitter microphones had been recovered before but never an actuator/transponder. This was a not-so-minor coup for the IC. The tissue box, held in place by a Velcro strip attached to the Malibuski rear window's carpeting, concealed an antenna that captured the OES conference room conversations into a recording device located under the front passenger seat of the vehicle.

Planting a transmitter in a restricted conference room was nothing new for the SVR. The SVR had attempted to bug a House of Representatives committee room during a public session hoping to later eavesdrop on classified conversations in the same room when it was closed for sensitive hearings. In an operation known as Flamingo, the SVR similarly introduced a transmitter into a conference room owned by Systems Planning Corporation (SPC) located in Arlington, Virginia. It was done during an open meeting attended by SPC officials and Russian representatives who had determined that Department of Defense and SPC officials would use the same conference room at a later date. Victor Lozenko, an SVR officer working under diplomatic cover, attached a transmitter to the underside of the SPC conference table that captured and broadcast conversations concerning sensitive US military operations to a vehicle with Russian diplomatic plates parked nearby. Sounds all too familiar. The SPC operation lasted ten months before the transmitter's batteries died.

Lozenko was subsequently awarded the Order of the Red Star for the feat. I wonder if Gusev returned to such high acclaim,

In August 1999, months after the discovery of the SVR device planted in the OES conference, an escort policy including restriction on foreign diplomats was reinstated.

EPILOGUE

On the well-guarded grounds of the Central Intelligence Agency in Langley, Virginia, sits a 1950s era, white-domed glass and steel structure designated officially as the Headquarters Auditorium but affectionately dubbed by the agency's employees as the "bubble." In many respects, it resembles an outsized igloo, but the odd shape has a more practical purpose as its design also affords protection against electronic eavesdropping. The seven thousand square foot auditorium is equipped with the latest in audio and video technology, seats 470 people, and is outfitted with ceiling-to-floor curtains to guarantee privacy from prying eyes. It also serves as the venue for award ceremonies.

I had visited the "bubble" before, but on August 30, 2000, my presence was much more personal—not just as a spectator but as the recipient of one of this nation's top counterintelligence honors. I was a bit nervous and humbled by the whole thing as the day's events would, among other awards, recognize our achievement in unmasking the SVR's installation of a transmitter inside the HST. In the past, I would have elected to avoid such functions, but under the circumstances, the ceremony's secrecy, atmospherics, and overall hoopla were just too damn appealing to pass up.

With my hand over my heart, I stood tall and proud next to John Tello, my immediate supervisor for the past two years, as "The President's Own" United States Marine Corps Band String Quartet played the national anthem to open that year's Intelligence Community Awards Ceremony. At the conclusion of "The Star Spangled Banner," George J. Tenet, the director of the CIA, confidently strode onto the stage to officiate at one of the very few federal ceremonies to which journalists and media reporters were never invited. Not surprisingly, spooks of all shades and stripes are a bit uncomfortable in such company.

As the master of ceremony, Director Tenet asked the award recipients, intelligence community officials, and invited guests to sit down. He was resplendently turned out in a ubiquitous Washington power suit of dark gray, a white button down shirt, and a red striped tie. He stood behind a large lectern at center stage, flanked by the American and CIA flags.

He began his speech by briefly reminding the audience of the importance of the intelligence community's mission in safeguarding our nation's security and the reasons why the director of central intelligence established the Intelligence Community awards to honor those federal employees who provided exceptional service on behalf of the United States. It was an impressive, forceful speech heavily tinged with red, white, and blue symbolism, and it tugged at the patriotic heartstrings of all in attendance.

After his introductory comments, the ceremony moved on to the presentation of individual honors, starting with the National Intelligence Certificates of Distinction to those individuals working for the National Imagery and Mapping Agency, the Federal Bureau of Investigation, Defense Intelligence Agency, and United States

Air Force. In each instance, the individual's name was announced along with a brief and cryptic synopsis of his or her work. One award that grabbed my attention was the National Intelligence Medal of Achievement for meritorious conduct "of an especially difficult duty in a clearly exceptional manner . . . to provide the intelligence required for national security policy determinations."

As the middle-aged man mounted the steps to the stage, I concluded that only his announced employment with the NSA was true and that his faux beard, toupee, and pseudonym were merely props to protect his real identity. When officially honoring superior performance in protecting the nation's security—even inside a secure facility, located on restricted grounds, with invited guests only—the IC sometimes demanded extraordinary anonymity. Tenet continued by awarding several National Intelligence Distinguished Service Medals and one Intelligence Community Seal Medallion.

It is unfortunate the public is not allowed to witness or share in this ceremony honoring the successes of our intelligence officers in the same public spirit as we do with our soldiers who are awarded medals for bravery and service. I believe that the American public would be very proud of their public servants who must, by the very nature of the job, work in secrecy and obscurity.

Tenet's final act was to present the National Intelligence Meritorious Unit Citations that are bestowed on "a unit or group of individuals whose accomplishments were of a clearly superior nature and of significant benefit to the Intelligence Community." The standard protocol for this award was different from the previous ones in that, as Tenet read the citation, a designated representative proceeded to the lectern and shook the director's hand while accepting the award on behalf of the others who remained standing in the audience. It was now our turn to be recognized. Tenet began the seventh group citation by stating,"Operation Sacred Ibis is awarded a National Intelligence Meritorious in recognition of its collective superior performance from June 1999 through February 2000. Throughout this period, the superb cooperation between the Federal Bureau of Investigation, the Central Intelligence Agency, and the Department of State Bureau of Diplomatic Security resulted in the successful conclusion of a joint technical counterintelligence operation. This effort, which will serve as a case study of how future technical operations should be executed, was the ultimate search for the proverbial 'needle in the haystack.' However, one of the great successes of the operation was not the discovery of the audio device in the chair rail at the main headquarters of the Department of State—"

With the mention of the State Department and a technical penetration in the same sentence, there were several groans and guffaws from the audience as well as some rueful head-shaking. The image of SVR officers traipsing undetected on the seventh floor of the HST and stealthily installing a "bug" inside a restricted conference room was the ultimate proof that the Black Dragons simply didn't take security matters seriously. The old quip about the State Department being "the only ship that leaks at the top" crossed my mind.

As we stood at attention and enjoyed the moment, John and I gave each other a sideways glance, knowing full-well that other significant security lapses had plagued the IC over the years. And it wasn't always the State Department who suffered intelligence defeats although we had experienced more than our fair share, due largely to lax security standards, lack of enforcement, and failure to hold employees personally accountable for their indiscretions. One thoroughly confounding incident occurred when the CIA inadvertently sent a shipping container loaded with classified papers to a foreign port, and it went undetected for months. That event, dubbed "Conex of documents" by those of us involved, required my presence on the Hill to testify in a closed meeting before a Congressional committee. That situation and many others had mercifully remained out of the press, unlike the State Department bugging incident.

Tenet continued, "—but the discovery instead showed how far the spirit of teamwork can unite officers from different backgrounds and cultures who are dedicated to a common cause.

"The unselfish and extremely valuable contributions made to the national security of the United States by the members of Operation Sacred Ibis reflect credit upon their respective agencies and the Intelligence Community."

Polite and perfunctory applause followed Tenet's comments as FBI agent Andy, the designated Sacred Ibis recipient, walked to the stage to accept the award. Director Tenet shook his hand, and as the young FBI agent left the podium, the Sacred Ibis team took their seats.

Thirteen years later, the FBI continues to pursue leads in the Sacred Ibis case as it tries to determine if the SVR had help from the inside.

★★★

Sacred Ibis wasn't the high point of my career, but it certainly was the most satisfying. I would continue working with the FBI and CIA for the next three years in joint investigations to identify and neutralize foreign intelligence agencies trying to compromise and recruit State Department officers.

As I approached my fiftieth birthday in late 2002, I reminded Peter Bergin, the principal deputy assistant secretary of state for DS, that I had always promised myself I would retire in the month I turned fifty. He had often heard me state, sometimes in not so eloquent or subtle terms, that I would retire at fifty years of age regardless of professional or personal circumstances. Peter knew there were no incentives to offer, either grade promotions or assignments of greater responsibilities or fanciful promises of great career possibilities, that would change my mind. To his credit, he did not try to dissuade me for one second, and I appreciated the respect he always afforded me. Peter left DS in 2003 to assume the position of senior director with Pepsico.

Why the urgency to go? My daughter Chloe was ten years old at the time, and my wife was a partner at a major international law firm with a demanding six-day-plus work week that included both domestic and foreign travel. Chloe, who had an au pair to take care of her since we returned from Paris in 1995, now needed a parent full time when she was not in school. My wife needed a partner to be more home oriented. Now was the time for me to be a father and spouse. This was the promise I had made during our Catholic pre-marriage classes in 1989.

In September 2002, I surrendered my special agent credentials, boxed up my personal items, and walked out of the counterintelligence office where I had worked for the past seven-plus years. As I left the department, NSB clandestine intelligence officer Isabelle Cheng had just recently arrived in Washington, DC, and was about to be introduced to Principal Deputy Assistant Secretary of State Donald Keyser. At the same time, INR analyst Kendall Myers was preparing secretly to fly to South America to meet his Cuban handlers.

By 2003, not without some hesitation, I returned as a part-time DS/CI contractor at the request of senior DS officials. For the next seven years, I still dropped Chloe off at school every day and left DS/CI in time to pick her up.

ACKNOWLEDGMENTS

I have been fortunate to have the guidance, support, and camaraderie of many fine people throughout my career and the writing of this book.

Lance Putney, the late Dave Roberts, the late Clark Dittmer, Genta Hawkins-Holmes, George Larson, Gordon Harvey, the late John Kwaitkowski, Gary Caldwell, Burley Fuselier Jr., William Armor, Peter Gallant, Thomas McKeever, Peter Bergin, Nanette Kreiger, John Tello, David Carpenter, Patrick Donovan, and Barry Moore were excellent bosses or DS seniors with supervisory responsibility for me. Many of them were key mentors, teaching me investigative and other skills and helping temper my sometimes excessive exuberance about my cases or frustrations with the bureaucracy. They always were willing to hear me out, respected my judgment, and supported me in making the tough calls.

My fellow DS agents and colleagues—Giovanna Cavalier, Jane Colon, the late Mike Considine, John Fitzsimmons, Bob Franks, Paul Gaffney, Steve Jenkins, Andy Koropeckyj, Tom Lalley, the late Joan Lombardi, Chris Lyons, Mark McMahan, Hal Orbits, Mike Posillico, Bill Stowell, Barbara Shields, Dick Tatum, and Kevin Warrener—and FBI colleagues—Kate Alleman, Lauren Anderson, Tim Bereznay,

Tony Buckmeier, Sheila Horan, Brett Kamarsic, Greg Leylegian, R.J. Porath, Matt Rader, Donna Mauer, Don Sullivan, and Rachel Vaccaro—constitute an amazing collection of talent. Their dedication to righting wrongs, respect for the law, unstinting perseverance, consummate professionalism, and unfailing good humor were inspirational and kept me going for thirty plus years.

Jim Bamford, Fred Burton, and Joel Swerdlow provided me with crucial insights into the world of publishing and encouraged me to tell my story. Dave Major, George Larson, Lori Sostowski, and Bill Strong provided valuable feedback on the manuscript, in some cases after slogging through multiple drafts. Tim Boswell, my developmental editor at Brown Books, deftly guided me in bringing the manuscript to life as the stories of flesh and blood people. Janet Harris, my senior editor at Brown Books, provided crucial insights regarding the organization of the book and making its "Inside the Beltway" aspects transparent for the general public. Kathy Penny, my project manager at Brown Books, kept everyone on track. Ted Johnson served as my personal photographer. Amy Baker and Randy Baker, my New Hampshire IT gurus, patiently launched me into the world of urls, blogs, and sundry other technology tools.

Besides their specific contributions, the friendship and encouragement extended by all of the foregoing persons as well as by members of my family and my dear friends have made my life and the writing of this book a much richer experience.

GLOSSARY

ADX—Administrative Maximum Facility Florence

AIPAC—American Israeli Public Affairs Committee

A/S—Assistant Secretary of State

AFSA—American Foreign Service Association, State Department

AIT—American Institute in Taiwan

AUSA—Assistant United States Attorney

BEX—Board of Examiners, State Department

Black Dragon—Senior career Foreign Service Officer in leadership/management position

BQA—better qualified applicant

CIA—Central Intelligence Agency

CuIS—Foreign Intelligence Service, Cuba

Clandestine intelligence (CI) officer—commonly called a "spy"

CODEL—Congressional delegation

CO—Corrections officer

DAS—Deputy Assistant Secretary of State, State Department

DASS—Deputy Assistant Secretary of State for Security

DIA—Defense Intelligence Agency

DAO—Defense Attaché Office

DOD—Department of Defense

DOJ—Department of Justice

DRL—Bureau of Democracy, Human Rights and Labor, State Department

DS—Diplomatic Security

DS/CI—Diplomatic Security, Office of Counterintelligence, State Department

DGSE—Direction Générale de la Sécurité Extérieure, Foreign Intelligence Service, France

EAP—East Asia and Pacific Affairs, State Department

FAM—Foreign Affairs Manual, State Department

FBI—Federal Bureau of Investigation

FSI—Foreign Service Institute, State Department

FSO—Foreign Service Officer, State Department

GIB—General Investigations Bureau, China (predecessor of the MSS)

GRU—Main Intelligence Directorate of the General Staff of the Armed Forces of the Russian Federation

GWU—George Washington University

HR—Office of Human Resource, State Department

HST—Harry S. Truman building, State Department headquarters

IC—Intelligence Community (CIA, DIA, FBI, NSA, and others)

ICE—Immigration and Customs Enforcement, Department of Homeland Security

INR—Bureau of Intelligence and Research, State Department

IO—Intelligence Officer

IRA—Irish Republican Army

JEH—John Edgar Hoover, FBI Director from 1924–1972

KGB—Komitet Gosudarstvennoy Bezopasnosti, Committee for State Security, Foreign Intelligence Service, Russia

Main State—Harry S. Truman building, Washington, DC

MFA—Ministry of Foreign Affairs

Mossad—HaMossad le Modi'in ule Tafkidim Meyuhadim, Foreign Intelligence Service, Israel

MSS—Ministry for State Security, Foreign Intelligence Service, China

NID—National Intelligence Daily, the CIA's daily report containing reports of NSA, CIA, and DOD, including National Reconnaissance Office satellite photography

NKVD—Narodnyy Komissariat Vnutrennik Del (The People's Commissariat for Internal Affairs), Russia

NODIS—Caption stamped on State Department documents meaning "no distribution outside the department and limited distribution inside the department to specific addressees"

NSA—National Security Agency

NSB—National Security Bureau, Foreign Intelligence Service, Taiwan

NSC—National Security Council

NSDD—1991 National Security Directive establishing the State Department "Pass-Through" program

OES—Bureau of Oceans, International Environment and Scientific Affairs, State Department

OFB—Old Furniture Building at Lorton Reformatory

OIG—Office of the Inspector General, State Department

PDAS—Principal Deputy Assistant Secretary of State, State Department

penetration agent—commonly called a "mole"

PEPCO—Potomac Electric Power Company

PRC—Peoples' Republic of China

PRCMUN—Permanent Mission of the Peoples' Republic of China to the United Nations

RSO—Regional Security Officer

SA—Special Agent

Sacred Ibis—code name for the investigation of the Russian technical penetration of the State Department

SAIS—Johns Hopkins School of Advanced International Studies

SCI—Special Compartmented Information, an additional access within Top Secret

SCIF—Sensitive Compartmented Information Facility

SF 86—Standard Form 86, federal agency employee security questionnaire

SIPR net—Secure Internet Protocol Router network, encrypted government e-mail system

SIB—Special Investigations Branch (Internal Affairs), State Department

S/P—Policy Planning Staff, State Department

SSA—Supervisory Special Agent

State Department—Department of State of the United States of America,

SVR—Sluzhba Vneshney Razvedki, Foreign Intelligence Service, Russia (Successor to the KGB)

SY—Office of Security, State Department (Predecessor to the Bureau of Diplomatic Security)

SY File—Security file for State Department employees

TECRO—Taipei Economic and Cultural Representative Office

UK—United Kingdom

UN—United Nations

UPI—United Press International

USAID—United States Agency for International Development

USC—United States Code, federal laws

USLO—United States Liaison Office, Beijing, China

USSS—United States Secret Service

USUN—United States Mission to the United Nations

WFO—Washington Field Office

WSJ—Wall Street Journal

Vision Quest—code name for the Kendall Myers investigation

YR—Country code for "Russia" appearing on license plates issued by the Office of Foreign Missions, State Department, to Russian diplomats

SOURCES

Introduction

History of the Bureau of Diplomatic Security of the United States Department of State, Printed October 2011, Global Publishing Solutions, First Edition. Also available online at www.state.gov/m/ds/rls/rpt/c47602.htm and www.state.gov/documents/organization/176589.pdf.

Part 1, Chapter 1

Affidavit of FBI Special Agent Katharine G. Alleman in support of Criminal Complaint, Arrest Warrants, and Search Warrants. *United States of America v. James M. Clark, Theresa M. Squillacote, and Kurt A. Stand* (United States Court for the District of Eastern Virginia, Criminal Action 98-0061), October 1997.

Harnden, Toby. "Spying for Fidel: The Inside Story of Kendall and Gwen Myers," *Washingtonian,* October 2009.

Indictment. *United States of America v. Walter Kendall Myers, aka Agent 202, and Gwendolyn Steingraber Myers, aka Agent 123, and Agent E-634* (United States District Court for the District of Columbia Criminal Action 09-150), June 4, 2009.

Interviews of Walter Kendall Myers and others by Robert Booth, February through May 2010.

Part 1, Chapter 2

Baldwin, Tom. "The policy of hugging America close has been a failure for the British, a US State Department analyst claims," *Timesonline*, November 30, 2006.

Criminal Complaint. *United States of America v. Walter Kendall Myers, aka Agent 202, and Gwendolyn Steingraber Myers, aka Agent 123, and Agent E-634* (United States District Court for the District of Columbia Criminal Action 09-150), June 4, 2009.

Harnden, Toby. "Spying for Fidel: The Inside Story of Kendall and Gwen Myers," *Washingtonian*, October 2009.

___________. "State Department official who mocked Britain is arrested as Cuban spy," http://blogs.telegraph.co.uk/toby_harnden/blog/2009/06/05/state_department_official_who_ mocked_ britain_is_arrested_as_cuban_spy, *The Telegraph*, June 6, 2009.

Indictment. *United States of America v. Walter Kendall Myers, aka Agent 202, and Gwendolyn Steingraber Myers, aka Agent 123, and Agent E-634* (United States District Court for the District of Columbia Criminal Action 09-150), June 4, 2009.

Interviews of Walter Kendall Myers and others by Robert Booth February through May 2010.

Murray, Tom. "My Professor, the Spy," *The Daily Beast*, June 11, 2009.

Popkin, Jim. "Woman Indicted in Cuba Spy Case is in Sweden and Out of U.S. Reach," *Washington Post*, April 23, 2013.

Reuters. "U.S.-British 'special relationship' questioned," http://www.infowars.com/articles/us/us_british_special_relationship_questioned.htm, December 1, 2006.

State of South Dakota v. Gwendolyn Steingraber and Walter Kendall Myers, 296 N.W.2d 543 (Supreme Court of South Dakota), September 17, 1980.

United States Department of Justice Office of Public Affairs. "Unsealed Indictment Charges Former U.S. Federal Employee with Conspiracy to Commit Espionage for Cuba," Press Release, April 25, 2013.

Part 1, Chapter 3

Betrayed: The Trusted Insider. FBI Academy Studios, Video, 2011.

Criminal Complaint. *United States of America v. Walter Kendall Myers, aka Agent 202, and Gwendolyn Steingraber Myers, aka Agent 123, and Agent E-634* (United Stated District Court for the District of Columbia Criminal Action 09-150), June 4, 2009.

Evrard, Paul. "Why did Cuba jail USAID contractor Alan Gross?" http://realcuba.wordpress.com/2012/02/04/why-did-cuba-jail-usaid-contractor-alan-gross/, Realcuba's Blog, February 4, 2012.

Indictment. *United States of America v. Walter Kendall Myers, aka Agent 202, and Gwendolyn Steingraber Myers, aka Agent 123, and Agent E-634* (United States District Court for the District of Columbia Criminal Action 09-150), June 4, 2009.

Interviews of Walter Kendall Myers and others by Robert Booth February through May 2010.

Part 1, Chapter 4

Betrayed: The Trusted Insider. FBI Academy Studios, Video, 2011.

Goldberg, Jeffrey. "Fidel: 'Cuba Model Doesn't Even Work For Us Anymore'" *The Atlantic*, September 8, 2010.

Harnden, Toby. "Spying for Fidel: The Inside Story of Kendall and Gwen Myers," *Washingtonian*, October 2009.

Interviews of Walter Kendall Myers and others by Robert Booth February through May 2010.

Transcript of Sentencing Before the Honorable Judge Reggie B. Walton, United States District Judge. *United States of America v. Walter Kendall Myers and Gwendolyn Steingraber Myers* (United States District Court for the District of Columbia Criminal Action 09-150), July 16, 2010.

Part 2, Chapter 5

Department of the Treasury, United States Customs Service. Customs Declaration of Donald W. Keyser, September 7, 2003.

Discussions between Robert Booth and Paul Doumitt in Paris, France, 1994 to 1995.

Ignatius, David. "Spy World Success Story," *Washington Post*, May 2, 2004.

Interviews of DS Special Agent Kevin Warrener by Robert Booth in March 2007 and March 2014.

Kalugin, Oleg, and Penn Montaigne. *The First Directorate: My 32 Years in Intelligence and Espionage Against the West*, St. Martin's Press, 1994.

Kamen, Al. "Rangel, Rumsfeld and Bygones," *Washington Post*, December 14, 2005.

Lilley, James, and Jeffrey Lilley. *China Hands: Nine Decades of Adventure, Espionage, and Diplomacy in Asia*, Public Affairs, 2004.

Marquis, Christopher. "Security Faces Review After a Laptop Vanishes," *New York Times,* April 22, 2000.

Mufson, Steven. "State Dept. Computer with Secrets Vanishes," *Washington Post,* April 17, 2000.

____________. "[ISN] Senior Diplomat Resigns to Protest Albright's Action," *Washington Post*, December 5, 2000.

Office of Inspector General, United States Department of State U.S. Information Agency. Report of Inspection – Inspection of Moscow, Russia and Constituent Posts and U.S. Information Service Russia (ISP/I-98-19), March 1998.

Schweisberg, David R. "Chinese Try to Recruit American as Embassy Spy," United Press International, November 1, 1988.

Snyder, Charles, "Confusion over Keyser deepens," *Taipei Times,* http://www.taipeitimes.com/News/taiwan/archives/2004/09/23/2003203983, September 23, 2004.

Statement of Facts. *United States v. Donald W. Keyser*, United States District Court for the Eastern District of Virginia, Crim. No. 1:05CR543, December 12, 2005.

The White House, Office of the Press Secretary. "President Clinton Names Donald W. Keyser for Rank of Ambassador as Special Negotiator for Nagorno-Karabakh and New Independent States Regional Conflicts," April 16, 1999.

United States Department of State Foreign Affairs Manual, 3 FAM 4100, Appendix B.

United States Department of State Foreign Affairs Manual, 12 FAM 26.

US Department of State. Outgoing Telegram from DASS Dikeos to Ambassador USLO Peking, June 5, 1978.

PART 2, CHAPTER 6

Affidavit of FBI Special Agent David R. Farrell, Jr. in Support of Criminal Complaint and Arrest Warrant. *United States v. Donald Willis Keyser*, United States District Court for the Eastern District of Virginia, Crim. No. 1:04M803, September 15, 2004.

Ambassade de France à Washington, E-mail to Office of Mr. Donald Keyser, July 2, 2003.

Defense Personnel and Security Research Center, Office of the Secretary of Defense & Defense Intelligence Agency, summary of Frederick Christopher Hamilton case, http://www.dhra.mil. perserec/espionagecases/secretary.html.

Gerstein, Josh. "Heritage Foundation Official Fingered as Possible Spy Recruit," *New York Sun*, http://www.nysun.com/national/heritage-foundation-official-fingered-as-possible/37834/, August 14, 2006.

Howe, Robert F. "Va. Man Pleads Guilty to Leaking US Secrets," *Washington Post*, February 6, 1993.

Interviews of DS Special Agent Giovanna Cavalier by Robert Booth in 2007 and 2014.

Interviews of DS Special Agent Kevin Warrener by Robert Booth in 2007 and 2014.

Interviews of FBI Special Agents [Names redacted at request of FBI] by Robert Booth in 2004 through 2006.

Memorandum in Support of Motion to Find Defendant in Material Breach of Plea Agreement and to Release the Government from its Pleas Obligations and Exhibits 2, 3, 4, 11, 12, 13, 14, 29, 30, 34, 36, 37, 38, 39, 40, 41, 42, 44, 47, 53, 54, 59, 61, and 63 thereto. United States District Court for the Eastern District of Virginia, Crim. No. 1:05CR543, July 5, 2006.

"NSB clarifies 'not involved' in intelligence in United States," *The China Post,* October 16, 2007.

Secretary of State, Washington, DC. "Guidelines on Contacts with Taiwan Unclassified," October 2, 2000.

Statement of Facts. *United States v. Donald W. Keyser*, United States District Court for the Eastern District of Virginia, Crim. No. 1:05CR543, December 12, 2005.

United States Department of State Foreign Affairs Manual, 12 FAM 26.

Warrant for Arrest. *United States v. Donald Willis Keyser*, United States District Court for the Eastern District of Virginia, Crim. No. 1:04M803, September 15, 2004.

Part 2, Chapter 7

E-mail from Kevin P. Warrener to Robert Booth including picture of magnet "Beware of Female Spies," March 26, 2014.

Interviews of DS Special Agent Giovanna Cavalier by Robert Booth in 2007 and 2014.

Interview of DS Special Agent Kevin Warrener by Robert Booth in 2007 and 2014.

Interviews of FBI Special Agents [Names redacted at request of FBI] by Robert Booth in 2004 through 2006.

Memorandum in Support of Motion to Find Defendant in Material Breach of Plea Agreement and to Release the Government from its Pleas Obligations and Exhibits 15, 47, and 48. United States District Court for the Eastern District of Virginia, Crim. No. 1:05CR543, July 5, 2006.

Statement of Facts. *United States v. Donald W. Keyser*, United States District Court for the Eastern District of Virginia, Crim. No. 1:05CR543, December 12, 2005.

Part 2, Chapter 8

Burger, Timothy J., and Adam Zagorin. "A Steamy Spy Scandal at the State Department," *Time* magazine, http://www.time.com/time/world/article/0,8599,1214911,00.html, July 15, 2006.

Chen, Melody. "Envoy to EU commends NSB official," *Taipei Times*, http://www.taipeitimes.com/News/taiwan/archives/2004/09/24/2003204120, September 24, 2004.

"Cheng denies links with U.S.'s Keyser," *China Post*, http://www.chinapost.com/tw/2007/10/15/126719/Cheng-denies.htm.

China Policy Institute Blog. "Happy Holidays," http://blogs.nottingham.ac.uk/chinapolicyinstitute/2013/12/10/happy-holidays, December 10, 2013.

CNN.com. "Accused double agent pleads to tax charge," http:www.cnn.com/2005/LAW/12/16/spy.compromise, December 16, 2005.

Criminal Complaint and Affidavit of FBI Special Agent Scott Freeman. *United States of America v. Benjamin Pierce Bishop*, United States District Court for the District of Hawaii, Case No. 13-0207, March 14, 2013.

Defendant's Opposition to Government's Motion to Find Defendant in Material Breach of Plea Agreement and to Release the Government from its Plea Obligations. United States District Court for the Eastern District of Virginia, Crim. No. 1:05CR543, October 27, 2006.

Docket Entry 110, Order (certified copy) signed by Judge Gerald Bruce Lee on September 20, 2006, that 1:06-mc-59 be consolidated with 1:05-cr-543 as to Donald Willis Keyser, United States District Court for the Eastern District of Virginia, Crim. No. 1:05CR543, July 5, 2006.

Eggen, Dan. "Handling of Secrets in Spy Cases Debated; Fear of Disclosures Affects Pursuit of Alleged Double Agent," *Washington Post*, May 7, 2003.

Gerstein, Josh. "In a Reversal, Taiwan Officials Seek to Block U.S. Spy Investigation," *New York Sun*, http://www.nysun.com/article/40501, September 28, 2006.

Goodenough, Patrick. "Secret Document Case May Affect US-Taiwan Relations," cnsnews.com, http://cnsnews.com/news/article/secret-document-case-may-affect-us-taiwan-relations, July, 7, 2008.

Interview of United States District Court Judge Paul Friedman, October 4, 2006.

Interviews of DS Special Agent Giovanna Cavalier by Robert Booth in 2007 and 2014.

Interviews of FBI Special Agents [Names redacted at request of FBI] by Robert Booth in 2004 through 2006.

Lefebvre, Stéphanie. "The Case of Donald Keyser and Taiwan's National Security Bureau," *International Journal of Intelligence* 20, No. 3 (2007): 512–526. doi:10.1080/08850600701249832.

Litchblau, Eric. "F.B.I. Agent Pleads Guilty in Deal in Chinese Spy Case," *New York Times*, May 13, 2004.

Litchblau, Eric, and David E. Sanger. "State Dept. Official Arrested in Inquiry on Taiwan Contact," *New York Times*, http://www.nytimes.com/2004/09/16/politics/16spy.html?_r=0, September 16, 2004.

Markon, Jerry. "Powell Aide Gave Papers To Taiwan, FBI Says," *Washington Post,* http://www.washingtonpost.com/wp-dyn/articles/A24703-2004Sep15.html, September 16, 2004.

Memorandum in Support of Motion to Find Defendant in Material Breach of Plea Agreement and to Release the Government from its Pleas Obligations and Exhibits 8, 13, 40, 41, 42, and 70, United States District Court for the Eastern District of Virginia, Crim. No. 1:05CR543, July 5, 2006.

Motion of Taipei Economic and Cultural Representative Office for Return of Seized Property and for Injunction Barring Use of Information, September 20, 2006.

Plea Agreement. *United States v. Donald W. Keyser*, United States District Court for the Eastern District of Virginia, Crim. No. 1:05CR543, December 12, 2005.

Remarks by Philp T. Reeker, Deputy Spokesman, Bureau of Public Affairs, Dept. of State. http://hongkong.usconsulate.gov/ustw/state/2003/080101.htm, August 1, 2003.

Reuters. "Taiwan Says Security Officers Did Not Hurt U.S. Ties," September 27, 2004.

Transcript of Plea Proceedings Before the Honorable T.S. Ellis, III, United States District Judge. *United States v. Donald W. Keyser*, United States District Court for the Eastern District of Virginia, Crim. No. 1:05CR543, December 12, 2005.

US Attorney's Office, District of Hawaii. "Defense Contractor Charged in Hawaii with Communicating Classified Information to Person Not Entitled to Receive Such Information," Press Release, March 18, 2013.

US Department of State. Nomination for Award of Kevin P. Warrener, December 12, 2012 and approval thereof, February 7, 2013 (Robert Booth private papers).

Warrant for Arrest. *United States v. Donald Willis Keyser,* United States District Court for the Eastern District of Virginia, Crim. No. 1:04M803, September 15, 2004.

Part 3, Chapter 9

Boadle, Anthony. "Brazil's Rousseff calls off state visit to U.S. over spying," Reuters, http://www.reuters.com/article/2013/09/17/us-usa-security-snowden-brazil-idUSBRE98G0VW20130917, July 17, 2013.

Chernow, Ron. *Washington: A Life,* Penguin Press, 2010.

Elkins, Stanley M. and Eric McKitrick. *The Age of Federalism: The Early American Republic, 1788–1800,* New York Oxford University Press, 1993.

France 24.com. "France tells US to stop spying 'immediately,'" http://www.france24.com/en/20130701-france-hollande-snowden-us-spying-unacceptable-germany-asylum, July 2, 2013.

Interviews of Elijah Kelly Jr. (April 10, 1986), William Walker (April 11, 1986), James Michel (April 11, 1986), Bob Loftis (April 11, 1986), Robert Kagan (April 11, 1986), Richard H. Solomon (April 7, 1986), Lloyd Richardson (April 11, 1986), Elliott Abrams (April 17, 1986), Nicholas Platt (April 11, 1986), Brunson McKinley (April 11, 1986), Kenneth Quinn (April 11, 1986), "Confidential Source A" (April 15, 1986), "Confidential Source B" (April 15, 1986) by Robert Booth.

Johnston, David. "Bush Pardons 6 in Iran Affair, Aborting a Weinberger Trial; Prosecutor Assails 'Cover-Up,'" *New York Times*, http://www.nytimes.com/books/97/06/29/reviews/iran-pardon.html, December 24, 1992.

Leigh, David. "How 250,000 US embassy cables were leaked," *The Guardian*, http://www.theguardian.com/world/2010/nov/28/how-us-embassy-cables-leaked, November 28, 2010.

Letter from Lawrence S. Eagleburger to Bernard W. Aronson (Robert Booth private papers), July 17, 1991.

Lynch, Colum. "U.S. Backed U.N. General Despite Evidence of Abuses," *Washington Post*, http://www.washingtonpost.com/wp-dyn/content/article/2008/09/20/AR2008092001801.html, September 21, 2008.

Olson, Alexandra. "WikiLeaks' First Casualty: Carlos Pascual, U.S. Ambassador to Mexico, Resigned Over Leaked Cables," *The World Post*, http://www.huffingtonpost.com/2011/03/24/wikileaks-carlos-pascual_n_840049.html, March 24, 2011.

Romero, Simon. "Ecuador Expels U.S. Ambassador Over WikiLeaks Cable," *New York Times*, http://www.nytimes.com/2011/04/06/world/americas/06ecuador.html, April 5, 2011.

Sherdan, Mary Beth. "Calderon: WikiLeaks caused severe damage to U.S.-Mexico relations," *Washington Post*, http://www.washingtonpost.com/wp-dyn/content/article/2011/03/03/AR2011030302853.html, March 3, 2011.

Surk, Barbara . "U.S. soldier linked to Iraq video charged," *Washington Times*, http://www.washingtontimes.com/news/2010/jul/6/us-soldier-linked-iraq-attack-video-charged/, July 6, 2010.

Traynor, Ian, Philip Oltermann, and Paul Lewis. "Angela Merkel's call to Obama: are you bugging my mobile phone," *The Guardian*, http://www.theguardian.com/world/2013/oct/23/us-monitored-angela-merkel-german, October 23, 2013.

Tyler, Patrick E. "Ambassador Assails O'Neill Delegation," *Washington Post*, April 10, 1986.

US Department of State Office of the Historian. "A Short History of the Department of State," https://history.state.gov/departmenthistory/short-history/framework.

Walker, Peter. "Amnesty International hails WikiLeaks and Guardian as Arab Spring 'catalysts,'" *The Guardian*, http://www.theguardian.com/world/2011/may/13/amnesty-international-wikileaks-arab-spring, May 12, 2011.

Part 3, Chapter 10

CNN.com Politics. "Bush commutes Libby's prison sentence," http://www.cnn.com/2007/POLITICS/07/02/libby.sentence/index.html?iref=allsearch, July 2, 2007.

Department of State Daily Press Briefing, May 16, 1986.

Interviews of "Mr. Penn" by Robert Booth and Mark McMahan on April 23, 1986, and June 3,1986.

Watson, Jerome R. "Employee Fired by State Dept. for News Leak," *Chicago Sun-Times*, May 17, 1986.

Part 3, Chapter 11

Devroy, Ann. "Ex-Bush Aide Quits as Zimbabwe Envoy," *Washington Post*, October 17, 1990.

E-mail correspondence from Sid Balman Jr. (Robert Booth private papers), May 13, 2014.

Epstein, Edward Jay. "Embassy cables – How the U.S. Embassy Reported an Economic Crisis in Kuwait to the State Department," *The Atlantic,* May 1983.

Interview of Sy Oglesby by Robert Booth, May 17, 1983 and other dates in 1983.

Interview of William Sherman by Robert Booth, January 9, 1985.

Interview of "Edgar" by Robert Booth, January 10, 1985.

Interview of Peter Gallant by Robert Booth, June and July 1985.

Interview of "Mr. Reaves" by Robert Booth, July 11, 1985.

Interview of Hume Horan by Robert Booth, July 25, 1985.

Powers, Charles T. "U.S. Evacuates Ethiopian Jews. Last Group of Falashas Airlifted from Sudan to Israel," *Los Angeles Times*, http://articles.latimes.com/1985-03-23/news/mn-21077_1_ethiopian-jews, March 25, 1985.

_______________. "Ethiopian Rescue: An All U.S. Operation: Airlift Plan Came from Officer in Sudan, not Israel," *Los Angeles Times*, http://articles.latimes.com/1985-03-27/news/mn-20004_1_sudanese-government, March 27, 1985.

_______________. "Saga of Secret Airlift Ethiopian Jews: Exodus of a Tribe," *Los Angeles Times*, http://articles.latimes.com/1985-07-07/news/mn-9368_1_gondar, July 7, 1985.

Randal, Jonathan C. "Trial Tests Sudan-U.S. Relations," *Washington Post*, January 28, 1986.

Witcher, S. Karene. "Mexico's Belt Tightening Could Cause Social Unrest," *Wall Street Journal*, January 1, 1982.

_______________. "Havana's Efforts to Reschedule Its Debt Meeting Difficulties, U.S. Officials Say," *Wall Street Journal*, September 13, 1982.

______________. "U.S. Banks Reportedly Felt Threatened into Joining 4 Billion Credit to France," *Wall Street Journal*, October 22, 1982.

______________. "U.S. Preparing a Rescue Package for Yugoslavia," *Wall Street Journal*, December 7, 1982.

______________. "Turkey Asks for more Relaxed IMF Pact; U.K. Faults Cuba's Plan to Reschedule," *Wall Street Journal*, December 27, 1982.

______________. "Jamaica Reportedly at Odds with the IMF; Economic Growth Could be Depressed," *Wall Street Journal*, March 11, 1983.

______________. "Venezuela Seen About to Seek IMF Loan As Oil Price Decline Buffets Its Economy," *Wall Street Journal*, April 15, 1983.

Part 3, Chapter 12

Interviews of Charles Wrice, Corrections Officer, Lorton Reformatory by Robert Booth and DS Special Agent Michael Considine, November 4 and 9, 1983.

Knight, Athelia. "Lorton Search Uncovers More Classified Data," *Washington Post*, November 10, 1983.

Lippman, Thomas W. "Agents Investigate State Department Security Breach," *Washington Post*, March 9, 1998.

Mufson, Steven. "Security Clearance of U.S. Ambassador to Israel is Suspended," *Washington Post*, September 23, 2000.

Pincus, Walter. "State Department Official Resigns Amid Allegations," *Washington Post*, reprinted in *The Tech Online Edition*, http://tech.mit.edu/V116/N34/state.34w.html, August 26, 1996.

Schweid, Barry. "U.S. Ambassador Regains Security OK," http://www.apnewsarchive.com/2000/U-S-Ambassador-Regains-Security-OK/id-8d8d3502bedc9f61af12e5321a09b823, October 10, 2000.

Telephone interview of Charles Wrice, Corrections Officer, Lorton Reformatory by Robert Booth, November 14, 1983.

United Press International. "Schultz Orders Hunt for Person who Let Secret Papers Go to Jail," *Washington Times*, November 10, 1983.

Part 4, Chapter 13

Anderson, Jack, and Dale Van Atta. "Delayed Memo May Have Cost a Life," *Washington Post*, August 10, 1998.

Associated Press. "Embassy Guard Who Spied for Soviets is Freed," *Los Angeles Times*, February 28, 1996.

Federal Bureau of Investigation. "The Year of the Spy," http://www.fbi.gov/about-us/history/famous-cases/the-year-of-the-spy.

Gertenzang, James, and Jonathan Eig. "Two Slain Near Schultz's Office: Gunman Foils Security, Kills Mother, Himself," *Los Angeles Times*, June 22, 1985.

Ignatius, David. "Bugged at the State Department," *Washington Post*, December 22, 1999.

Memorandum from Doug Langan to James W. Sandlin, April 2, 1992.

Oberdorfer, Don. "Marine Guards Spy Scandal Snowballed, Then Melted Away," *Washington Post*, January 17, 1988.

Office of Inspector General, United States Department of State, Security and Intelligence Oversight Audit, "Protecting Classified Documents at State Department Headquarters," SIO/A-99-46, September 1999.

"State Dept. Tightens Security in Wake of Killings," *New York Times*, http://www.nytimes.com/1985/06/23/us/state-dept-tightens-security-in-wake-of-killings.html, June 23, 1985.

State Department Domestic Security Lapses and Status of Overseas Domestic Enhancements: Hearings before the Committee on International Relations, House of Representatives, One Hundred Sixth Congress, Second Session, May 11 and May 17, 2000, U.S. Government Printing Office, 2000.

US Department of State. *History of the Bureau of Diplomatic Security of the United States Department of State*, First Edition, Global Publishing Solutions, October 2011.

US Department of State, Bureau of Management. "Reinventing government: change at State," September 1993.

US Department of State, Department Notice, "New Visitor Escort Requirements," November 17, 1998.

US Department of State, Bureau of Diplomatic Security Uniformed Protection Branch, "Escort of Russian and Romanian Diplomats No Longer Needed," Circular 92-19, June 24, 1992.

Part 4, Chapter 14

Gerstein, Josh. "Leniency for AIPAC leaker," *Politico*, http://www.politico.com/news/stories/0609/23671.html, June 11, 2009.

Johnston, David. "Israel Lobbyists Facing Charges in Secrets Case," *New York Times*, http://www.nytimes.com/2005/08/05/politics/05inquire.html?fta=y&pagewanted=all, August 5, 2005.

______________. "Pentagon Analyst Gets 12 Years for Disclosing Data," *New York Times*, http://www.nytimes.com/2006/01/20/politics/20cnd-franklin.html, January 20, 2006.

Lewis, Neil A., and David Johnston. "U.S. to Drop Spy Case Against Pro-Israel Lobbyists," *New York Times*, http://www.nytimes.com/2009/05/02/us/politics/02aipac.html, May 1, 2009.

Markon, Jerry. "Defense Analyst Guilty in Israeli Espionage Case," *Washington Post,* http://www.washingtonpost.com/wp-dyn/content/article/2005/10/05/AR2005100501608.html, October 6, 2005.

____________. "US Drops Case Against Ex-Lobbyists," *Washington Post,* http://www.washingtonpost.com/wp-dyn/content/article/2009/05/01/AR2009050101310.html, May 2, 2009.

Schweid, Barry. "Audit: Visitors Roaming State Dept.," *Yahoo News*, http://www.agaphil.com/AuditingArticles/Good/us_russia_spy_26.html, December 15, 1999.

Superseding Indictment. *United States of America v. Lawrence Anthony Franklin, Steven J. Rosen, Keith Weissman*, United States District Court for the Eastern District of Virginia, Criminal No. 1:05CR225, August 4, 2005.

Part 4, Chapter 15

Andrew, Christopher, and Mitrokhin Vasili. *The Sword and the Shield: The Mitrokhin Archive and the Secret History of the KGB*, Basic Books, 1999.

BBC News. "US 'spy' recalled," http://news.bbc.co.uk/2/hi/europe/546422.stm, December 2, 1999.

Gordon, Michael. R. "Russians Briefly Detain U.S. Diplomat, Calling her a Spy," *New York Times*, http://www.nytimes.com/1999/12/01/world/russians-briefly-detain-us-diplomat-calling-her-a-spy.html, December 1, 1999.

Kalugin, Oleg, and Penn Montaigne. *The First Directorate: My 32 Years in Intelligence and Espionage Against the West*, St. Martin's Press, 1994.

Raum, Tom. "U.S. Agents Helped Suspected Spy," *Yahoo News*, http://dailynews.yahoo.com/h/ap/20000/wl/russian_spy_1.html, February 11, 2000.

Shannon, Elaine. "It's Still Spy v. Spy," *Time* magazine, http://www.cnn.com/ALLPOLITICS/time/1999/12/13/spy.html, December 13, 1999.

Shenon, Philip. "A Spy's Bug Set Artfully in Woodwork, U.S. Concedes," *New York Times*, http://www.nytimes.com/1999/12/11/world/a-spy-s-bug-set-artfully-in-woodwork-us-concedes.html, December 11, 1999.

Unclassified Cable, FBIS 117-Dec 10, "Russia Protests to US Envoy Over Diplomat's Expulsion," Interfax, December 10, 1999.

Unclassified S/NIS Press Guidance Cable, December 9, 1999.

US Department of State, Office of the Spokesman. On-the-Record Briefing, Assistant Secretary of State for Diplomatic Security David Carpenter and Assistant Director in Charge of the FBI National Security Division Neil J. Gallagher, December 9, 1999.

Vise, David A., and Steven Mufson. "Russian May Have Monitored 50 to 100 Meetings," *Washington Post*, December 10, 1999.

______________________________. "State Department Employees Questioned: Officials Trying to Pinpoint How Listening Device Got in Molding," *Washington Post*, December 11, 1999.

Additional Reading

Andrew, Christopher, and Vasili Mitrokhin. *The Sword and the Shield: The Mitrokhin Archive and the Secret History of the KGB*, Basic Books, 1999.

Bok, Sissela. *Secrets: On the Ethics of Concealment and Revelation*, Vintage Books New York, December 1989.

Collins, Bernhard B., Jr. "The Diplomatic Security Service: Partner in National Security," U.S. Army War College, February 18, 1992.

Executive Order 12958: Classified National Security Information. 60 F.R. 19825, April 20, 1995.

Executive Order 13292: Classified National Security Information. 68 FR 15315 (March 28, 2003).

Executive Order 13526: Classified National Security Information. 75 FR 707, January 5, 2010, Correction Page 75 FR 1013, January 8, 2010.

Grimes, Sandra, and Jeanette Vertefeuille. *Circle of Treason: A CIA Account of Traitor Aldrich Ames and the Men He Betrayed*, Naval Institute Press, Annapolis, MD, 2012.

Haynes, John Earl, and Harvey Klehr. *Early Cold War Spies: The Espionage Trials That Shaped American Politics*, Cambridge University Press, New York, 2006.

Huslin, Anita. "If These Walls Could Talk . . . SCIF Rooms Play It Safe with U.S. Secrets," *Washington Post*, May 28, 2006.

Kulish, Nicholas. "A Diplomat Reflects on Taiwan's Isolation," *New York Times*, http://www.nytimes.com/2007/06/24/world/asia/24taiwan.html, June 24, 2007.

Lefebvre, Stéphanie. "The Case of Donald Keyser and Taiwan's National Security Bureau," *International Journal of Intelligence* 20, No. 3 (2007): 512–526. doi:10.1080/08850600701249832.

Lilley, James, and Jeffrey Lilley. *China Hands: Nine Decades of Adventure, Espionage, and Diplomacy in Asia*, PublicAffairs, 2004.

Ross, Gary. *Who Watches the Watchmen? The Conflict Between National Security and Freedom of the Press*, NI Press, Washington, DC, July 2011.

de Toledano, Ralph. *Spies, Dupes, & Diplomats*, Arlington House, New Rochelle, New York, 1967.

United States Code Title 18, Section 2 (Aiding and Abetting and Causing an Act to be Done). United States Code Title 18, Section 371 (Conspiracy).

United States Code Title 18, Section 951 (Agent of Foreign Government). United States Code Title 18, Section 982 (Forfeiture).

United States Code Title 18, Section 1001(a) (Making False Statements).

United States Code Title 18, Section 1343 (Wire Fraud).

US Department of State. "Adjudicative Guidelines for Determining Eligibility for Access to Classified Information," http://www.state.gov/m/ds/clearances/60321.htm., February 3, 2006.

US Department of State. "FAQs" [regarding security clearances], http://www.state.gov/m/ds/clearances/c10977.htm.

INDEX OF NAMED INDIVIDUALS

J

K

L

M

N

O

P

Q

R

S

T

U

V

W

Y

Z

ABOUT THE AUTHOR

Robert Booth served as a Special Agent with the State Department's Bureau of Diplomatic Security from 1974 to 2002. His overseas assignments included Beijing, Geneva, Tokyo, Haiti, and Paris. He was Deputy Director, Office of Counterintelligence from 1996–2002 and a consultant for the Office of Counterintelligence from 2003–2012. His numerous meritorious service awards include a nomination for the FBI Director's Group Award and a State Department Group Superior Honor Group Award for his role in the Kendall Myers spy case.

Born in Johnson City, Tennessee, he is married and has one daughter. He holds a BA from the University of Tennessee, Knoxville, and a Training Specialist Certificate from Georgetown University. He was a professor with the CI Centre in Washington, DC, from 2003–2012. He currently resides in Hanover, New Hampshire, where he is a guest speaker and audits courses at Dartmouth College.

CPSIA information can be obtained
at www.ICGtesting.com
Printed in the USA
BVHW070718151221
624022BV00010B/766